PRAYERS AND THE CONSTRUCTION
OF ISRAELITE IDENTITY

ANCIENT ISRAEL AND ITS LITERATURE

Thomas C. Römer, General Editor

Editorial Board:
Susan Ackerman
Thomas B. Dozeman
Cynthia Edenburg
Shuichi Hasegawa
Konrad Schmid
Naomi A. Steinberg

Number 35

PRAYERS AND THE CONSTRUCTION OF ISRAELITE IDENTITY

Edited by
Susanne Gillmayr-Bucher and Maria Häusl

SBL PRESS

Atlanta

Copyright © 2019 by Society of Biblical Literature

All rights reserved. No part of this work may be reproduced or transmitted in any form or by any means, electronic or mechanical, including photocopying and recording, or by means of any information storage or retrieval system, except as may be expressly permitted by the 1976 Copyright Act or in writing from the publisher. Requests for permission should be addressed in writing to the Rights and Permissions Office, SBL Press, 825 Houston Mill Road, Atlanta, GA 30329 USA.

Library of Congress Cataloging-in-Publication Data

Names: Gillmayr-Bucher, Susanne, 1962– editor.
Title: Prayers and the construction of Israelite identity / edited by Susanne Gillmayr-Bucher and Maria Häusl.
Description: Atlanta : SBL Press, 2019. | Series: Ancient Israel and its literature ; Number 35 | Includes bibliographical references and index.
Identifiers: LCCN 2019000482 (print) | LCCN 2019005096 (ebook) | ISBN 9780884143673 (ebk.) | ISBN 9781628372434 (pbk. : alk. paper) | ISBN 9780884143666 (hbk. : alk. paper)
Subjects: Bible—Prayers—History and criticism. | Bible. Old Testament—Criticism, interpretation, etc. | Jews—Identity. | Identification (Religion).
Classification: LCC BS1199.P68 (ebook) | LCC BS1199.P68 P73 2019 (print) | DDC 221.6—dc23
LC record available at https://lccn.loc.gov/2019000482

Printed on acid-free paper.

Contents

Abbreviations vii

Introduction
    Susanne Gillmayr-Bucher and Maria Häusl 1

Shaping Biblical Books through Prayer

Rhetorically and Ideologically Shaping the Narrative
    through Direct and Indirect Prayer Speech in Chronicles 11
    Michael D. Matlock

Prayers in the Book of Jonah: Reflections on Different
    "Israelite" Identities?
    Dirk J. Human 33

"So I Prayed to the God of Heaven" (Neh 2:4): Praying and
    Prayers in the Books of Ezra and Nehemiah
    Maria Häusl 53

Identity and Social Justice in Postexilic Yehud: Reading
    Nehemiah 9 in an African Liberationist Perspective
    Ndikho Mtshiselwa 83

(Re)modeling Biblical Figures through Prayers

Testing Tales: Genesis 22 and Daniel 3 and 6
    Christo Lombaard 113

Glory and Remorse: Transitions in Solomon's Prayer
    (1 Kgs 8)
    Susanne Gillmayr-Bucher 125

Hannah's Prayer(s) in 1 Samuel 1–2 and in Pseudo-Philo's
    Liber antiquitatum biblicarum 147
    Hannes Bezzel

(Re-)constructing Identity in the Prayers of the Psalter

Psalm 37 and the Devotionalization of Instruction in the
    Postexilic Period
    Scott C. Jones 167

To Sanction and to Subvert: The Reuses of Psalm 132 in
    the Hebrew Bible
    Melody D. Knowles..189

Aspects of Dynamic Remembering and Constructing in Psalm 145:
    A Contribution to the Study of Prayer in Persian and Hellenistic
    Times
    Nancy Rahn...203

List of Contributors..229
Ancient Sources Index...231
Modern Authors Index..240
Subject Index..244

Abbreviations

1QH^a	1QHodayot^a
AASF	Annales Academiae Scientiarum Fennicae
AB	Anchor Bible
ABD	Freedman, David Noel, ed. *Anchor Bible Dictionary*. 6 vols. New York: Doubleday, 1992.
ABS	Archaeology and Biblical Studies
AcBib	Academia Biblica
AG	*Amt und Gemeinde*
AGJU	Arbeiten zur Geschichte des antiken Judentums und des Urchristentums
AIL	Ancient Israel and Its Literature
A.J.	Josephus, *Antiquitates judaicae*
ATANT	Abhandlungen zur Theologie des Alten und Neuen Testaments
ATD	Das Alte Testament Deutsch
ATS	Artscroll Tanach Series
b.	Babylonian Talmud
BBB	Bonner biblische Beiträge
BCESS	Bibliothèque des Centres d'Études Supérieures Spécialisés
BE	Biblische Enzyklopädie
Ber.	Berakot
BETL	Bibliotheca Ephemeridum Theologicarum Lovaniensium
BEvT	Beiträge zur evangelische theologie
BHT	Beiträge zur historischen Theologie
Bib	*Biblica*
BibInt	Biblical Interpretation Series
BibSem	The Biblical Seminar
BibS(N)	Biblische Studien (Neukirchen, 1951–)
BJS	Brown Judaic Studies
BKAT	Biblischer Kommentar, Altes Testament

BLS	Bible and Literature Series
BN	*Biblische Notizen*
BRLJ	Brill Reference Library of Judaism
BThAT	Beiträge zur Theologie des Alten Testaments
BThSt	Biblisch-theologische Studien
BTZ	*Berliner Theologische Zeitschrift*
BZAW	Beihefte zur Zeitschrift für die alttestamentliche Wissenschaft
CBC	Cambridge Bible Commentary
CBQ	*Catholic Biblical Quarterly*
CBQMS	Catholic Biblical Quarterly Monograph Series
CHANE	Culture and History of the Ancient Near East
Chr	Chronicler
ConBOT	Coniectanea Biblica: Old Testament Series
CurTM	*Currents in Theology and Mission*
CV	*Communio Viatorum*
DCLS	Deuterocanonical and Cognate Literature Studies
DJD	Discoveries in the Judaean Desert
DSD	*Dead Sea Discoveries*
Dtr	Deuteronomist
DtrH	Deuteronomistic History
EJL	Early Judaism and Its Literature
EP	*Ekklesiastikos Pharos*
ETS	Erfurter theologischen Studien
EvT	*Evangelische Theologie*
ExpTim	*Expository Times*
FAT	Forschungen zum Alten Testament
FJTC	Flavius Josephus: Translation and Commentary
FOTL	Forms of the Old Testament Literature
GBT	Gender and the Biblical Tradition
HBM	Hebrew Bible Monographs
HBS	History of Biblical Studies
HCOT	Historical Commentary on the Old Testament
HFK	Historisk-Filosofisk Klasse
HSM	Harvard Semitic Monographs
HSS	Harvard Semitic Studies
HThKAT	Herders Theologischer Kommentar zum Alten Testament
HTS	*Harvard Theological Studies*
HUCA	*Hebrew Union College Annual*

HvTSt	*Hervormde teologiese studies*
IBC	Interpretation: A Bible Commentary for Teaching and Preaching
ICC	International Critical Commentary
IEJ	*Israel Exploration Journal*
Int	*Interpretation*
JANESCU	*Journal of the Ancient Near Eastern Society of Columbia University*
JBL	*Journal of Biblical Literature*
JBTh	Jahrbuch für Biblische Theologie
Jdt	Judith
JHebS	*Journal of Hebrew Scriptures*
JJS	*Journal of Jewish Studies*
JNES	*Journal of Near Eastern Studies*
JNSL	*Journal of Northwest Semitic Languages*
JSHRZ	Jüdische Schriften aus hellenistisch-römischer Zeit
JSJ	*Journal for the Study of Judaism*
JSNTSup	Journal for the Study of the New Testament: Supplement Series
JSOT	*Journal for the Study of the Old Testament*
JSOTSup	Journal for the Study of the Old Testament Supplement Series
JSP	*Journal for the Study of the Pseudepigrapha*
JSS	*Journal of Semitic Studies*
KAI	Donner, Herbert, and Wolfgang Röllig. *Kanaanäische und aramäische Inschriften*. Wiesbaden: Harrassowitz, 1962–2002.
KAT	Kommentar zum Alten Testament
KHC	Kurzer Hand-Commentar zum Alten Testament
KST	Kohlhammer-Studienbücher Theologie
LAB	Pseudo-Philo, Liber antiquitatum biblicarum
LAI	Library of Ancient Israel
LASBF	*Liber Annuus Studii Biblici Fransciscani*
LBS	Library of Biblical Studies
LHBOTS	Library of Hebrew Bible/Old Testament Studies
LNTS	Library of New Testament Studies
LSTS	Library of Second Temple Studies
LTK	Kasper, Walter, et al., eds. *Lexikon für Theologie und Kirche*. 3rd ed. 11 vols. Freiburg: Herder, 1993–2001.

LXX	Septuagint
MJT	Marburger Jahrbuch Theologie
MS B	Manuscript B of Ben Sira
MT	Masoretic Text
NCB	New Century Bible
NCBC	New Cambridge Bible Commentary
NEchtB	Neue Echter Bibel
Neot	Neotestamentica
NGTT	*Nederduitse gereformeerde teologiese tydskrif*
NIB	New Interpreter's Bible
NICOT	New International Commentary on the Old Testament
NIV	New International Version
NJB	New Jerusalem Bible
NRSV	New Revised Standard Version
OBO	Orbis Biblicus et Orientalis
OBT	Overtures to Biblical Theology
OTE	*Old Testament Essays*
OTL	Old Testament Library
OTR	Old Testament Readings
OtSt	Oudtestamentische Studien
PEQ	*Palestine Exploration Quarterly*
PFES	Publications of the Finnish Exegetical Society
POuT	De Prediking van het Oude Testament
PSPR	*Personality and Social Psychology Review*
RHPR	*Revue d'histoire et de philosophie religieuses*
SBLDS	Society of Biblical Literature Dissertation Series
SBLMS	Society of Biblical Literature Monograph Series
SBS	Stuttgarter Bibelstudien
SC	Sources chrétiennes
ScEs	*Science et esprit*
SEÅ	*Svensk exegetisk årsbok*
Sem	*Semitica*
SemeiaSt	Semeia Studies
SI	*Social Identities*
Siphrut	Siphrut: Literature and Theology of the Hebrew Scriptures
Sir	Ben Sira
SNVAO	Skrifter utgitt av det Norske Videnskaps-Akademi i Oslo
SRA	Studies of Religion in Africa
SSEJC	Studies in Scriptures in Early Judaism and Christianity

SSH	Social Science History
SSN	Studia Semitica Neerlandica
STDJ	Studies on the Texts of the Desert of Judah
STR	Studies in Theology and Religion
TDOT	Botterweck, G. Johannes, Helmer Ringgren, and Heinz-Josef Fabry, eds. *Theological Dictionary of the Old Testament*. Translated by John T. Willis et al. 15 vols. Grand Rapids: Eerdmans, 1974–2006.
ThWAT	Botterweck, G. Johannes, Helmer Ringgren, and Heinz-Josef Fabry, eds. *Theologisches Wörterbuch zum Alten Testament*. 10 vols. Stuttgart: Kohlhammer, 1970–2000.
T&K	*Texte & Kontexte*
TRE	Krause, Gerhard, and Gerhard Müller, eds. *Theologische Realenzyklopädie*. Berlin: de Gruyter, 1977–
TW	Theologische Wissenschaft
TynBul	*Tyndale Bulletin*
VetE	*Verbum et Ecclesia*
VT	*Vetus Testamentum*
VTSup	Supplements to Vetus Testamentum
WAW	Writings from the Ancient World
WBC	Word Biblical Commentary
Wis	Wisdom of Solomon
WMANT	Wissenschaftliche Monographien zum Alten und Neuen Testament
WUNT	Wissenschaftliche Untersuchungen zum Neuen Testament
y.	Jerusalem Talmud
ZAW	*Zeitschrift für die Alttestamentliche Wissenschaft*
ZKT	*Zeitschrift für katholische Theorie*
ZLG	*Zeitschrift der Luther-Gesellschaft*
ZTK	*Zeitschrift für Theologie und Kirche*

Introduction

Susanne Gillmayr-Bucher and Maria Häusl

The growing elaboration of prayers in postexilic biblical writings indicates that this genre, as well as its literary presentation, became increasingly important in this period.[1] During that time, a transformation took place: from short, individual prayers to longer theological and historical reflections, ritualized recitations, instructions reciting normative values and commandments, confirmations of hope, prophecy, and penitential prayers. These texts clearly show not only that prayers are a communication between the people and their deity but also that the community, who heard or repeated these prayers, must be considered as another important aspect of prayers and their communicative intentions.[2] In their prayers, people addressed God but also spoke about God, presenting their concerns to the deity and, simultaneously, addressing the community and encouraging a common reflection or action. In this way, prayers mirror challenges and needs, as well as hopes and fears, but also convictions, beliefs, and shared traditions. Prayers not only assume different functions; they are an entity of their own, presenting distinct and diverse anthropological and theological discourses. The prayers in the biblical texts are part of this development, which can also be observed in the numerous prayers from the Dead Sea Scrolls.[3]

---

1. See Judith H. Newman, *Praying by the Book: The Scripturalization of Prayer in Second Temple Judaism*, EJL 14 (Atlanta: Scholars Press, 1999).

2. See, e.g., Andreas Wagner, "Strukturen des Gebets im Alten Testament," in *Orakel und Gebete: Interdisziplinäre Studien zur Sprache der Religion in Ägypten, Vorderasien und Griechenland in hellenistischer Zeit*, ed. Markus Witte and Johannes F. Diehl, FAT 2/38 (Tübingen: Mohr Siebeck, 2009), 197–215.

3. For an overview, see Eileen Schuller, "Psalms, Hymns, and Prayers in Late Second Temple Judaism," in *Functions of Psalms and Prayers in the Late Second Temple*

Due to the increased presence of elaborated prayers, it is reasonable to assume that prayers also participate in discourses on identity—on an individual level, but also on a collective level. Prayers play an important role for the identity of a group, as they evoke a sense of belonging to specific groups (e.g., the righteous, the pious, the poor, Israel) and add emotional significance to this affiliation.[4] Furthermore, they confirm common values, encourage joint actions, and offer a view on the past, justifying these attitudes and perspectives.[5] Such constructions of identity can confirm already existing concepts, or they may initiate a change. Not only can membership loyalties be revised or the meaning given to social categories be modified, but identity constructions also need to be adapted as social, political, or economical situations change or as the identity of a group is challenged by rival groups.[6] For biblical prayers, such challenges occur especially in exilic and postexilic times. On a national level, Israel has to reconstruct its identity without a king and a monarchy of its own.[7] This is

---

Period, ed. Mika S. Pajunen and Jeremy Penner, BZAW 486 (Berlin: de Gruyter, 2017), 5–23.

4. According to Henri Tajfel, these are the basic elements of identity: "Identity is that part of an individual's self-concept which derives from his knowledge of his membership in a social group (or groups) together with the value and emotional significance attached to that membership" (*Human Groups and Social Categories: Studies in Social Psychology* [Cambridge: Cambridge University Press, 1981], 255).

5. Marc Zvi Brettler recently used the sociopsychological conception of collective identity of David Ohad and Daniel Bar-Tal. Their schema of generic features and content-based features offers a helpful pattern for analyzing the construction of collective identity in biblical prayers (Brettler, "Those Who Pray Together Stay Together: The Role of Late Psalms in Creating Identity," in Pajunen and Penner, *Functions of Psalms and Prayers*, 277–304; Ohad and Bar-Tal, "A Sociopsychological Conception of Collective Identity: The Case of National Identity as an Example," *PSPR* 13 [2009]: 354–79).

6. See Anna de Fina, "Group Identity, Narrative and Self Representations," in *Discourse and Identity*, ed. Anna de Fina, Deborah Schiffrin, and Michael Bamberg (Cambridge: Cambridge University Press 2006), 351–75; Denis-Constant Martin, "The Choices of Identity," *SI* 1 (1995): 5–20.

7. See Hans-Peter Mathys, "Israel und die Völker in der Achämenidenzeit: Bekanntes und weniger Bekanntes," in *Die Identität Israels: Entwicklungen und Kontroversen in alttestamentlicher Zeit*, ed. Hubert Irsigler, Herders biblische Studien 56 (Freiburg im Breisgau: Herder, 2009), 145–56; John W. Rogerson, "Die Neubesinnung auf die Identität Israels in der exilischen Epoche," in *Die Identität Israels: Entwicklungen und Kontroversen in alttestamentlicher Zeit*, ed. Hubert Irsigler, HBS 56 (Freiburg im Breisgau: Herder, 2009), 101–9.

not, however, a uniform process; quite the contrary: competing groups try to reconstruct and solidify an Israelite identity.[8] It is therefore not one but a "patchwork of concepts that make up the chequered history of ideas."[9] The biblical prayers collected, edited, or written during this period often show traces of such different identity constructions.

The collected essays of this book provide exemplary insights into various identity discourses reflected in the biblical prayers of postexilic times. They explore the role and function of various prayers from different biblical books as impetus for and as expression of identity discourses of this era.[10]

The first section of the book compiles four essays studying prayers that play a key role for an entire biblical book and its (re)construction of the people's history and identity. Michael D. Matlock focuses on the function of prayers in the books of Chronicles in his chapter, "Rhetorically and Ideologically Shaping the Narrative through Direct and Indirect Prayer Speech in Chronicles." Using a synchronic narrative-critical examination of the numerous recorded and reported prayers in 1–2 Chronicles, he shows how the content, location, and integration into the narrative of each prayer largely determine the forceful rhetorical function of prayer within the narrative contexts of 1–2 Chronicles. In this way, this chapter illustrates the important role prayers have in the Chronicler's reshaping of the new Israel for the colonial, exilic, and liturgical realities of the late Persian-period Yehudite community.

The next chapter, "Prayers in the Book of Jonah: Reflections on Different 'Israelite' Identities?," by Dirk J. Human, examines different prayers in the book of Jonah in order to reconstruct aspects of Israelite or Hebrew identity. Not only the prayers of Jonah (2:3–10; 4:2–3, 9) but also the prayers and allusion to prayer by the foreign sailors (1:14) or Assyrians

---

8. For an overview of different approaches to defining Israelite identity, see Jon L. Berquist, "Constructions of Identity in Postcolonial Yehud," in *Judah and the Judeans in the Persian Period*, ed. Oded Lipschits and Manfred Oeming (Winona Lake, IN.: Eisenbrauns, 2006), 53–66; see also Brettler, "Those Who Pray," 85.

9. Stefan C. Reif, "The Place of Prayer in Early Judaism," in *Ancient Jewish Prayers and Emotions*, ed. Stefan Reif and Renate Egger-Wenzel, DCLS 26 (Berlin: de Gruyter, 2015), 13.

10. The collected essays are based on papers presented in the research group "Israel and the Production and Reception of Authoritative Books in the Persian and Hellenistic Period" at the 2015 Annual Meeting of the European Association of Biblical Studies in Cordoba.

(1:8) are thereby read in the context of the whole book. Through the perspectives of these prayers, different Israelite identities become visible, pointing to two quite different postexilic communities. The prayers in the book of Jonah thus provide stimulating indicators for understanding and reconstructing the discourse(s) on an Israelite identity.

Maria Häusl deals with the different prayers in the books of Ezra and Nehemiah in "'So I Prayed to the God of Heaven' (Neh 2:4): Praying and Prayers in the Books of Ezra and Nehemiah." Besides the three penitential prayers in Ezra 9 and Neh 1:5–11 and 9, she also focuses on Nehemiah's short formulaic prayers (Neh 3:36–37; 5:19; 6:14; 13:14, 22, 29, 31) and several narrated acts of praying (e.g., Ezra 3:11–12; 8:21, 23; Neh 2:4–5; 4:3). She describes the specific function of these prayers in the context of the narration and emphasizes how these prayers became the decisive form of communication between God and Israel in the books of Ezra and Nehemiah. Her analysis points out that people not only express their concerns in prayers, but they also try to reveal God's will and intention in prayers.

The fourth contribution, by Ndikho Mtshiselwa, continues with the book of Nehemiah and focuses on the penitential prayer in Neh 9. In his chapter, "Identity and Social Justice in Postexilic Yehud: Reading Nehemiah 9 in an African Liberationist Perspective," he uses an African liberationist approach to highlight the oppressive ideologies of the dominant social class at the time of the production and transmission of the prayer Neh 9:6–37. He argues that remembering Israel's history in this prayer not only serves the purpose of raising concerns for social justice in postexilic Yehud but also advances a (re)construction of the Judeans' identity.

The second part of the book addresses the question of how biblical figures are remodeled by their prayers. By adding prayers to the characters in a narration, their own internal viewpoints—their opinions, beliefs, hopes, or fears—can be introduced. In this way, new, sometimes even contradictory discourses on identity emerge, mirroring the changing historical, social, and cultural backgrounds. Three chapters offer exemplary insights into this aspect.

Christo Lombaard's "Testing Tales: Genesis 22 and Daniel 3 and 6" takes a close look at the function of prayers in these texts. The verses widely, though not universally, accepted as additions to Gen 22—namely, 22:1b and 15–18—show interesting parallels to Dan 3 and 6 on the concept of a God who tests the faith of heroes. According to this theological development in Hellenistic Israel, God did in some instances deliberately examine the depth of these figures' faith. Although the idea of God testing faith is known from other Hebrew Bible texts, the idea is strongly narrativized in the texts of Gen 22 and Dan 3 and 6. Thus the image of a God who tests is underlined by the context of prayer.

The next chapter turns to King Solomon's prayer. In "Glory and Remorse: Transitions in Solomon's Prayer (1 Kgs 8)," Susanne Gillmayr-Bucher focuses on the transformation of Solomon's royal image and the reinterpretation of the temple through the perspective of his prayer in 1 Kgs 8. While the narration depicts a splendid king at the height of his reign, the prayer presents him as a prudent man speaking of sin and asking for forgiveness. At the grand finale of the temple building, the royal prayer looks ahead and already anticipates further developments in the time of the exile and beyond. Solomon's prayer points to several transitions—in the concept of the temple, the importance of prayer, and the characterization of the king—that are important for the changing identity discourses of postexilic times.

Hannes Bezzel's contribution takes Hannah's prayer as an example that shows how the reworking of a prayer may change a figure and his or her effect as a role model. In "Hannah's Prayer(s) in 1 Samuel 1–2 and in Pseudo-Philo's Liber antiquitatum biblicarum," he first focuses on the diachronic development of Hannah and her prayer in the biblical text and then demonstrates how her prayer—although it seemingly was left aside in Pseudo-Philo's rewritten Bible, the Liber antiquitatum biblicarum—has been transformed into a narrative in order to fit into Pseudo-Philo's neo-Deuteronomistic interpretation of Israel's history.

The third part, finally, addresses the Psalms. The three exemplary studies in this section point out different ways in which psalms from postexilic times shape, reflect, and modify discourses on identity.

In "Psalm 37 and the Devotionalization of Instruction in the Postexilic Period," Scott C. Jones argues that this psalm can be read as an exercise in identity construction through reflection but also through pious praxis. He substantiates this thesis in three ways. First, he shows that the term "the poor" in Ps 37 is not so much a marker of group identity as it is an ethical term for those who strive to conform their lives to God's will through righteous living. Second, he analyzes the hopes of the poor—namely, the hope for justice and possession of the land—and, in connection with these hopes, the psalm's focus on the fate of one's descendants. Third, he points out that Ps 37 is a practical wisdom instruction that views justice as being socially embedded. In this way, Ps 37 offers a guideline for everyday life in the postexilic community.

In "To Sanction and to Subvert: The Reuses of Psalm 132 in the Hebrew Bible," Melody Knowles focuses on Ps 132, which has been adapted twice into biblical texts from the Persian and Hellenistic periods. Ancient editors included it in the collection of Psalms of Ascent (Pss 120–134), and the Chronicler employed a version of Ps 132:8–10 to conclude Solomon's dedicatory prayer (2 Chr 6:41–42). Strikingly, even as they hold some values in common, these receptions of Ps 132 also promote very different programs of communal identity. In the Psalms of Ascent, the text gives a rare account of how David and Jerusalem were chosen by God and valorizes the prayer of the human community as having an active influence on divine activity. In the Chronicler's work, the text also promotes the city and its temple as the center of God's rule on earth and the people's identity. Yet even as it sanctions a similar program of religious practice and community identity, the reuse in Chronicles also subverts aspects of Ps 132.

Nancy Rahn's "Aspects of Dynamic Remembering and Constructing in Psalm 145: A Contribution to the Study of Prayer in Persian and Hellenistic Times" explores Ps 145 in depth, analyzing the ways in which theological and anthropological insights are offered in form of a prayer. The chapter first focuses on different aspects of prayer, paying special attention to the psalm's superscription, תהלה, which reveals a perspective focused on praise without ignoring lament. It then moves on to the construction of images of God and humanity, human and divine power, emphasizing the unique concept of God's kingdom in Ps 145. The detailed study of the different aspects of this psalm shows how its theological work is aimed at the reassessment of well-known traditions by remembering and (re)constructing them in a prayer.

These studies both individually and collectively show through selected examples that prayers play an essential part in the various discourses on identity. They frequently offer new theological and anthropological reflections or anticipate developments relevant for the construction of Israelite identity. In this way, prayers not only introduce new discourses but are also used to (re)shape biblical characters and even entire books in the light of current identity discourses in postexilic times.

Bibliography

Berquist, Jon L. "Constructions of Identity in Postcolonial Yehud." Pages 53–66 in *Judah and the Judeans in the Persian Period*. Edited by Oded Lipschits and Manfred Oeming. Winona Lake, IN.: Eisenbrauns, 2006.

Brettler, Marc Zvi. "Those Who Pray Together Stay Together: The Role of Late Psalms in Creating Identity." Pages 277–304 in *Functions of Psalms and Prayers in the Late Second Temple Period*. Edited by Mika Pajunen and Jeremy Penner. BZAW 486. Berlin: de Gruyter, 2017.

Denis-Constant, Martin. "The Choices of Identity." *SI* 1 (1995): 5–20.

Fina, Anna de. "Group Identity, Narrative and Self Representations." Pages 351–75 in *Discourse and Identity*. Edited by Anna de Fina, Deborah Schiffrin, and Michael Bamberg. Cambridge: Cambridge University Press 2006.

Mathys, Hans-Peter. "Israel und die Völker in der Achämenidenzeit: Bekanntes und weniger Bekanntes." Pages 145–56 in *Die Identität Israels: Entwicklungen und Kontroversen in alttestamentlicher Zeit*. Edited by Hubert Irsigler. Herders biblische Studien 56. Freiburg im Breisgau: Herder, 2009.

Newman, Judith H. *Praying by the Book: The Scripturalization of Prayer in Second Temple Judaism*. EJL 14. Atlanta: Scholars Press, 1999.

Ohad, David, and Bar-Tal, Daniel. "A Sociopsychological Conception of Collective Identity: The Case of National Identity as an Example." *PSPR* 13 (2009): 354–79.

Reif, Stefan C., "The Place of Prayer in Early Judaism." Pages 1–18 in *Ancient Jewish Prayers and Emotions*. Edited by Stefan Reif and Renate Egger-Wenzel. DCLS 26. Berlin: de Gruyter, 2015.

Rogerson, John W. "Die Neubesinnung auf die Identität Israels in der exilischen Epoche." Pages 101–9 in *Die Identität Israels: Entwicklungen und Kontroversen in alttestamentlicher Zeit*. Edited by Hubert Irsigler. HBS 56. Freiburg im Breisgau: Herder, 2009.

Schuller, Eileen. "Psalms, Hymns, and Prayers in Late Second Temple Judaism." Pages 5–23 in *Functions of Psalms and Prayers in the Late Second Temple Period*. Edited by Mika S. Pajunen and Jeremy Penner. BZAW 486. Berlin: de Gruyter, 2017.

Tajfel, Henri. *Human Groups and Social Categories: Studies in Social Psychology*. Cambridge: Cambridge University Press, 1981.

Wagner, Andreas. "Strukturen des Gebets im Alten Testament." Pages 197–215 in *Orakel und Gebete: Interdisziplinäre Studien zur Sprache der Religion in Ägypten, Vorderasien und Griechenland in hellenistischer Zeit*. Edited by Markus Witte and Johannes F. Diehl. FAT 2/38. Tübingen: Mohr Siebeck, 2009.

Shaping Biblical Books through Prayer

Rhetorically and Ideologically Shaping the Narrative through Direct and Indirect Prayer Speech in Chronicles

Michael D. Matlock

1. Introduction

Mindful of the axiomatic concept that all literature builds upon prior literature, the Chronicler (Chr) exhibits an unquestionable, heavy dependence upon the reporting found in the books of Samuel and Kings. The Chr updates Israel's prior history and provides a new hermeneutic for his community to use in facing challenges and opportunities that arise from the shared lives of faith in YHWH's goodness. Beyond Samuel and Kings, the Chr also draws upon the other books of the Deuteronomistic History (DtrH), the five books of the Torah, numerous psalms, Isaiah, Jeremiah, and Zechariah (and possibly Ezra and Nehemiah).[1] As with every faith community that must recontextualize its own religious teachings to meet new situations, the message of the Chr seeks to address new political, social, cultural, and religious realities. Thus the Chr addresses the new colonial, exilic, and liturgical realities of the late Persian period Yehudite community. As the Chr remembers Israelite history, he is reshaping the new Israel who lives in Yehud with his pro-restoration agenda.

Within the last several decades, scholars researching the books of Chronicles have moved from categorizing them as banal and imitative texts to treating them as significant and captivating texts in their own right. This study seeks to make an additional literary-rhetorical and ideological contribution through the study of the genre of prayer in Chronicles. As

---

1. Chronicles, Ezra, and Nehemiah share texts, but dependency is more difficult to assert.

such, prayer will be analyzed in both its recorded (indirect) and reported (direct) speech forms throughout the larger narrative.[2]

Samuel E. Balentine, Pancratius C. Beentjes, and Otto Plöger have well demonstrated the Chr's prevalent use of the genre of prayer.[3] The thesis of this essay is that the Chr seeks to restore hope to a population negatively impacted by the Babylonian conquest and the ensuing realities by persuading his readers to pray in and toward the temple in order to receive YHWH's favor, his *shalom*, and prosperity through the ideology of the prosaic and poetic prayers in Chronicles. This primary narratological aim is clearly demonstrated through Solomon's recorded temple-dedication prayer (2 Chr 6:14–42), in connection with many other prayers in Chronicles, by means of the literary device of expectancy and remembrance. Because much has been written about Solomon's lengthy prayer in Chronicles (and Kings), I will discuss only salient features that impact prayer speech throughout Chronicles. In addition, the reported prayer of Manasseh provides the paradigmatic means for reversing a negative exilic state for a king and his subjects. The other twenty-eight direct and indirect prayers and psalms in 1–2 Chronicles also function as a means to restore hope and to receive YHWH's ongoing favor in the late Persian Yehudite community. I will treat the thesis of my essay in three sections: (1) the allocation of prayer speech in Chronicles, (2) the role of the reported prayer of Manasseh (2 Chr 33:12–13) and Solomon's recorded prayer (2 Chr 6:14–42) in the overall narrative, and (3) additional functions of the Chr's prayer-oriented *Sondergut* (original creations).

---

2. See Cynthia L. Miller, *The Representation of Speech in Biblical Hebrew Narrative: A Linguistic Analysis*, HSM 55 (Atlanta: Scholars Press, 1996).

3. Samuel E. Balentine, "'You Can't Pray a Lie': Truth and Fiction in the Prayers of Chronicles," in *Chronicler as Historian*, ed. M. Patrick Graham, Kenneth Hoglund, and Steven McKenzie (Sheffield: Sheffield Academic, 1997), 246–67; Pancratius C. Beentjes, "'Give Thanks to Yhwh. Truly He Is Good': Psalms and Prayers in the Book of Chronicles," in *Tradition and Transformation in the Book of Chronicles*, SSN 52 (Leiden: Brill, 2008), 141–76; Otto Plöger, "Speech and Prayer in the Deuteronomistic and the Chronicler's Histories," in *Reconsidering Israel and Judah: Recent Studies on the Deuteronomistic History*, ed. J. Gordon McConville and Gary Knoppers (Winona Lake, IN: Eisenbrauns, 2000), 31–46.

2. The Distribution and Location of Indirect and Direct Prayer Speech in Chronicles[4]

The narrative of Chronicles has a three-part structure: (1) the story of Israel as told through genealogies (1 Chr 1–9), (2) the story of Israel during the united kingdom (1 Chr 10–2 Chr 9), and (3) the story of Israel during the divided kingdom and the exilic and postexilic periods (2 Chr 10–36). The prayer and psalm speeches are distributed in the three-part structure of Chronicles as shown in the following graph.

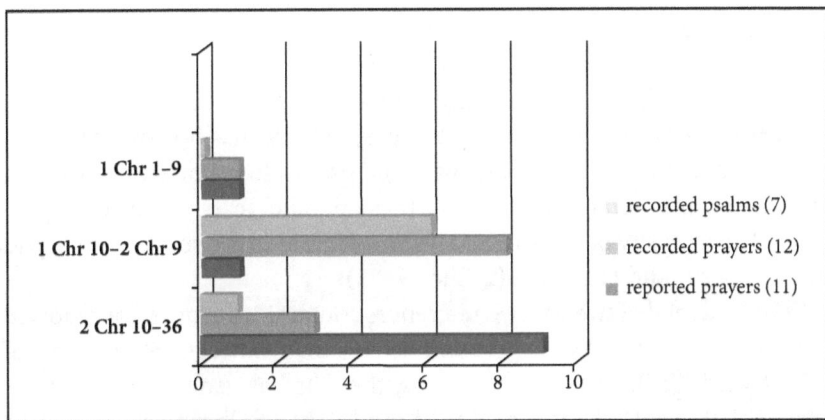

2.1. Eleven Indirect (Reported) Prayers

The Chr includes in his narrative eleven reported prayers: 1 Chr 5:20; 21:26; 2 Chr 12:6; 13:14; 18:31; 20:26; 30:27; 31:8; 32:20, 24; 33:12–13. Of these eleven occurrences, the Chr's *Sondergut* totals nine: 1 Chr 5:20; 2 Chr 12:6; 13:14; 20:26; 30:27; 31:8; 32:20, 24; 33:12–13. Thus only two of these eleven contain observable sources: 1 Chr 21:26 // 2 Sam 24:25 and 2 Chr 18:31 // 1 Kgs 22:32.

2.2. Nineteen Direct (Recorded) Prayers and Psalms

As for recorded prayers in Chronicles, I observe twelve occurrences: 1 Chr 4:10; 14:10; 17:16–27; 21:8, 17; 29:10–20; 2 Chr 1:8–10; 6:3–11, 14–39; 14:10;

---

4. I am drawing upon Beentjes, "'Give Thanks to Yhwh,'" 141–43; and Balentine, "You Can't Pray a Lie," 251–52.

20:5–12; 30:18–19. Moreover, there are seven recorded psalms, 1 Chr 16:8–36, 41; 2 Chr 5:13; 6:40–42; 7:3, 6; 20:21. Of these nineteen occurrences of recorded prayers and psalms (the latter marked with an asterisk), the Chr's *Sondergut* totals ten: 1 Chr 4:10; 16:41*; 29:10–20; 2 Chr 5:13*; 7:3*, 6*; 14:10; 20:5–12, 21*; 30:18–19. Thus there are nine prayers and psalms that possess sources: 1 Chr 14:10 // 2 Sam 5:19; 1 Chr 16:8–36* // Ps 96; 105–106; 1 Chr 17:16–27 // 2 Sam 7:18–29; 1 Chr 21:8 // 2 Sam 24:10; 1 Chr 21:17 // 2 Sam 24:17; 2 Chr 1:8–10 // 1 Kgs 3:6–9; 2 Chr 6:3–11 // 1 Kgs 8:14–21; 2 Chr 6:14–42 // 1 Kgs 8:22–53; 2 Chr 6:40–42* // Ps 132:8–10.

2.3. Other Placement and Numerical Considerations

Nine times the Chr has adopted the reported or recorded prayers from his parent text(s) in 2 Samuel and 1 Kings; twice he has borrowed (or created?) psalms to create (by borrowing?) a psalm. In *all* cases, however, in one way or another, he has adapted these parallel texts for his own purposes. The majority of the adopted texts are found in the sections on David (1 Chr 11–29) and Hezekiah (2 Chr 29–32).

Out of a total of twenty-two references containing recorded or reported prayers, the Chr himself has created no less than thirteen (59 percent) of them (*Sondergut*). In terms of psalms, the Chr has generated five of the seven (71 percent). Thus a reader of the books of Chronicles should be aware that precisely in those occurrences of prayer that are the author's *Sondergut*, the Chr's theology contains newly developed features. The Chr has created an exceptional narrative feature by placing sixteen occurrences (73 percent) of prayer on only four kings' lips: David, Solomon, Jehoshaphat, and Hezekiah. These four kings figure the most prominently in Chronicles. On the other hand, only one of the seven recorded or reported psalms is appropriated to a king—namely, Solomon in 2 Chr 6:40–42. The other six psalms are presented by cultic personnel or by "all Israel" in a cultic manner.

3. Overarching Considerations of the Narrative in Chronicles Illustrated with One Reported and One Recorded Prayer

3.1. Characterization

The Chr wrote to encourage the postexilic community and forge their new identity in three primary areas: (1) the reestablishment of the Davidic throne,⁵ (2) the reimposition of temple personnel and employment,⁶ and (3) the reinstitution and reordering of YHWH's people under the Mosaic torah.⁷ Identity formation in each area is indispensable for the full restoration of postexilic Yehudites. Ehud Ben Zvi notes, "Chronicles, in turn, influenced the balance of social memory towards an increased mindshare for the closely related themes of David and Davidic temple, and associated both with proper worship at the temple. By doing so, Chronicles not only appropriated the memory of Moses, but associated it with that of David."⁸

---

5. See 1 Chr 17:1–27; 22:7–13; 28:2–10; 2 Chr 1:8–10; 6:3–17, 40–42; 7:17–22; 13:1–22; 21:2–7; 23:1–3. For a helpful redactional analysis regarding the reestablishment of the Davidic throne in the King Jehoram account (2 Chr 21:2–22:1), see Louis Jonker, "Textual Identities in the Books of Chronicles: The Case of Jehoram's History," in *Community Identity in Judean Historiography: Biblical and Comparative Perspectives*, ed. Gary N. Knoppers and Kenneth A. Ristau (Winona Lake, IN: Eisenbrauns, 2009), 206–15. Note also Hugh G. M. Williamson, "The Dynastic Oracle in the Book of Chronicles," in *Isaac Leo Seeligmann Volume: Essays on the Bible and the Ancient World*, ed. Alexander Rofe and Yair Zakovitch, 3 vols. (Jerusalem: Rubinstein, 1983), 3:305–18; Williamson, "Eschatology in Chronicles," *TynBul* 28 (1977): 133–42.

6. Edward Curtis and Albert Madsen, *A Critical and Exegetical Commentary on the Books of Chronicles*, ICC (Edinburgh: T&T Clark, 1910), 7–17; Sara Japhet, *The Ideology of the Book of Chronicles and Its Place in Biblical Thought* (Winona Lake, IN: Eisenbrauns, 2009), 170–94; Ralph W. Klein, *1 Chronicles: A Commentary*, Hermeneia (Minneapolis: Fortress, 2006), 45. Yeong Seon Kim states that, "among historians who seek to understand how the Temple was administered in the Achaemenid era, the book of Chronicles is a central resource" (*The Temple Administration and the Levites in Chronicles*, CBQMS 51 [Washington, DC: Catholic Biblical Association of America, 2013], 2; see further 1–3, 18–26).

7. See 2 Chr 23:18; 25:4; 30:16; 34:14; 35:12; also note תורת יהוה in 1 Chr 16:40; 22:12; 2 Chr 12:1; 17:9; 31:3–4; 35:26. Gary Knoppers argues this point in his commentary, *I Chronicles, 1–9: A New Translation with Introduction and Commentary*, AB 12 (New York: Doubleday, 2003), 83. Georg Steins, "Torah-Binding and Canon Closure: On the Origin and Canonical Function of the Book of Chronicles," in *The Shape of the Writings*, ed. Julius Steinberg and Timothy Stone, Siphrut 16 (Winona Lake, IN: Eisenbrauns, 2015), 249–70. García López remarks that "for the Chronicler, the tôrâ is the great pillar on which his work rests" (*TDOT*, 15:639, s.v. "tôrâ").

8. Ehud Ben Zvi, "On Social Memory and Identity Formation in Late Persian Yehud: A Historian's Viewpoint with a Focus on Prophetic Literature, Chronicles, and the Deuteronomistic Historical Collection," in *Texts, Contexts, and Readings in Postexilic Literature: Explorations into Historiography and Identity Negotiation in Hebrew Bible and Related Texts*, ed. Louis Jonker, FAT 2/53 (Tübingen: Mohr Siebeck, 2011), 97.

Moreover, it is difficult to overstate how the Chr's treatment of royal figures evidences his convictions concerning Israel's future. Deeply embedded within the relationship of divine promise and the institution of kingship, the Chr found hope in the continuing importance of the concept of the Davidic throne for his community.[9] In the area of characterization, the Chr regularly presents striking profiles of a character's moral, political, and religious dispositions. He dexterously crafted the literary techniques of status, appearance, speech, actions, and authorial comments to help his readers understand, assess, and react to characters' priorities and values.[10]

Royal figures occupy center stage in Chronicles.[11] Richard Pratt points out that "the most obvious feature of plot in the chronicler's history is the centrality of royal figures."[12] There are three basic types of royalty characterizations in these books.[13] First, a number of kings cast a shadow of moral darkness over themselves. Jehoram (2 Chr 21:4–20), Ahaziah (22:1–9), Ahaz (28:1–27), Amon (33:21–25), Jehoahaz (36:2–4), Jehoiakim (36:5–8), Jehoiachin (36:9–10), and Zedekiah (36:11–14) have either no or negligible redeeming qualities. All of these depictions of the first type already appear in the books of Kings; the Chr has not altered any of these characterizations to the point of moving them out of the realm of moral failure. He does, however, add certain details that portray these men as even greater failures. Thus, in the case of King Jehoram, the Chr includes new unfavorable familial details (2 Chr 21:4) and an unusual and gruesome death (21:18–19).[14]

A second category of royal portraits exhibits both negative and positive elements.[15] The Chr follows the books of Kings closely for some of these blended portraits. Thus Asa (2 Chr 14:2–16:14) and Jehoshaphat

---

9. Yisca Zimran, "'The Covenant Made with David': The King and the Kingdom in 2 Chronicles 21," *VT* 64 (2014): 305–25.

10. Richard Pratt, "First and Second Chronicles," in *A Complete Literary Guide to the Bible*, ed. Leland Ryken and Tremper Longman (Grand Rapids: Zondervan, 1993), 193–205.

11. See Mark A. Throntveit, *When Kings Speak: Royal Speech and Royal Prayer in Chronicles*, SBLDS 93 (Atlanta: Scholars Press, 1987).

12. Pratt, "First and Second Chronicles," 199.

13. Pratt, "First and Second Chronicles," 195. I will remain in close dialogue with Pratt's analysis for the remainder of my discussion on the characterization of royalty.

14. For possible reasons the Chr includes these features of characterization, see Zimran, "Covenant Made with David," 307–24.

15. Pratt, "First and Second Chronicles," 195.

(17:1–21:3) emerge as mixed characters in Kings as well as in Chronicles. On the other hand, other examples of these portraits are the Chr's unique creations. He presents more balanced accounts than those found in the books of Kings for the reigns of Rehoboam (10:1–12:16), Joash (22:10–24:27), Amaziah (25:1–28), Uzziah (26:1–23), Josiah (34:1–36:1), and Manasseh (33:1–20).

Lastly, the Chr portrays certain kings in a chiefly positive manner in a third category of royal characterizations.[16] He describes a number of kings as models of devotion and obedience by excluding failures recorded in the books of Kings and increasing examples of positive accomplishments and divine blessings. David (1 Chr 11:1–29:30), Solomon (2 Chr 1:1–9:31), Abijah (2 Chr 13:1–14:1), Jotham (2 Chr 27:1–9), and Hezekiah (2 Chr 29:1–32:33) receive astonishingly positive descriptions in Chronicles. In the books of Samuel and Kings, the portrayals of David, Solomon, and Hezekiah are mixed, whereas the descriptions of Abijah and Jotham are predominantly negative. Nonetheless, the Chr elevates all these kings as highly positive representatives for his readers.

3.2. Presenting Manasseh and His Reported Prayer (2 Chr 33:12–13)

No king in the first group is portrayed as praying in Chronicles. Thus, apparently, kings who possess few, if any, redeeming qualities are also sovereigns who do not engage in prayer with YHWH. Generally, the Chr holds the prevailing notion that these kings are not in close communion with YHWH, the absolute sovereign, which is marked by the conspicuous absence of piety in their character.

We will now consider one example from the second group of kings (mixed portrait)—namely, King Manasseh, who is described in 2 Chr 33 and 2 Kgs 21. The Chr repeated the readily available positive detail that King Manasseh enjoyed the longest reign in Judah: fifty-five years (2 Kgs 21:1; 2 Chr 33:1).[17] Other than this positive detail, the Chr created an "*exceptional* sequence that as such cannot but draw attention to itself, to the figure of Manasseh *as evoked by Chronicles*, and to the messages that this

---

16. Pratt, "First and Second Chronicles," 195.

17. Although the term "length of days" (ארך ימים; Deut 30:20; Prov 3:2) is not used explicitly, the concept is implied through the high number of regnal years. The Chr and his community deemed a long life to be a divine physical blessing from their theological and social perspective because YHWH rewards the good works of his people.

figure/site of memory communicated to the remembering community."[18] The primary exceptional point of Manasseh's account in Chronicles is that Manasseh demonstrates the rare exception of a bad king turned good and hence serves as a remarkable example of repentance.[19]

When there are long parallel accounts in Scripture, as in the case of the two great narratives of Israel's history, the author has at his disposal many opportunities to quote and allude to the source texts. Not surprisingly, in the versions of the reign of Manasseh, Hezekiah's son and the seventeenth king of Judah (687–642 BCE), the Chr reproduces the portrayal of 2 Kgs 21 closely in biographical details. Both the Deuteronomist (Dtr) and the Chr attribute to Manasseh a laundry list of heinous actions: rebuilding high places, erecting altars to Baal and making an Asherah pole, bowing down to the starry hosts and worshiping them, sacrificing his son in a fire, practicing divination, seeking omens, and consulting mediums and spiritists (2 Kgs 21:2–7; 2 Chr 33:2–7). Beyond these transgressions, there are many other points of comparisons between the two accounts. Thus these profuse details of Manasseh's dismal, destructive, immoral, and evil behavior provide the author of the prayer of Manasseh many opportunities to create intertextual associations.[20]

But the Chr adds some surprising information about Manasseh. The Chr's presentation contains a more balanced presentation than found in Kings. William M. Schniedewind notes that "the Chr's Manasseh is a paradigm of a contrite sinner, whereas according to the Deuteronomist, Manasseh was the archetypal sinner who was ultimately responsible for the Babylonian exile."[21] Whereas the historian of 2 Kgs 21:11–18 (cf. Jer 15:4)

---

18. Ehud Ben Zvi, "Reading Chronicles and Reshaping the Memory of Manasseh," in *Chronicling the Chronicler: The Book of Chronicles and Early Second Temple Historiography*, ed. Paul Evans and Tyler Williams (Winona Lake, IN: Eisenbrauns, 2013), 123–26, emphasis original.

19. Ben Zvi, "Reading Chronicles," 130–31.

20. See my essay "The Prayer of Manasseh: A Pithy Penitential Text Recasting Scripture through a Vast Intertextual Repertoire," in *Intertextual Explorations in the Deuterocanonical and Cognate Literature*, ed. Geoffrey Miller and Jeremy Corley, DCLS 31 (Berlin: de Gruyter, 2019), 99–126.

21. William M. Schniedewind, "The Source Citations of Manasseh: King Manasseh in History and Homily," *VT* 41 (1991): 450. See also Gary Knoppers, "Saint or Sinner? Manasseh in Chronicles," in *Rewriting Biblical History: Essays on Chronicles and Ben Sira in Honour of Pancratius C. Beentjes*, ed. Jeremy Corley and Harm van Grol, DCLS 7 (Berlin: de Gruyter, 2011), 211–19.

conveys many more of Manasseh's detestable actions and the Lord's judgment, in 2 Chr 33:11–20, we are told that Manasseh was captured by the king of Assyria and taken prisoner to Babylon, where something amazing occurs. In this foreign Babylonian prison, Manasseh prays a penitential prayer, and the Lord responds and brings Manasseh back to Judah (vv. 12–13). Thereafter, Manasseh bolsters his newly found moral orientation by seeking much-needed physical and spiritual restoration through pious prayer. In verses 18–19, the MT text indicates that the events of Manasseh's reign, particularly his penitential prayer, were written in two sources: "annals of the kings of Israel" (דברי מלכי ישראל) and the "accounts of the seers" (דברי חוזי). These two sources authenticate Manasseh's astonishingly redemptive action and link the seemly unredeemable king's action to the prophetic tradition ("words of the seers," דברי חוזי) and the Chr's larger agenda. Indeed, several early Jewish interpreters take up or modify these important details in their writings, indicating the high value placed upon Manasseh's pious actions.[22]

To ask a larger narratological question: How does Manasseh's reported prayer enhance primary ideologies contained in the narrative of Chronicles? From a narrative-critical perspective, the primary interpretive significance in reported prayers rests in the action and framing of the prayer. Recorded prayers, such as Solomon's discussed below, contain these two features as well, but they also have the weighty aspect of the supplicant's words.

Through his own *Sondergut*, the Chr designates Manasseh's penitential prayer as the last of eleven instances of reported prayer (and specifically of the nine reported prayers in the third and final part of the book, 2 Chr 10–36). The vast majority (only three are prayers of blessing: 2 Chr 20:26; 30:27; 31:8) of reported prayers focus upon the dire conditions of the supplicant. Thus Manasseh's prayer is the climax of reported prayers concerning one's dire circumstances.

Shortly after Shalmaneser V's and Sargon II's capture and exile of the Israelites living in the Northern Kingdom (722–721 BCE), Manasseh offers a prayer toward the end of his failing, covenant-bound Southern Kingdom. The prayer contains an explicit request for a reversal of his exiled

---

22. Ben Zvi points out that "Chronicles reminded the readers that Manasseh's prayer was worth remembering for generations and, since the book does not provide the text of the prayer, it opened the prayer's contents to the imagination of the readers" ("Reading Chronicles," 122).

state. The Chr reports the king's exilic experience by indicating that the Assyrians apprehend him, put him in bronze fetters (נחשתים), and took him off to Babylonian prison. Notably, the Chr only uses נחשת within the semantic domain of "capture" in one other place (out of twenty-five occurrences): the very last chapter. Toward the conclusion of the Chr's epic story of Israel, Nebuchadnezzar takes King Jehoiakim in a manner similar to Manasseh's capture (2 Chr 36:6). Thus Manasseh's experience foreshadows the fate of one of the Southern Kingdom's final three kings, who serve while the Babylonians exile the Judeans, and the possibility of reversing this fate. Manasseh's penitential prayer is a banner of hope for the readers of the book.

Moreover, by comparing Manasseh's prayer with the earliest reported prayer in the third major section of Chronicles—namely, Rehoboam and his officers' prayer (2 Chr 12:6)—the profile of Manasseh's prayer becomes even more instructive for understanding the ideology of the Chr. Like Manasseh, the Chr characterizes Rehoboam with a mixture of both positive and negative traits. This contrasts with the Dtr, who employs only negative traits for both kings. In accord with Manasseh, Rehoboam and his officials also humble themselves (כנע) in light of YHWH's punishment through a foreign king (2 Chr 12:7). The Chr's last use of כנע comes in the final chapter. The last of the three final kings, King Zedekiah, who serves while the Babylonians exile the Judeans, would not submit himself to Jeremiah, the prophet who spoke YHWH's instructions to him. Manasseh's prayer, offered in submission to YHWH's torah, indicates his willingness not only to dialogue with YHWH but also to make the essential course correction in his behavior.

3.3. Presenting Solomon and His Recorded Temple Dedication Prayer and Psalm (2 Chr 6:14–42)

The lengthy account of King Solomon contains a convenient example of the Chr's group of highly praised kings. In 1 Kgs 1–11, Solomon is presented with positive and negative features. He rises in greatness (1:1–2:46), then attains blemishes (3:1–10:29), then plummets in status, receiving a forcefully negative assessment by the Dtr (11:1–40). The Dtr describes Solomon in a realistic manner and as a round character. In short, the Dtr's presentation balances his high esteem of the Davidic line with his justification of the forced exile. On the other hand, as with the packaging of Manasseh, the Chr offers a more positive characterization of Solomon. Solomon's characterization contains virtually no flaws.²³ Thus the portrayal of the king has shifted from realistic in the DtrH to idealistic in Chronicles, with the removal of negative elements and addition of new positive features to Solomon's character.

To grasp the significance of these changes, let us review four ideologically charged omissions by the Chr.²⁴ First, concerning YHWH's promise through Nathan, both Dtr and Chr state אני אהיה־לו לאב והוא יהיה־לי לבן ("I will be his father, and he will be my son"; 2 Sam 7:14; 1 Chr 17:13). Yet, the Chr deletes Nathan's next words found in 2 Samuel, directed to David regarding Solomon, אשר בהעותו והכחתיו בשבט אנשים ובנגעי בני אדם ("When he does wrong, I will punish him with the rod of men, with human floggings inflicted by men").²⁵ The Chr's omission of Solomon's punishment exemplifies his idealized characterization and the hope of unity for YHWH's people attached to Solomon's reign.

The Chr also deletes the account of Solomon's use of force to establish his kingdom noted in 1 Kgs 1:1–2:46. By deleting this material, the Chr depicts the transfer of kingship from David to Solomon as an orderly history of Israelite dynastic succession. In the Chr's portrait, Solomon's kingdom initially lacked detractors, and he is depicted as having a greater measure of divine approval. This omission also promotes the unity of YHWH's people. Moreover, the Chr bolsters his idealization of Solomon by omitting the reference to Solomon's Egyptian wife near the beginning of Solomon's reign (1 Kgs 3:1–3; compare with the placement at 2 Chr 8:11). The torah only explicitly prohibited marriage to Canaanite women (Exod 34:16; Deut 7:3), and the list of foreign wives who influenced the downfall of Solomon did not include Egyptians (1 Kgs 11:1). The Dtr hints, however, at Solomon building an Egyptian alliance in the early stages of his reign in order to secure horses (1 Kgs 4:26; 10:28), a metonym for war strength. YHWH strictly prohibits all Israelite kings from accumulating horses, particularly from Egypt (Deut 17:16). Thus this omission suggests that Solomon, according to the Chr, is wholly dependent upon YHWH's leadership and strength. This dependency motif is heightened in the Chr's account of Solomon's temple dedication prayer and psalm (2 Chr 6:14–42).

Solomon's final collapse and YHWH's disapproval of him in 1 Kgs 11:1–40 receives no mention in Chronicles. As noted above, the Chr does

---

23. Roddy L. Braun, "Solomonic Apologetic in Chronicles," *JBL* 92 (1973): 503–16.
24. Pratt, "First and Second Chronicles," 198.
25. Unless otherwise noted, all translations are mine.

not hide the fact that Solomon had an Egyptian wife (2 Chr 8:11), but he does omit the lengthy discussion of Solomon's many wives for fear that it might mar the king's character as an ideal king. The torah explicitly prohibits an Israelite king from marrying many women, with a goal of preventing idolatry in the worship of foreign gods (Deut 17:17). This purity motif will factor in the temple dedication prayer and psalm as well.

These omissions dramatically illustrate the Chr's ideology in his presentation of Solomon. As far as the Chr's account indicates, Solomon faithfully brought his people into a closer, righteous relationship with YHWH. The Chr excludes any flaws Solomon may have had because these flaws would have detracted from his two larger ideological purposes, dependency upon YHWH and purity in relationship with YHWH. Solomon functions as a virtuous royal ideal. Moreover, the Chr portrays Solomon as an amazing political leader in that his subjects offer their widespread support for his rule. When he summons his people for worship in Gibeon, the narrator describes those in attendance by repeating כל four times: "all Israel," "all the leaders of all Israel," and "all of the assembly" (2 Chr 1:2–3). In addition, at Solomon's second coronation, the Chr notes that "all Israel" obeyed him and that he was highly exalted before "all Israel" (1 Chr 29:23, 25).

The Chr insists on idealizing Solomon's religious leadership as well. In terms of space allocated, in six of nine chapters the Chr reports Solomon's cultic activities as demonstrations of his wisdom (2 Chr 2:1–7:22). This selectivity places the focus largely on Solomon constructing and arranging the temple of YHWH. Solomon thus provides an almost flawless model of dependency, purity, and worship centered upon YHWH for the late Persian period Yehudite community.

Solomon's reported temple dedication prayer in (2 Chr 6:14–42) forms the centerpiece of his characterization; it is also the most detailed, theologically packed prayer of the eight recorded ones in the second major unit of the book detailing the united kingdom (1 Chr 10–2 Chr 9). Heavily borrowing from the Dtr's account of Solomon's prayer (1 Kgs 8:22–53), the Chr shaped his record of subsequent events so that they could be properly understood only through the words of Solomon's recorded prayer.[26] The

---

26. For analysis of Solomon's prayer in 1 Kgs 8 and early Jewish versions of this prayer, see my "Prayer Changes Things or Things Change Prayer: Innovations of Solomon's Temple Prayer in Early Jewish Literature," in *The Letters and Liturgical Traditions*, vol. 2 of *"What Does the Scripture Say?": Studies in the Function of Scripture*

Chr deploys a literary method of anticipation and recollection even more extensive than the threefold application in the books of Kings: Jehoshaphat enacts 1 Kgs 8:44–45 (petition 6), Hezekiah fulfills 1 Kgs 8:37–40 (petition 4), and Jehoiachin enacts 1 Kgs 8:46–53 (petition 7).[27] The Chr expands the application of Solomon's seven petitions in the accounts of the first four kings of Judah (Rehoboam, Abijah, Asa, and Jehoshaphat). In each case, the kings face a military threat, call out in prayer, and receive God's blessing of protection and victory (2 Chr 12:2–12; 13:13–21; 14:9–15; 18:28–19:1; petition 6).

In addition to the prayers for deliverance from these first kings of Judah, the Chr recollected Solomon's prayer in the reign of Hezekiah. He mentions Hezekiah's prayer during the Sennacherib invasion (2 Chr 32:20; cf. 2 Kgs 19:15–29) and his prayer for healing (2 Chr 32:24; cf. 2 Kgs 20:2–3), but he only reports their occurrences. On the other hand, the Chr places greater emphasis on Hezekiah's prayer for the impure at the great Passover celebration (2 Chr 30:18–19). This *Sondergut* prayer harkens back to the general petitionary part (2 Chr 6:19–21) of Solomon's dedication prayer, in which the supplicant begs YHWH to heed the cry and prayer voiced by David's heirs. The prayer indicates how Hezekiah's Passover celebration symbolically reunited Israel and Judah in worship as one people under their Davidic king.[28] Again, the motif of the necessity of a unity forged in YHWH's people is evident, as is the theme of placing higher value on an upright heart in worship than on mistakes in ritual purity.

4. The Narrative in Chronicles Considered through the Remaining Reported Prayers and Recorded Prayers and Psalms

4.1. The Chronicler's *Sondergut* Regarding Recorded Prayers

A considerable part of what is said by characters in biblical narrative falls into the category of directive speech and is intended to compel someone to

---

in *Early Judaism and Christianity*, ed. Craig Evans and Daniel Zacharias, LNTS 470 (London: T&T Clark, 2012), 159–86.

27. Richard Pratt, "Royal Prayer and the Chronicler's Program" (ThD diss.: Harvard University, 1987), 261–64.

28. H. G. M. Williamson, *1 and 2 Chronicles*, NCB (Grand Rapids: Eerdmans, 1982), 350–51.

action.[29] In petitionary prayer, the supplicant addresses God to compel the divine to action. Moreover, the narrator utilizes this type of prayer speech to persuade readers to perform some type of action as well. The *Sondergut* prayers are 1 Chr 4:10 (Jabez), 29:10–20 (David), 2 Chr 14:10 (Asa), 20:5–12 (Jehoshaphat), and 30:18–19 (Hezekiah).

Jabez's prayer is the only prayer recorded by nonroyal person. It is the first prayer that appears in the entire book, and it is located in a prominent place, inserted alongside the genealogy of the tribe of Judah (1 Chr 2:3–4:23). As the leading prayer, it is utilized by the Chr as part of an etiological story to set the stage for the efficacy of prayer. Because it interrupts the "bureaucratic character of the genealogies," the prayer provided an excellent example of the Chr's religious concepts.[30] The Chr employs dramatic effect through wordplay with the name Jabez (יעבץ) and the infinitive construct "harm" or "sorrow" (עצבי), and the word "pain" (עצב) in the previous verse (1 Chr 4:9).[31] The wordplay indicates a radical reversal of fortunes for this representative of all Israel, from birth pains and hardship (עצב) in his early experiences to a place of honor. William Johnstone notes that "verse 10a is a model of what makes for acceptable prayer: it is a cry to God (1 Chr 5:20; 16:8; 21:26; 2 Chr 6:33; 14:11), an expression of fundamental trust and outright dependence on the part of the petitioner."[32] Thus Jabez's prayer inspires the Yehudite community by showing that a life of sorrow may be replaced with greater happiness and an honored reputation.

The late Persian period Yehudite community needed YHWH's material aid. It is not difficult to imagine the community longing for more land, since a reduction in territory accompanied the exile, as well as a reduction in pain induced by the experience of exile. Jabez's prayer picks up on a major theme in Chronicles, namely, seeking YHWH and resisting dependence on weak humans. He prays for YHWH's blessing and protection, which are major aspirations of the Persian period Yehudite community. Since Jabez is from the tribe of Judah, these elements add to the image of longstanding piety in David's tribe and bolster the Chr's larger vision of a reestablished Davidic throne.

---

29. Shimon Bar-Efrat, *Narrative Art in the Bible*, BLS 17 (Sheffield: Almond Press, 1989), 72.

30. Sara Japhet, *I and II Chronicles*, OTL (Louisville: Westminster, 1993), 110–11.

31. See Japhet's discussion in *I and II Chronicles*, 108–11.

32. William Johnstone, *1 Chronicles 1–2 Chronicles 9 Israel's Place among the Nations*, vol. 1 of *1 and 2 Chronicles* (Sheffield: Sheffield Academic, 1997), 61.

Of the four recorded *Sondergut* royal prayers in Chronicles, David's supplication appears first. David's thanksgiving (מודים) prayer is both a blessing (ויברך ... ברוך) and praise (מהללים) for the large voluntary offerings given to build the first temple (1 Chr 29:10–20). The major stress of the prayer is on the omnipotence of God over against the dependence of humanity, and more particularly on the divine supervision of Solomon and those whom he rules.[33] As the preeminent leader of Israel's past laudable achievements, David's words are utilized by the Chr to inspire the current leaders' motivations—particularly the Levites, who were taking a growing role in leadership—toward love and trust in YHWH.

The Chr locates Asa's prayer (2 Chr 14:10) in his enlarged, more balanced portrayal of the king. As part of the Chr's rhetorical strategy, he presents Asa through a "parallel plot structure"[34] in which the Chr describes a negative ledger (his shortcomings in war, his condemnation of a prophet and his resulting sin, and his unfortunate sickness and death) after he first reports a positive ledger (his victory in war, his approval of a prophet and reform, and his early years of prosperity). Asa prays in order to invite and insist on God's help to defeat the Ethiopians in war. His prayer bolsters the portrait of how he is good and righteous from YHWH's (and the Chr's) perspective (14:1) and how he seeks the Lord (14:3, 6). Thus the king exhibits piety in crisis and notes the proper distinction between human weakness and divine strength, a thread running through most prayers in Chronicles.

Jehoshaphat's prayer (2 Chr 20:5–12) appears toward the end of his reign in a military context, when Moab, Ammon, and Edom prepare to wage war against him and the Judeans. His prayer shares much in common with a corporate lament (see, e.g., Pss 44; 60; 74; 79; 83; 89). The king affirms his trust by appealing to the general petitionary section, the third petition, and the sixth petition in Solomon's temple dedication prayer (2 Chr 20:9; cf. 2 Chr 6:19–21, 28–31, 34–35). Like Asa, Jehoshaphat exhibits piety in crisis and displays the contrast between human weakness and divine strength. Asa offers a very strong, courageous faith statement in 20:6 (ואין

---

33. Throntveit rightly contends that the Sondergut prayers in Chronicles (1 Chr 17:16; 29:15; 2 Chr 14:10; 20:6, 12) contain a particular theological *Tendenz* to stress the omnipotence of God over against the dependence of humanity (*When Kings Speak*, 62–75, 88, 93–96). Plöger argued that the prayers in Chronicles as a whole show a thread of human guilt and human powerlessness ("Speech and Prayer," 45).

34. Pratt, "First and Second Chronicles," 200–201. A parallel plot structure is similar to a chiasm but not identical.

עמד להתיצב) and 20:12 (אין בנו כח). This ideology goes to the center of the Chr's message by noting that YHWH's people are powerless in themselves but that YHWH has no enemy that can defeat him or his people.

Hezekiah's special prayer in Chronicles comprises his intercession for the impure people at the great Passover celebration (2 Chr 30:18–19). As noted above, this prayer reinforces the Chr's ideology because it symbolizes the reunification of Judah and Israel into one worshiping body. The Chr conveys his strong conviction that a posture seeking to worship YHWH proceeding from the heart has a higher value than one's inability to keep strict torah observance. Moreover, the compassion prayer also contains the inclusive *Tendenz* of the Chr to unite all of Israel and a desire to help those who need special provisions in order to be included. Thus the primary benefactors of YHWH's healing (רפא) are Israelites from four northern tribes—Ephraim, Manasseh, Issachar, and Zebulun—who want to worship during the Passover at the Jerusalem temple.

4.2. The Chronicler's *Sondergut* Reported Prayers

In addition, the Chr exhibits a strong preference for inserting into the larger narrative reported prayers not found in the DtrH. As discussed above, Manasseh's prayer is the last, climactic one found in 1–2 Chronicles and was the most significant *Sondergut* reported prayer, due to the prayer's explicit depiction of a reversal of exile. As for the other eight *Sondergut* reported prayers, two are nonroyal (1 Chr 5:20; 2 Chr 13:14). The tribes of Reuben and Gad and the half-tribe of Manasseh offer the first reported prayer in Chronicles (1 Chr 5:20); the prayer addresses their human weakness in war against their Transjordanian enemies, the Hagrites. God grants their supplication, which came in response to their trust in the ability of God's power to deliver. The status of the two and a half tribes is significant, being perhaps the most vulnerable tribes of the twelve due to their Transjordanian location. Vulnerability is a dominant characteristic of the late Persian period Yehudite community. Klein writes that Yehud had a "population of fifty thousand or less, perhaps as small as twenty thousand. Yehud was therefore a tiny entity in the mighty Persian Empire, which extended from Libya and Egypt in North Africa in the west and to India in the east."[35] The community was vulnerable but divinely protected.

---

35. Ralph Klein, "1–2 Chronicles," in *The Old Testament and Ethics: A Book-by-*

If the first recorded prayer (Jabez) fortifies the reestablishment of the Davidic throne, then the first *reported* prayer fortifies another key theme in the book: the reestablishment of all Israel.[36] The Judeans' prayer (2 Chr 13:14) also addresses human weakness and the need to rely on YHWH's power to defeat the Northern Kingdom Israelites. The Judeans trust in the Lord, and YHWH delivers them as a result. Their success comes specifically because they relied (נשענו) upon YHWH, a major motif in the book. A third type of reported prayer, all of which are the Chr's *Sondergut*, functions as a hybrid composite of a royal and a nonroyal prayer. For the first example, Rehoboam and his officers are the supplicants (2 Chr 12:6). In conjunction with the reshaping of Rehoboam's characterization, the Chr includes the praying officers to indicate that humble prayers must be offered by other spiritual leaders in addition to the king in order for the nation to receive the favor of the Lord. Regarding the other three examples, prayers by Jehoshaphat and the plunder collectors (2 Chr 20:26), by Hezekiah and his officers (2 Chr 31:8), and by Hezekiah and the prophet Isaiah (2 Chr 32:20) are examples of this hybrid type of prayer. These hybrid prayers are part of the Chr's penchant for democratizing, in which the people share kingly power and responsibilities.[37] There is an interesting intertextual connection regarding Jabez's prayer for blessing (ברך תברכני) and Jehoshaphat and the people who find plunder among the Ammonites, Moabites, and inhabitants of Mount Seir, calling the spoils and place "blessing" (ברכה). No king exists for the late Persian period Yehudite community; these identity-forming prayers subtly bridge the experience of a kingless people who who need to offer prayer in contrast with their existence under the rule of a monarch.

The other six reported prayers contain two prayers with sources and four *Sondergut*-type prayers. I will briefly mention the three reported Hezekian prayers (2 Chr 31:8; 32:20; 32:24). After David, Hezekiah ranks second in terms of the number of prayers invoked by a person in Chronicles. Hezekiah's four prayers, the first with text and the final three without text, help shape the climactic purposes in the book as

---

Book Survey, ed. Joel B. Green and Jacqueline E. Lapsley (Grand Rapids: Baker Academic, 2013), 80.

36. Williamson's *Israel in the Books of Chronicles* (Cambridge: Cambridge University Press, 1977) contains an excellent treatment of this topic.

37. Sara Japhet, *The Ideology of the Book of Chronicles and Its Place in Biblical Thought* (Winona Lake, IN: Eisenbrauns, 2009), 325–33; Japhet, *I and II Chronicles*, 47.

well. I have discussed the recorded prayer and its significance above. The three reported prayers are offered by (1) Hezekiah and his officers, (2) Hezekiah and the prophet Isaiah, and (3) Hezekiah alone, respectively. Collectively, these prayers bolster the significance of prayer for king, prophet, and other leaders or prayer for the whole of "Israel"—namely, those who engage in the proper worship of YHWH. The Chr is spreading the spiritual responsibilities among the various leaders in the late Persian Yehudite community.

4.3. The Chronicler's *Sondergut* Psalms

The Chr displays five original recorded psalms, none of which are found in the DtrH (1 Chr 16:41; 2 Chr 5:13; 7:3, 6; 20:21); these psalms are pithy but potent in promoting the Chr's ideology. If the prayers in Chronicles proclaim "YHWH, you are our God," then the psalms proclaim the same but with the caveat that "YHWH is good and his חסד endures forever."[38] To the rhetorical elements of speaking prayer, the Chr adds the dramatic effect of singing prayer.

Whereas kings dominate in terms of those who offer prayers, non-royal persons are dominant in offering psalms. More precisely, and perhaps expectedly, the worship personnel consisting of priests and Levites predominate in praying psalms. This emphasis on psalm prayer strengthens another main theme of the Chr: the reimposition of temple personnel and employment. Interestingly, of the seven psalms, four (including the non-*Sondergut* 2 Chr 6:40–42) occur in the section where Solomon dedicates the temple (2 Chr 5:2–7:11), but only one of these four is offered by King Solomon. Unlike in Solomon's dedicatory prayer in 1 Kgs 8, the Chr concludes Solomon's long prayer with a psalm. Solomon's psalm parallels a portion of one of the Songs of Ascent, Ps 132:8–10. In this particular psalm, the proper resting place of the ark of the covenant (namely, the temple) and the continuation of David's royal line are paired in the petition.[39] The Chr has captured these two themes well in three verses from Ps 132 (vv. 8–10) and thus bolstered his larger rhetorical plan to promote these two themes.

---

38. See Samuel E. Balentine, *Prayer in the Hebrew Bible: The Drama of Divine Human Dialogue*, OBT (Minneapolis: Fortress, 1993), 102.

39. One caveat indicated by Klein ("Psalms in Chronicles," *CurTM* 32 [2005]: 270–72): dynasty is downplayed, while temple and people are played up in the quotation by the Chr.

As for the first and also the lengthiest non-*Sondergut* psalm (1 Chr 16:8–36), David asks Asaph, one of the prominent leaders of the temple singers and musician guilds, to pray the psalm. The psalm contains the most extensive poetry in Chronicles. This psalm includes the confession that YWHW is good and his חסד endures forever and sets the rhetorical stage for the purpose of praying a psalm. The psalm consists of portions of three canonical psalms: Pss 105:1–15; 96:1–13; and 106:1, 47–48. There are thirty imperatival forms (imperatives and jussives) addressing the reader and encouraging participation.[40] The main features of the psalm are as follows: (1) the meaning and rationale for praising the Lord, (2) a call to praise God over all the nations and therefore over their gods and the whole earth, and (3) a summons to God's people as a whole to join the Levites' praise. As for the rhetorical function of singing a prayer, music always plays an important role in all mass movements, because it ties the people together and submerges the individual. This brings me to my last point. Prayer that is sung or chanted will sustain lasting prayer much longer than prayer without music. We might call this "praying through to praise," much like the canonical Psalter concludes on a note of praise.

5. Conclusion

In sum, the Chr exhibits a strong preference for inserting recorded prayers in the larger narrative, as also found in the DtrH, but five of these are the Chr's *Sondergut*. In addition, there are five original recorded psalms in Chronicles and nine newly created reported prayers. As the Chr incorporates these many prayers and psalms, he demonstrates the inclusivity of prayer, particularly for a people now without a king but not without a cult. While the royal prayers dominate and catch our attention on a first reading, it is the nonroyal prayers and the hybrid royal and nonroyal prayers that pave the way to a brighter, more contextually appropriate relationship with YHWH. Moreover, the Chr introduces the psalms to broaden the application and underscore the necessity of prayer for the late Persian period Yehudite community, which is dominated by the centrality of the cult without a king.

The Chr's prayers are meant to encourage a new political, social, cultural, and religious perspective and nourish the faith of the late Persian

---

40. Beentjes, "Give Thanks to Yhwh," 171.

period Yehudite community. The prayers serve as a banner of hope for the readers of the book, who must submit to and dialogue with YHWH and learn to make essential course corrections in their behavior. The Yehudites are called to become more dependent and desirous of right worship in their relationship with YHWH. Through the prayers in the book, the Chr seeks the reunification of Israel and Judah in worship as one people and wants there to be more shared responsibility in this endeavor. Ultimately, the Chr wants his community to trade their lives of sorrow for greater happiness and an honorable reputation.

Bibliography

Balentine, Samuel E. *Prayer in the Hebrew Bible: The Drama of Divine Human Dialogue*. OBT. Minneapolis: Fortress, 1993.

———. "'You Can't Pray a Lie': Truth and Fiction in the Prayers of Chronicles." Pages 246–67 in *Chronicler as Historian*. Edited by M. Patrick Graham, Kenneth Hoglund, and Steven McKenzie. Sheffield: Sheffield Academic, 1997.

Bar-Efrat, Shimon. *Narrative Art in the Bible*. BLS 17. Sheffield: Almond Press, 1989.

Beentjes, Pancratius C. "'Give Thanks to Yhwh. Truly He Is Good': Psalms and Prayers in the Book of Chronicles." Pages 141–76 in *Tradition and Transformation in the Book of Chronicles*. SSN 52. Leiden: Boston: Brill, 2008.

Ben Zvi, Ehud. "On Social Memory and Identity Formation in Late Persian Yehud: A Historian's Viewpoint with a Focus on Prophetic Literature, Chronicles, and the Deuteronomistic Historical Collection." Pages 95–148 in *Texts, Contexts, and Readings in Postexilic Literature: Explorations into Historiography and Identity Negotiation in Hebrew Bible and Related Texts*. Edited by Louis Jonker. FAT 2/53. Tübingen: Mohr Siebeck, 2011.

———. "Reading Chronicles and Reshaping the Memory of Manasseh." Pages 121–40 in *Chronicling the Chronicler: The Book of Chronicles and Early Second Temple Historiography*. Edited by Paul Evans and Tyler Williams. Winona Lake, IN: Eisenbrauns, 2013.

Braun, Roddy L. "Solomonic Apologetic in Chronicles." *JBL* 92 (1973): 503–16.

Curtis, Edward, and Albert Madsen. *A Critical and Exegetical Commentary on the Books of Chronicles*. ICC. Edinburgh: T&T Clark, 1910.

Japhet, Sara. *I and II Chronicles*. OTL. Louisville: Westminster, 1993.

———. *The Ideology of the Book of Chronicles and Its Place in Biblical Thought*. Winona Lake, IN: Eisenbrauns, 2009.

Johnstone, William. *1 Chronicles 1–2 Chronicles 9 Israel's Place among the Nations*. Vol. 1 of *1 and 2 Chronicles*. Sheffield: Sheffield Academic, 1997.

Jonker, Louis. "Textual Identities in the Books of Chronicles: The Case of Jehoram's History." Pages 197–217 in *Community Identity in Judean Historiography: Biblical and Comparative Perspectives*. Edited by Gary N. Knoppers and Kenneth A. Ristau. Winona Lake, IN: Eisenbrauns, 2009.

Kim, Yeong Seon. *The Temple Administration and the Levites in Chronicles*. CBQMS 51. Washington, DC: Catholic Biblical Association of America, 2013.

Klein, Ralph. *1 Chronicles: A Commentary*. Hermeneia. Minneapolis: Fortress, 2006.

———. "1–2 Chronicles." Pages 79–81 in *The Old Testament and Ethics: A Book-by-Book Survey*. Edited by Joel B. Green and Jacqueline E. Lapsley. Grand Rapids: Baker Academic, 2013.

———. "Psalms in Chronicles." *CurTM* 32 (2005): 264–75.

Knoppers, Gary N. *I Chronicles, 1–9: A New Translation with Introduction and Commentary*. AB 12. New York: Doubleday, 2003.

———. "Saint or Sinner? Manasseh in Chronicles." Pages 211–29 in *Rewriting Biblical History: Essays on Chronicles and Ben Sira in Honour of Pancratius C. Beentjes*. Edited by Jeremy Corley and Harm van Grol. DCLS 7. Berlin: de Gruyter, 2011.

Matlock, Michael D. "Prayer Changes Things or Things Change Prayer: Innovations of Solomon's Temple Prayer in Early Jewish Literature." Pages 159–86 in *The Letters and Liturgical Traditions*. Vol. 2 of *"What Does the Scripture Say?": Studies in the Function of Scripture in Early Judaism and Christianity*. Edited by Craig Evans and Daniel Zacharias. LNTS 470. London: T&T Clark, 2012.

———. "The Prayer of Manasseh: A Pithy Penitential Text Recasting Scripture through a Vast Intertextual Repertoire." Pages 99–126 in *Intertextual Explorations in the Deuterocanonical and Cognate Literature*. Edited by Geoffrey Miller and Jeremy Corley. DCLS 31. Berlin: de Gruyter, 2019.

Miller, Cynthia L. *The Representation of Speech in Biblical Hebrew Narrative: A Linguistic Analysis*. HSM 55. Atlanta: Scholars Press, 1996.

Plöger, Otto. "Speech and Prayer in the Deuteronomistic and the Chronicler's Histories." *Reconsidering Israel and Judah: Recent Studies on the Deuteronomistic History*. Edited by J. Gordon McConville and Gary Knoppers. Winona Lake, IN: Eisenbrauns, 2000.

Pratt, Richard. "First and Second Chronicles." Pages 193–205 in *A Complete Literary Guide to the Bible*. Edited by Leland Ryken and Tremper Longman. Grand Rapids: Zondervan, 1993.

———. "Royal Prayer and the Chronicler's Program." ThD diss.: Harvard University, 1987.

Schniedewind, William M. "The Source Citations of Manasseh: King Manasseh in History and Homily." *VT* 41 (1991): 450–61.

Steins, Georg. "Torah-Binding and Canon Closure: On the Origin and Canonical Function of the Book of Chronicles." Pages 237–80 in *The Shape of the Writings*. Edited by Julius Steinberg and Timothy Stone. Siphrut 16. Winona Lake, IN: Eisenbrauns, 2015.

Throntveit, Mark A. *When Kings Speak: Royal Speech and Royal Prayer in Chronicles*. SBLDS 93. Atlanta: Scholars Press, 1987.

Williamson, Hugh G. M. *1 and 2 Chronicles*. NCB. Grand Rapids: Eerdmans, 1982.

———. "The Dynastic Oracle in the Book of Chronicles." Pages 305–18 in vol. 3 of *Isaac Leo Seeligmann Volume: Essays on the Bible and the Ancient World*. Edited by Alexander Rofé and Yair Zakovitch. 3 vols. Jerusalem: Rubinstein, 1983.

———. "Eschatology in Chronicles." *TynBul* 28 (1977): 115–54.

———. *Israel in the Books of Chronicles*. Cambridge: Cambridge University Press, 1977.

Zimran, Yisca. "'The Covenant Made with David': The King and the Kingdom in 2 Chronicles 21." *VT* 64 (2014): 305–25.

Prayers in the Book of Jonah:
Reflections on Different "Israelite" Identities?

Dirk J. Human

1. Introduction

The genre of prayer probably reveals the most intimate and innermost aspects of the self in the relationship between a worshiper and his or her deity.[1] Not only are theological convictions, inner faith, fears, anger, wrath, joy, gratitude, depression, or other emotions displayed in prayers, but facets of a supplicant's religious, social, ethnic, or political identity, whether it applies to personal or group identity, are as well.[2] Prayer in Israel and the ancient Near East displays, despite certain differences, several resemblances regarding terminology, postures, mode, or form.[3]

To establish a few perspectives on Israelite identity, this chapter uses the prayers in the book of Jonah to reconstruct aspects of "Israelite" identity/identities in the postexilic period.[4] Not only the prayers of Jonah (2:3–10;

---

1. See Melanie Köhlmoos, *Altes Testament* (Tübingen: Francke, 2011), 305–6; Otto Wahl, "Gebet, biblisch-theologisch," *LTK* 4:309; see also Patrick D. Miller, *They Cried to the Lord: The Form and Theology of Biblical Prayer* (Minneapolis: Fortress, 1994), 1.

2. For a definition of prayer, see Martin Leuenberger, "Gebet/Beten (AT)," WiBiLex, released October 2010, http://www.bibelwissenschaft.de/stichwort/19002/.

3. Miller provides a description of these resemblances (*They Cried to the Lord*, 5–31). See also Rainer Albertz, "Gebet—Altes Testament," *TRE* 1.12:34–42.

4. Several scholars date the book of Jonah in the postexilic period—see the arguments in, e.g., Hans-Christoph Schmitt, *Arbeitsbuch zum Alten Testament: Grundzüge der Geschichte Israels und der alttestamentlichen Schriften*, 2nd ed., Uni-Taschenbuch 2146 (Göttingen: Vandenhoeck & Ruprecht, 2007), 389; Ernst A. Knauf, "Jona," in *Einleitung in das Alte Testament: Die Bücher der Hebräischen Bibel und die alttestamentlichen Schriften der katholischen, protestantischen und orthodoxen Kirchen*, ed.

4:2–3; 4:9) but also the prayers or references to prayer by the foreign sailors (1:14) or the Assyrians (1:8) are interpreted within the context of the whole book. If this prophetical book reflects an understanding of Israelite identity in the historical context of postexilic time(s), then this late picture of Israelite identity can be placed in discussion with or be seen as different from an earlier self-understanding of Israel's identity, as reflected in other text(s).

This essay is thus an endeavor to determine whether or not this prophetic book depicts an understanding of Israelite identity in the postexilic period that is different from an earlier Israelite self-understanding. The question is: What does a later (or postexilic) understanding of Israelite identity entail, and how is this identity related to the Israelite God, YHWH, or to the foreigners and their gods? The discussion also touches on questions regarding the relationship between inclusivity and exclusivity in the Israelite community.[5] Was the postexilic Israelite community historically assumed behind the book of Jonah an exclusive or inclusive group with regard to identity? In order to outline aspects of such Israelite identities, the prayers in Jonah, in dialogue with the rest of this prophetic book, might provide some guiding perspectives.

2. The Book of Jonah: A Postexilic Novelette

A discussion of Israelite identity through the lens of prayers in the book of Jonah requires that one should determine the historical setting (*Sitz im Leben*) of this book more closely. It is, furthermore, important to separate and distinguish the *character* Jonah in the book from the *historical*

Thomas Römer, Jean-Daniel Macchi, and Christophe Nihan, trans. Christine Henschel, Julia Hillebrand, and Wolfgang Hüllstrung (Zürich: TVZ, 2013), 477; Walter Dietrich, "Jona," in *Die Entstehung des Alten Testaments*, ed. Walter Dietrich et al., TW 1 (Stuttgart: Kohlhammer, 2014), 438. It was especially in the postexilic period that the Israelites prayed for divine intervention to redeem them from their enemies (see Wahl, "Gebet, biblisch-theologisch," 309).

5. See Susanne Gillmayr-Bucher, "Jonah and the Other: A Discourse on Interpretative Competence," in *Imagining the Other and Constructing Israelite Identity in the Early Second Temple Period*, ed. Ehud Ben Zvi and Diana V. Edelman, LHBOTS 456 (London: Bloomsbury, 2014), 201–18; Dirk J. Human, "Sensitivity towards Outsiders in Late Second Temple Judaism and its Relation to New Testament," in *Sensitivity to Outsiders: Exploring the Dynamic Relationship between Mission and Ethics in the New Testament and Early Christianity*, ed. Jakobus Kok et al., WUNT 364 (Tübingen: Mohr Siebeck, 2014), 41–58.

prophet with the same name behind the book. These two figures are probably worlds apart from one another in the mind of the author of the book of Jonah. Ultimately, the historical prophet Jonah, the character Jonah, and the book of Jonah engage critically with each other in order to differentiate the understanding of Israelite identity as YHWH's people in different times (or contexts).

Jonah is probably not only the latest Old Testament prophetical book but also the latest addition to the prophetical Book of the Twelve.[6] This assumption places the Jonah novelette with more certainty in the Israelite postexilic period. Although opinions are divided, with suggestions for the fifth, fourth, and third centuries BCE, there are strong arguments for its dating in the postexilic period.[7] Evidence for this date include the appearance of phrases and terminology taken from late Old Testament literature (e.g., the Chronistic History, Qoheleth, and Daniel); Aramaisms from late biblical and extrabiblical texts (see, e.g., the relative particle –ש *še*, the term "God of heaven," and the reference to "the nobles" in 1:9); the comprehensive knowledge of the narrator, who engages with slightly older biblical texts like Joel (e.g., Jonah 3:9a; 4:2b with Joel 2:13b, 14a—concern; 4:10–11. with Joel 2:17—compassion) or older traditions and themes (Jonah 4:8b with 1 Kgs 19:4–5—the Elijah narrative; Jonah 2 with the book of Psalms); the dependence of Jonah on Jeremiah (the Deuteronomistic *Umkehr* [conversion] theology of Jeremiah, Jonah 3:8–10 with Jer 18:7/26:3); and a clear distance of the book from preexilic information regarding historical names, data, and social or religious rites of the Persian period (3:7a).[8] All

---

6. Jörg Jeremias is of the opinion that the book of Jonah belongs to the Ptolemaic period, on account of its many Aramaisms and the author's comprehensive knowledge of the scriptures. For him, the Ptolemies are the hidden *Chiffre* behind the Assyrians in the book. See Jeremias, *Die Propheten Joel, Obadja, Jona, Micha*, ATD 24.3 (Göttingen: Vandenhoeck & Ruprecht, 2007), 80. Aaron Schart supports the view that Jonah is the latest addition to the Book of the Twelve with the intertextual discussion between the book of Jonah and the prophetic books of Joel and Malachi (1:11, 14). See, among others, Schart, *Die Entstehung des Zwölfprophetenbuchs: Neubearbeitungen von Amos im Rahmen schriftenübergreifender Redaktionsprozesse*, BZAW 260 (Berlin: de Gruyter, 1998), 289–90, 315.

7. See Hans Walter Wolff, *Obadja und Jona*, vol. 3 of *Dodekapropheton*, BKAT 14.3 (Neukirchen-Vluyn: Neukirchener Verlag, 1977), 54–57; Jeremias, *Die Propheten*, 80.

8. For the dependence on Jeremiah, see Konrad Schmid, "Das Jonabuch," in *Grundinformation Altes Testament: Eine Einführung in Literatur, Religion und Geschichte des Alten Testaments*, ed. Jan Christian Gertz, 4th ed., Uni-Taschenbuch 2745 (Göttingen:

of these lines of evidence support placing the origin of the book in the late Persian period, most probably in the second part of the fourth century BCE.

Nonetheless, other convincing voices advocate an early Hellenistic period for the book of Jonah's origin. Both the appearance of the fish, the sun myth, and extrabiblical sea motifs in Jonah 2 and allusions to the Greek mythologies, such as the Perseus, Heracles, or Jason sagas, are convincing evidence for an early Hellenistic origin instead.[9] An additional reason for dating it to this epoch is that the Persians had not been perceived negatively at all in the Hebrew Scriptures, as was the case with the Assyrian and Babylonian powers. Throughout the Old Testament they are portrayed only in a positive manner. This perspective makes the Ptolemies a better candidate for the historical enemy behind the *Chiffre* of "Nineveh" than the Persians, because of the former's oppressive rule.[10] Thus the prevailing consensus among a majority of scholars suggests that Jonah as a uniform literary composition can be dated between the second half of the fourth century and the beginning of the third century BCE for most of the above reasons.[11]

Jonah recalls the name of the eighth-century preexilic prophet (2 Kgs 14:25–27) with the same name. This Northern Kingdom prophet prophesied to Jeroboam II (787–747), who had done evil in the eyes of YHWH. In this biblical context, Jonah was a prophet of salvation for Israel but a prophet of doom for the enemy, the Aramaeans. The Israelite king Jeroboam restored Israel's boundaries, and YHWH redeemed Israel through this prophet's prophecy from their Aramaean enemy, while the enemy lost their territory. With a message of salvation, according to 2 Kgs 14:25–27, Jonah is portrayed as a successful, nationalistic prophet after proclaiming YHWH's word to Jeroboam, the unfaithful king. Jonah proclaimed a prophecy of hope and redemption, whereafter YHWH had bestowed mercy on his suffering people.

Vandenhoeck & Ruprecht, 2010), 393–94. On historical distance from preexilic information, see Wolff, *Obadja und Jona*, 54–55; Adam S. van der Woude, *Jona/Nahum*, POuT (Nijkerk: Callenbach, 1978), 10.

9. See Schmid, "Jonabuch," 394; see also Hans Walter Wolff, *Studien zum Jonabuch: Mit einem Anhang von Jörg Jeremias; Das Jonabuch in der Forschung seit Hans Walter Wolff*, 3rd ed. (Neukirchen-Vluyn: Neukirchener Verlag, 2003), 20–28.

10. See Schmid, "Jonabuch," 393.

11. See Erich Zenger, "Das Buch Jona," in *Einleitung in das Alte Testament*, ed. Christian Frevel, 8th ed., KST 1.1 (Stuttgart: Kohlhammer, 2012), 660. Zenger summarizes the scholarly consensus and arguments for this suggested date.

The historical Jonah behind the text of 2 Kgs 14:25 and the literary Jonah of the prophetic novelette are not the same.[12] A world of almost four to five centuries separates the two. The former Jonah relates much more with other preliterary prophets, such as Samuel, Nathan, Gad, and Elijah, whose prophecies could be characterized as unconditional and irrevocable.[13] In the case of these early prophets, even repentance could not have changed someone's fate, as was described in 1 Kgs 21:27–29. Divine punishment could not have been canceled after a prophetic message of doom; it could only be delayed. This was probably the result of a rigid view on YHWH and his actions with his people, owing to a rigid understanding of wisdom teaching and the retribution principle. In the case of Ahab (1 Kgs 21), the latter had shown remorse for his wickedness, but although his punishment was postponed, the prophet's word had been realized when Ahab later died. A rigid understanding of YHWH's word and the prophet's interpretation of it is reflected in this example.

The latter character, Jonah of the novelette, is most probably a fictitious character in the literary prophetic protest literature of the Hebrew Scriptures. In this novelette, the character Jonah's relationship with YHWH, his own people, his prophetic conduct, and the Other (foreign nations) is challenged by the author of the prophetic book.[14] Theological discourse between the role of the character and the author of the book provides evidence that there was most probably a diachronic difference in how Israelite identity was understood earlier and that there was also probably a synchronic difference in understanding of Israelite identity among different groups or communities in the same postexilic historical epoch (fourth to third century BCE). The novelette therefore poses a protest against a nationalistic, exclusivistic understanding of Israelite identity.[15]

---

12. See the description of Erik Eynikel, "Jonah," in *The International Bible Commentary: A Catholic and Ecumenical Commentary for the Twenty First Century*, ed. William R. Farmer (Collegeville, MN: Liturgical Press, 1998), 1147.

13. See Eynikel, "Jonah," 1147.

14. The book of Jonah also reflects characteristics of wisdom literature and might be seen as protest literature against a rigid understanding of the retribution principle; see Dirk J. Human, "Unbearable Lightness of Being (God): The Challenge of Wisdom Perspectives in the Theology of Jonah," in *Schriftprophetie: Festschrift für Jörg Jeremias zum 65. Geburtstag*, ed. Friedhelm Hartenstein, Jutta Krispenz, and Aaron Schart (Neukirchen-Vluyn: Neukirchener Verlag, 2004), 321–40.

15. Ferdinand E. Deist underscored that Jonah as didactic literature is directed to a postexilic and nationalistic Jewish community that was of the opinion that God was

3. Jonah: A Well-Structured Composition

The prophetic novelette of Jonah is well known.[16] This story is cast in the form of a literary artistic composition and painted with a variety of *Leitworte*, repetitions, stylistic figures, and literary techniques. With the author's application of these techniques, the story develops and the character of Jonah unfolds in his relationship with YHWH and the Other. The novelette rolls out in a symmetric, parallel structure consisting of two parts: 1:1–2:11 and 3:1–4:11, each introduced by the prophetic formula and divine commission for Jonah to go and preach ("call") against Nineveh because of its wickedness.[17]

In part 1 (1:1–2:11), Jonah was sent to Nineveh in the East, but he fled to Tarshish in the West. He went down to Joppa, down into the ship, down overboard, and down into the sea and into the fish's belly—away from YHWH and his commission. YHWH sent a great wind, which caused a life-threatening storm and havoc among Jonah and the sailors. After being identified through the casting of lots, Jonah seemed to be the culprit and acted heroically by suggesting that the sailors must throw him overboard. They nonetheless tried to save his life before casting him into the sea. These events caused the sailors to fear God increasingly, and ultimately they worshiped him with sacrifices and vows, while Jonah spent three days and three nights in the big fish's belly. From there, he directed a thanksgiving prayer to YHWH (2:1–11).

Part 2 (3:1–4:11) commences with a new beginning for Jonah. For the second time, the divine commission urged him to go and bring YHWH's word to the great city Nineveh. Jonah faithfully obeyed and delivered a message of doom to the Ninevites. Then they repented and changed their wicked conduct unexpectedly. They believed in God, and afterward the

---

relentlessly ("onverbiddelik") on their side (*Die God van Jona* [Kaapstad: Tafelberg, 1981], 9–10).

16. The text of Jonah is well preserved and requires few text-critical alterations; see Leslie C. Allen, *The Books of Joel, Obadiah, Jonah and Micah*, NICOT (Grand Rapids: Eerdmans, 1976), 191–92; James Limburg, *Jonah: A Commentary*, OTL (London: SCM, 1993), 33; W. Dennis Tucker, *Jonah: A Handbook on the Hebrew Text* (Waco, TX: Baylor University Press, 2006), 1–104.

17. These artistic characteristics and features are attested to by most scholars and specialists of the book of Jonah; see Wolff, *Studien zum Jonabuch*, 29–65; Dirk J. Human, "Jona se 'opstanding uit die dood': Perspektiewe op die 'opstandings-geloof' vanuit die Ou Testament," *HvTSt* 60.1–2 (2004): 223–27.

city's people and animals fasted and mourned. The king decreed that everyone call on God urgently. God relented with compassion and self-control, and he reversed his decision to destroy them. A displeased and angry Jonah blamed God for his compassion and mercy for the city. As an annoyed man, Jonah went to sit somewhere to the east of the city and built himself a shade. In the following series of events, God provided Jonah with a plant as shade, a worm to bite the plant, and a wind and sun that caused Jonah to faint. An angry Jonah was grateful for the mercy shown to him personally, but wished to die when God yielded mercy to the Ninevites. Ultimately, the rhetorical question at the end of the novelette (4:11) underscores YHWH's concern and care for thousands of Ninevites and their cattle. The question is left open for Jonah or the intended reader to answer—as well as for a nationalistic, exclusivistic audience to consider in self-reflection.

4. Prayers in Jonah

Prayer plays an integral part in the book of Jonah.[18] It "reflects and responds to his existential dilemma."[19] Furthermore, prayer does not occur only in chapter 2. Apart from this prayer-like psalm, notions of prayer with and without formulaic structure also appear in the rest of the novelette.

Part 1 (1:1–2:11) displays three prayer situations: the prayers of the sailors (1:5, 14), Jonah's lack of prayer upon request of the captain (1:6), and then Jonah's humble prayer of thanksgiving (2:3–10).

וייראו המלחים ויזעקו איש אל־אלהיו

All the sailors were afraid and each cried out to his own god. (1:5 NIV)

ויקראו אל־יהוה ויאמרו
אנה יהוה אל־נא נאבדה בנפש האיש הזה
ואל־תתן עלינו דם נקיא
כי־אתה יהוה כאשר חפצת עשית:

Then they cried out to the Lord,
"Please, Lord, do not let us die for taking this man's life.

---

18. T. A. Perry discusses the novelette as a book of prayer in which the soul of prayer carries the function of "existential force and dialogic desire" (*The Honeymoon Is Over: Jonah's Argument with God* [Peabody, MA: Hendrickson, 2006], 109–19, quote at 111).

19. See Perry, *Honeymoon is Over*, 111.

> Do not hold us accountable for killing an innocent man,
> for you, LORD, have done as you pleased." (1:14 NIV)

On the sea, where YHWH's storm and wind caused a life-threatening situation for both Jonah and the sailors, the foreign sailors prayed twice. Before the captain requested the prophet to call on his God (which he refused to do), each sailor "cried out to his own god" (1:5). These cries for help emphasize a situation of severe need and life-endangering distress. The sailors' recognition of and dependence on their unknown foreign gods expressed their absolute misery and helplessness. They did not want to die in a sea storm and called for the life-threatening endangerment to be changed by divine power.

The captain's urgent plea to Jonah to "call on his god" (1:6) underscores the prophet's reluctance to execute his prophetic office faithfully. After Jonah neglects his call to go to Nineveh, his uncaring behavior is further stressed by his refusal to pray to his own god and his ironic absence of insight into his own prophetic behavior.

In this context, Jonah's statement of his nationality and confession of his faith ("I am a Hebrew, and I fear YHWH, the God of heaven who made the sea and the land"; 1:9) seem to be rather boastful and presumptuous utterances. The content of Jonah's confession and how it relates with the execution of his office as prophet ironically do not coincide. His prophetic conduct testified against the expected behavior of the Israelite, Yahwistic prophetic office.

By contrast, the sailors' prayer in the following events (1:14) reflects a different picture.[20] The great wind, great storm, and increasingly life-endangering sea led them to turn for help to YHWH, the God of Jonah. They prayed in fear, while Jonah lost his fear.[21] Their supplication confirms their recognition of YHWH's ability to help, his power over life-threatening forces, and his sovereignty. In addition, the sailors had been concerned that they could be held accountable for an innocent Jonah's possible death. But, their dedicated devotion, which ultimately resulted in their great fear of YHWH and a sacrifice with vows (1:16), ironically yelled against Jonah's prophetic attitude and behavior. The sailors' behavior expressed concern

---

20. Miller illustrates that this prayer is structured with an *address* (to YHWH), *petition* ("do not let us..."), and *motivation* ("for you ... pleased") (*They Cried to the Lord*, 357). Then the divine response followed.

21. See Perry, *Honeymoon Is Over*, 109–10.

and mercy for the reluctant prophet, but the latter showed no prophetic concern for them.

If it happens that both Jonah and the sailors represent specific Israelite or Other communities or an understanding of a specific Israelite identity in the postexilic period, their behavior certainly represents different and distinct identities. Satirically, the reader experiences aversion to Jonah's selfish behavior, his arrogance, and his reluctance toward YHWH and the foreign sailors, all while he pretends to be a prophet of YHWH. The question is: Does he want the sailors to be excluded from YHWH's mercy? Is Jonah the representative of an (exclusive, nationalistic) Israelite community who wants to exclude an Other faith community from YHWH's grace?

Jonah's prayer (2:3–10), especially in relation to the rest of the narrative, provides insight into the psyche or behavior of both Jonah and the Other (foreign sailors). In this prayer, which has the profile of an artistically composed, individual thanksgiving song, Jonah's deepest theological convictions are embedded.[22]

ויתפלל יונה אל־יהוה אלהיו ממעי הדגה:
ויאמר קראתי מצרה לי אל־יהוה ויענני מבטן שאול שועתי שמעת קולי
ותשליכני מצולה בלבב ימים ונהר יסבבני כל־משבריך וגליך עלי עברו
ואני אמרתי נגרשתי מנגד עיניך אך אוסיף להביט אל־היכל קדשך:
אפפוני מים עד־נפש תהום יסבבני סוף חבוש לראשי:
לקצבי הרים ירדתי הארץ ברחיה בעדי לעולם ותעל משחת חיי יהוה אלהי:
בהתעטף עלי נפשי את־יהוה זכרתי ותבוא אליך תפלתי אל־היכל קדשך:
משמרים הבלי־שוא חסדם יעזבו:
ואני בקול תודה אזבחה־לך אשר נדרתי אשלמה ישועתה ליהוה: ס

From inside the fish Jonah prayed to the Lord his God.
He said: "In my distress I called to the Lord, and he answered me. From deep in the realm of the dead I called for help, and you listened to my cry. You hurled me into the depths, into the very heart of the seas, and the currents swirled about me; all your waves and breakers swept over me.
I said, 'I have been banished from your sight; yet I will look again toward your holy temple.'
The engulfing waters threatened me, the deep surrounded me; seaweed was wrapped around my head.

---

22. For a more detailed outline of this prayer, see Human, "Jona se 'opstanding uit die dood,'" 227–35.

> To the roots of the mountains I sank down; the earth beneath barred me in forever. But you, Lord my God, brought my life up from the pit.
> When my life was ebbing away, I remembered you, Lord, and my prayer rose to you, to your holy temple.
> Those who cling to worthless idols turn away from God's love for them. But I, with shouts of grateful praise, will sacrifice to you. What I have vowed I will make good. I will say, 'Salvation comes from the Lord.'"
> (2:2–10 NIV)

Interpreting this prayer in isolation from the rest of the narrative offers a different profile of Jonah's character and identity. There are several incongruities between the Jonah of the narrative and the Jonah praying in chapter 2. The situation of the prayer does not fit the broader narrative context. The prayer's language is different from the narrative, and the Jonah portrayed in the prayer is different from the Jonah in the narrative. Prayer descriptions seem to be inappropriate when viewing the prophet's situation in chapter 1.[23] Jonah was neither banished from YHWH's sight (2:4), nor was his life brought "up from the pit" (2:6). Not only does this highlight the irony and humor in the book, but it raises the question of the literary unity of the book: How integrated into the book is this prayer?[24] Was it originally part of the whole, or was it a later addition?[25] But in a canonical or holistic reading of this novelette, these differences and incongruities contribute to the portrayal of Jonah's character and identity.

This prayer, or individual thanksgiving song, displays a literary and thematic segmentation. Apart from an introduction (2:1–2) and conclusion (2:11), which forms an *inclusio* or frame, the structure includes an introductory theme, which emphasizes that YHWH answers prayers for

---

23. See John Collins, *Introduction to the Hebrew Bible*, 2nd ed. (Minneapolis: Fortress, 2014), 483.

24. The psalm seems to be displaced or inserted. On its own, the prayer was uttered in the temple, while in the context of the larger narrative, Jonah prayed from the belly of the fish. See Perry, *Honeymoon Is Over*, 118.

25. There are two opinions in this regard. First, there are scholars who reckon that the psalm was a composite, edited, later insertion in the narrative; see Wolff, *Obadja und Jona*, 103–6; Hans-Peter Mathys, *Dichter und Beter: Theologen aus spätalttestamentlicher Zeit*, OBO 132 (Göttingen: Vandenhoeck & Ruprecht; Freiburg: Universitätsverlag, 1994); Henk Potgieter, "Jonah's Prayer and the Post-exilic Editing of the Psalter" (PhD diss., University of Pretoria, 2015). Second, there are scholars who reckon "dass der Psalm zur ursprünglichen und insgesamt einheitlichen Erzählung gehört"; see Limburg, *Jonah*, 31; Zenger, "Das Buch Jona," 660.

redemption (2:3). The text comprises further a description of the distress (2:4–5) and a situation of inescapable death (2:6–7b). But YHWH redeems from death (2:7c). Jonah remembered YHWH for his salvation (2:8) and reacts with confessions, vows of praise, and sacrifice (2:9–10).[26]

In this situation of deadly distress, Jonah shows *humble dependence* on YHWH for help, which God provides. Similar to ancient Near Eastern mythological language and allusions, this situation of inescapable death is described with images of the fish, water, sea, Sheol, and under-earthly mountains. Jonah's pious devotion is further underscored by his thankful remembrance of YHWH's salvific deeds (2:7); his temple-oriented calls (2:4, 7); and cultic deeds of confession, vows of praise, and sacrifice (2:9). The portrait of a pious and faithful prophet in chapter 2 contradicts the reluctant prophetic behavior and conduct in chapter 1. Instead, this contrasting behavior of the Yahwistic prophet evokes ironic laughter.

Furthermore, in relation to chapter 1, the reader perceives Jonah's polemic utterance against the sailors and their foreign gods in his protest against those "who cling to worthless idols and turn away from God's love for them." This is not true. In the context of the prayer psalm, this protest (2:9–10) alludes to the foreign sailors who, to the contrary, increasingly feared YHWH and brought sacrifices and vows to Him. The statement (2:9) satirically confirms Jonah's blind spot and lack of insight into his own prophetic behavior, his unfaithfulness to YHWH, and his reluctance to pray for and with the foreigners. This self-satisfied prophet of the Yahwistic faith radiates traces of narrow-minded nationalism and exclusivism.

Part 2 (3:1–4:11) of the book of Jonah similarly displays three prayer situations: the king who urges the Ninevites to call on God (3: 8), Jonah's protest prayer against YHWH's compassion for Nineveh (4:2–3), and, ultimately, the angry Jonah's reluctance to answer God (after 4:9).

After Jonah's prophecy of doom to Nineveh (3:4), the city inhabitants believed God. The "word" (דבר) of doom was taken seriously by the king and ultimately the city's inhabitants. They responded with rituals of fasting, mourning, and the rectification of their evil and violent behavior. The king's encouragement to call on God (Elohim) signifies their recognition of and dependence on him, as well as the conviction of his salvific power. Their belief in him was supported by their religious rituals. That they repented

---

26. See Human, "Jona se 'opstanding uit die dood,'" 227–30.

seems obvious, although no explicit mention is made of their conversion. The Ninevites turned away from their wicked deeds toward God.

A surprising reaction from God and understanding of the wisdom-like retribution principle follow these events. After the Ninevites showed their belief, repented, and performed rituals, a change in the expected divine decision and behavior occurred. A relenting God had turned "from his fierce anger" and "did not bring on them the destruction he had threatened" (3:9–10). The deepest mystery that connects YHWH with his people Israel is now offered to heathen people.[27] Not only is a protest against the retribution principle evident here, but also the reality of a relenting God who does not act strictly rigid according to his word (3:4, 6, 10)—a God who bestows mercy and compassion inclusively on Israelites and non-Israelites. Such an understanding of God is not yet captured by Jonah.

ויקראו אל־אלהים בחזקה
Let everyone call urgently on God. (3:8 NIV)

Jonah's anger about YHWH's relenting compassion toward the Ninevites expresses his displeasure in God's application of Israel's faith statement regarding YHWH's compassion and anger, as described in the torah (Exod 34:6–7).[28] He expressed his displeasure in a prayer (4:2–3).[29]

ויתפלל אל־יהוה ויאמר אנה יהוה הלוא־זה דברי עד־היותי על־אדמתי על־כן
קדמתי לברח תרשישה כי ידעתי כי אתה אל־חנון ורחום ארך אפים ורב־חסד
ונחם על־הרעה:
He prayed to the Lord, "Isn't this what I said, Lord, when I was still at home? That is what I tried to forestall by fleeing to Tarshish. I knew that you are a gracious and compassionate God, slow to anger and abounding in love, a God who relents from sending calamity." (4:2 NIV)

---

27. Jörg Jeremias provides this description and calls it "Jahwes Selbstbeherrschung" (self-control) (*Die Reue Gottes: Aspekte alttestamentlicher Gottesvorstellung*, BibS(N) 65 [Neukirchen-Vluyn: Neukirchener Verlag, 1975], 105).

28. This description of YHWH is also found in Exod 34:6–7 and Deut 9. See also Num 14:18; Neh 1:5; 9:17; Joel 2:13; Pss 86:15; 103:8; 145:8.

29. Miller illustrates how the prayer shows a formulaic structure in an address ("O Lord"), petition ("Now Lord, take away…"), and motivation ("for it is better…") (*They Cried to the Lord*, 357). Then there is the divine response in 4:4 ("But the Lord replied, 'Is it right for you to be angry?'").

עתה יהוה קח־נא את־נפשי ממני כי טוב מותי מחיי:
Now, LORD, take away my life, for it is better for me to die than to live."
(4:3 NIV)

ויאמר היטב חרה־לי עד־מות
"It is," he said. "And I'm so angry I wish I were dead." (4:9 NIV)

Jonah's wish to die (4:3, 9) signifies anger and aversion toward YHWH because of the latter's grace and compassion for these foreigners. Jonah would rather have seen a rigid interpretation and application of this conditional faith statement (4:2) or retribution principle. YHWH's response questioned Jonah's anger and clearly acted beyond Jonah's expectations. Ironically, the prophet was very pleased when the same compassion and mercy were directed toward him (3:6). When this compassionate situation was turned around and Jonah almost fainted under the scorching wind and blazing sun, the prophet similarly wished to die when God's compassion was cut off from him. Blind to his own unfaithful prophetic behavior and selfish in his possessiveness of YHWH's mercy and salvation, Jonah focused on the exclusion of these foreigners from God's salvation and compassion. The prophet's narrow and inclusive, nationalistic mind is underscored by his anger and final death wish (4:9). He did not want to share God's mercy and compassion with the Other in creation.

Jonah's prophetic conduct negates the sovereignty of God, which the foreign sailors explicitly confessed earlier ("for you, O LORD, have done as you pleased"; 1:14). The Ninevites' rapid response to Jonah's prophetic word of doom and their willingness to react positively to this word illustrates their acceptance of God's divine authority, power, and sovereignty. YHWH's *Selbstbeherrschung* and changing of his initial intention to destroy the city, as well as his continuous compassion for Jonah, confirm his care for all his creation and creatures. YHWH's universal mercy and compassion for Israelite and foreigner (the Other) therefore become evident through the lens of these prayers. YHWH proved himself to indeed be "the God of heaven, who made the sea and the dry land" (1:9), according to the confession of Jonah.

5. Names of God in the Prayers

It is significant that the names of God alternate between YHWH, Elohim (God), and YHWH Elohim in the book of Jonah.[30] The suggestion that an Elohistic base layer in the book was reworked by a Yahwistic redactor has not been accepted by several scholars.[31] In the prayers of Jonah, the terms Elohim, El, and YHWH are used.

In the case of the sailors, who called on their gods, the term *Elohim* gives expression to the foreign gods (1:5). Furthermore, the king of Nineveh summoned everyone to call on God (Elohim), as reference to YHWH, the God of Israel (3:8). For this foreign monarch, the covenantal name YHWH would have been unknown or seen as a more distant god. But in the majority of cases in the rest of the prayers, the God of Israel is only addressed as YHWH.

The combination YHWH Elohim appears twice in Jonah (2:7; 4:6). In the first instance, Jonah referred to YHWH as "my God," thus indicating his personal and intimate relationship with YHWH. In the second instance, as provider of a small plant, the name YHWH Elohim alludes to the creator God in Gen 2. Elohim thus seems to qualify YHWH as personal and creator God in the prayers. As part of an old formulaic term, El depicts YHWH as "a gracious and compassionate God, slow to anger and abounding in love," from one of the oldest liturgical expressions in the Old Testament (Exod 34:6–7).

In the prayers of Jonah, the uses of God's name allude to the Israelite God, YHWH, as a personal God, a creator God, and a compassionate God with mercy—a relenting God.

6. Different Israelite Identities

In this section I distinguish between three Jonahs: the historical Jonah referred to in 2 Kgs 14:25; the character Jonah of the narrative; and the book Jonah (as represented by the author's perspective).[32] If each Jonah represents different Israelite prophetic perspectives in different epochs,

---

30. For YHWH, see Jonah 1:1–3:4; 4:1–5, 10–11; for Elohim, see 1:5 (as reference to foreign gods); 3:5–10; for YHWH Elohim, see 4:6.

31. See Zenger, "Das Buch Jona," 660; van der Woude, *Jona/Nahum*, 11.

32. One could even identify a fourth Jonah if the one of Jonah 2 is regarded as different from the Jonah of the narrative.

we could reckon with an eighth-century BCE preexilic and probably two postexilic, Persian-Hellenistic-period voices. Each voice reflects a different understanding of YHWH, a different Israelite faith community, and a different relationship with YHWH and the Other (foreigners). Both the sailors and Ninevites represent the outsider perspective, with the associated Assyrians as hated dominators who impose a yoke (Isa 9:3; 14:25; Nah 1:13) on subordinates, do evil (Nah 1:11; 2:1; 3:19), suppress others with violence and plundering (Nah 3:1,) and are arrogant (Zeph 2:13, 15). The *Chiffre* behind Nineveh and the Assyrians might therefore be the Greeks of the Hellenistic period at the end of the fourth century and beginning of the third century BCE.[33]

The historical Jonah of the eighth century BCE, from which the character and book of Jonah derived their name pseudonymously, was a Northern Kingdom prophet of salvation in Israel. Later history regarded this preliterary prophet as a prophet of doom to the nations (Aramaeans: see 2 Kgs 14:23–25), but a successful nationalistic prophet who brought to Israel a message of hope.[34] This cadre of preliterary prophets, including figures like Elijah, demonstrate a rigid understanding of YHWH's word or the interpretation of the torah (1 Kgs 21:27–29). For example, the prophecy of doom, like the one of Elijah to Ahab, could not be changed or reverted; it could only be delayed. Not even repentance could have made YHWH change his decision. Such a rigid understanding of the prophetic office or YHWH's word characterizes this early form of Israelite prophecy.

Although they represent different time periods, the fictitious character of the book of Jonah mirror images his preexilic historical counterpart. Not only do they share the same name, but the latter also discloses rigidity in his understanding of the torah (Exod 34:6–7) and of YHWH's mercy and compassion for his whole creation. Jonah of the book is a stubborn antiprophet and shows an unfaithful disrespect toward YHWH's mission. He shows a lack of insight into his own prophetic office and the foreigners' behavior. Compared to the historical Jonah, he is not a successful prophet. He retained God's grace and compassion for himself when praising God for his own salvation (2:3–10) or rejoicing about God's provision of a plant as shade against sun and wind (3:6), but he was displeased and angry with God concerning his mercy to the Ninevites by not destroying the city.

---

33. See the earlier discussion about dating the book in the late Persian/early Hellenistic period.

34. See Eynikel, "Jonah," 1147.

Jonah then wished to die rather than accept YHWH's love and mercy for hated foreigners.

The character Jonah in the book of Jonah seems to represent a voice that operated in a Southern Kingdom (Judah/Yehudite) context with a temple-oriented theology (2:5, 8). Jonah's reluctance to accept YHWH's compassion for the foreign Ninevites shows a nationalistic complacency and self-assurance as a Hebrew who reflects tendencies of particularism and exclusivism. Such an antiforeign attitude impacts the self-understanding of an Israelite religious community that is exclusive. Against this Jonah's voice, as representative of a postexilic Israelite religious community, the author of the book launches a didactic protest. The character really represents "a troubled perspective."[35]

The book of Jonah can be regarded as protest literature that reacts against stereotypes and rigidity in torah and prophetic interpretation.[36] With irony, satire, and humor, this narrative functions as a parody, which makes a caricature of the character and prophet Jonah.[37] The author was most probably an educated scribe in the early Hellenistic times, whose intention it was to convince his audience through wisdom perspectives of the universal love of the universal God YHWH for his whole creation.[38] This perspective impacts the understanding of an inclusive Israelite faith community, both ethnically (e.g., Hebrew, sailor, and Ninevite) and religiously. The only condition to be part of such an inclusive Israelite community is the recognition of and faith in YHWH as universal creator God.

The late Persian/early Hellenistic period provides a suitable *Sitz im Leben*, in which different Israelite groups or communities can be identified.[39] This epoch was characterized by internal differentiation and the rise of absolute monotheism. During this time period, several communities regarded themselves as Israel.[40] Applicable communities were those in

---

35. See the description in Gillmayr-Bucher, "Jonah and the Other," 204. Gillmayr-Bucher furthermore discusses the book in its dealing with the Other (204–18).

36. See Collins, *Introduction*, 440. Wisdom and wisdom perspectives play an important role in the story of Jonah as protest; see Deissler, *Obadja*, 150; Human, "Unbearable Lightness," 321–40.

37. See Knauf, "Jona," 477.

38. See Deissler, *Obadja*, 150; Schmid, "Jonabuch," 393.

39. There is a suggestion that the book might even date to the post-Achaemenid period; see Knauf, "Jona," 477.

40. See Köhlmoos, *Altes Testament*, 214–15.

Babylonia, Judah (Yehud), Samaria, Egypt (Elephantine), and the *gōlāh*, as well as those in the Persian heartland. It is evident that Israel or Israelite communities formed their understandings of themselves and their identities in interaction with foreigners or the Other.[41]

Antiforeign sentiments surely were part of the religious identity of the Judean (Yehudite) religious landscape. These communities likely defined themselves to some extent according to their exclusivity (particularism) or inclusivity (universalism). In Judah (Yehud) and Samaria, there had been attempts to revitalize the YHWH religion in the Persian period with a view to purifying it from foreign and syncretistic influences. Reflections of particularism or exclusivity are, inter alia, visible in the discouragement and annulment of mixed marriages (Ezra 9–10; Neh 8–10; 13:25), the purification of the priesthood (Neh 13:28–30), and the prevention of Samaritans from participating in the rebuilding of the temple (Ezra 4:2–3).[42] The character Jonah had become the *Chiffre* for the identity of such exclusivistic thinking Judean communities, while the book of Jonah represents a polemical and protesting voice that advocates for an inclusive identity for the Yahwist faith community. Support for this humane universalism and God's favor toward foreigners (the Other) is evident from other Old Testament texts (Isa 19:23–25; 56:3; Zeph 2:11; 3:9; Zech 14:9, 16).

7. Conclusion

Different Israelite identities become visible in the prayers in the book of Jonah. Prayer can be seen as a lens through which the inner selves of the different characters (foreign sailors, Jonah, and the Ninevites) and the change in their behavior become evident. Two kinds of postexilic Israelite communities, more specific in the late Persian/early Hellenistic period, are identified. One is represented by the character Jonah and the other by the author of the book of Jonah. These communities with their different identities might have been inside and outside Judah (Yehud) in the diaspora during this time period. The theological thrust of this book is a protest against an exclusivistic Israelite faith community in favor of an inclusive

---

41. See Human, "Sensitivity towards Outsiders," 52–53.
42. See David M. Carr, *An Introduction to the Old Testament: Sacred Texts and Imperial Contexts of the Hebrew Bible* (Chichester: Wiley-Blackwell, 2010), 235.

identity. The latter recognizes YHWH as a universal God who bestows compassion, mercy, and salvation on the whole of his creation, while the former restricts YHWH's mercy and grace exclusively to a clearly defined Israelite group. The rhetorical question at the end of the book ironically exposes the bias of a narrow-minded Jonah character and such postexilic Israelite communities.

Bibliography

Albertz, Rainer. "Gebet—Altes Testament." *TRE* 1.12:34–42.

Allen, Leslie C. *The Books of Joel, Obadiah, Jonah and Micah*. NICOT. Grand Rapids: Eerdmans, 1976.

Carr, David M. *An Introduction to the Old Testament: Sacred Texts and Imperial Contexts of the Hebrew Bible*. Chichester, UK: Wiley-Blackwell, 2010.

Collins, John. *Introduction to the Hebrew Bible*. 2nd ed. Minneapolis: Fortress, 2014.

Deissler, Alfons, *Obadja, Jona, Micha, Nahum, Habakuk*. Vol. 2 of *Zwölf Propheten*. NEchtB 8. Würzburg: Echter, 1984.

Deist, Ferdinand E. *Die God van Jona*. Kaapstad: Tafelberg, 1981.

Dietrich, Walter. "Jona." Pages 435–37 in *Die Entstehung des Alten Testaments*. Edited by Walter Dietrich, Hans-Peter Mathys, Thomas Römer, and Rudolf Smend. TW 1. Stuttgart: Kohlhammer, 2014.

Eynikel, Erik. "Jonah." Pages 1147–52 in *The International Bible Commentary: A Catholic and Ecumenical Commentary for the Twenty First Century*. Edited by William R. Farmer. Collegeville, MN: Liturgical Press, 1998.

Gillmayr-Bucher, Susanne. "Jonah and the Other: A Discourse on Interpretative Competence." Pages 201–18 in *Imagining the Other and Constructing Israelite Identity in the Early Second Temple Period*. Edited by Ehud Ben Zvi and Diana V. Edelman. LHBOTS 456. London: Bloomsbury, 2014.

Human, Dirk J. "Jona se 'opstanding uit die dood': Perspektiewe op die 'opstandings-geloof' vanuit die Ou Testament." *HvTSt* 60.1–2 (2004): 221–38.

———. "Unbearable Lightness of Being (God): The Challenge of Wisdom Perspectives in the Theology of Jonah." Pages 321–40 in *Schriftprophetie: Festschrift für Jörg Jeremias zum 65. Geburtstag*. Edited by Friedhelm Hartenstein, Jutta Krispenz, and Aaron Schart. Neukirchen-Vluyn: Neukirchener Verlag, 2004.

———. "Sensitivity towards Outsiders in Late Second Temple Judaism and Its Relation to the New Testament." Pages 41–58 in *Sensitivity to Outsiders: Exploring the Dynamic Relationship between Mission and Ethics in the New Testament and Early Christianity*. Edited by Jakobus Kok, Tobias Nicklas, Dieter T. Roth, and Christopher M. Hays. WUNT 364. Tübingen: Mohr Siebeck, 2014.

Jeremias, Jörg. *Die Propheten Joel, Obadja, Jona, Micha*. ATD 24.3. Göttingen: Vandenhoeck & Ruprecht, 2007.

———. *Die Reue Gottes: Aspekte alttestamentlicher Gottesvorstellung*. BibS(N) 65. Neukirchen-Vluyn: Neukirchener Verlag, 1975.

Kasper, Walter, Konrad Baumgartner, Horst Bürkle, Klaus Ganzer, Karl Kertelge, Wilhelm Korff, and Peter Walter, eds. *Lexikon für Theologie und Kirche*. Special edition 2009 of the 3rd ed. 10 vols. Freiburg im Breisgau: Herder, 2009.

Knauf, Ernst A. "Jona." Pages 474–80 in *Einleitung in das Alte Testament: Die Bücher der Hebräischen Bibel und die alttestamentlichen Schriften der katholischen, protestantischen und orthodoxen Kirchen*. Edited by Thomas Römer, Jean-Daniel Macchi, and Christophe Nihan. Translated by Christine Henschel, Julia Hillebrand, and Wolfgang Hüllstrung. Zürich: TVZ, 2013.

Köhlmoos, Melanie. *Altes Testament*. Tübingen: Francke, 2011.

Leuenberger, Martin. "Gebet/Beten (AT)." WiBiLex. Released October 2010. http://www.bibelwissenschaft.de/stichwort/19002/.

Limburg, James. *Jonah: A Commentary*. OTL. London: SCM, 1993.

Mathys, Hans-Peter. *Dichter und Beter: Theologen aus spätalttestamentlicher Zeit*. OBO 132. Göttingen: Vandenhoeck & Ruprecht; Freiburg: Universitätsverlag, 1994.

Miller, Patrick D. *They Cried to the Lord: The Form and Theology of Biblical Prayer*. Minneapolis: Fortress, 1994.

Müller, Gerhard, ed. *Theologische Realenzyklopädie*. 36 vols. Berlin: de Gruyter, 1993–2006.

Perry, T. A. *The Honeymoon Is Over: Jonah's Argument with God*. Peabody, MA: Hendrickson, 2006.

Potgieter, Henk. "Jonah's Prayer and the Post-exilic Editing of the Psalter." PhD diss., University of Pretoria, 2015.

Schart, Aaron. *Die Entstehung des Zwölfprophetenbuchs: Neubearbeitungen von Amos im Rahmen schriftenübergreifender Redaktionsprozesse.* BZAW 260. Berlin: de Gruyter, 1998.

Schmid, Konrad. "Das Jonabuch." Pages 392–94 in *Grundinformation Altes Testament: Eine Einführung in Literatur, Religion und Geschichte des Alten Testaments.* Edited by Jan Christian Gertz. 4th ed. Uni-Taschenbuch 2745. Göttingen: Vandenhoeck & Ruprecht, 2010.

Schmitt, Hans-Christoph. *Arbeitsbuch zum Alten Testament: Grundzüge der Geschichte Israels und der alttestamentlichen Schriften.* 2nd ed. Uni-Taschenbuch 2146. Göttingen: Vandenhoeck & Ruprecht, 2007.

Tucker, W. Dennis. *Jonah: A Handbook on the Hebrew Text.* Waco, TX: Baylor University Press, 2006.

Wahl, Otto. "Gebet, biblisch-theologisch." *LTK* 4:309–10.

Wolff, Hans Walter. *Obadja und Jona.* Vol. 3 of *Dodekapropheton.* BKAT 14.3. Neukirchen-Vluyn: Neukirchener Verlag, 1977.

———. *Studien zum Jonabuch: Mit einem Anhang von Jörg Jeremias; Das Jonabuch in der Forschung seit Hans Walter Wolff.* 3rd ed. Neukirchen-Vluyn: Neukirchener Verlag, 2003.

Woude, Adam S. van der. *Jona/Nahum.* POuT. Nijkerk: Callenbach, 1978.

Zenger, Erich. "Das Buch Jona." Pages 655–62 in *Einleitung in das Alte Testament.* Edited by Christian Frevel. 8th ed. KST 1.1. Stuttgart: Kohlhammer, 2012.

"So I Prayed to the God of Heaven" (Neh 2:4): Praying and Prayers in the Books of Ezra and Nehemiah

Maria Häusl

1. Prayers in a Narrative: The Question

The books of Ezra and Nehemiah are shaped as a narrative, both throughout their entire length and over broad passages of their text. Interwoven in the narrative are a large number of nonnarrative texts. Along with the letters and edicts (Ezra 4:7–16, 17–22; 5:7–17; 6:2–12; 7:11–26) are various lists (Ezra 2:1–70 // Neh 7:6–72; Ezra 7:1–5; 8:1–14, 18–20; 10:18–44; Neh 3:1–32; 10:1–28; 11:3–36; and 12:1–26), as well as the content of the contract in Neh 10:31–40 and the three long prayers in Ezra 9:5–15 and Neh 1:5–11 and 9:6–37. The nonnarrative texts cannot be described adequately in narrative analyses.[1] This essay is concerned with the prayers and their functions in the narrative texts of the books of Ezra and Nehemiah. It is based on my 2010 article on the prayers in the book of Nehemiah and supplements my research done on the prayers in the book of Ezra.[2]

If one takes a general view of praying and prayers in the books of Ezra and Nehemiah, then one notices immediately a different distribution of prayers within them. In Neh 1–13, there are many different prayer

---

1. See, e.g., the studies by Barbara Schmitz on Judith (*Gedeutete Geschichte: Die Funktion der Reden und Gebete im Buch Judith*, HBS 40 [Freiburg im Breisgau: Herder, 2004]) and by Johanna Rautenberg on Tobit (*Verlässlichkeit des Wortes: Gemeinschaftskonzepte in den Reden des Buches Tobit und ihre Legitimierung*, BBB 176 [Göttingen: Vandenhoeck & Ruprecht, 2015]).

2. See Maria Häusl, "'Ich betete zum Gott des Himmels' (Neh 2:4): Zur kontextuellen Einbettung der Gebete in Neh 1–13" in *Studien zu Psalmen und Propheten: Festschrift für Hubert Irsigler*, ed. Carmen Diller, HBS 64 (Freiburg im Breisgau: Herder, 2010), 47–64.

texts. Along with the so-called great penitential prayers in Neh 1:5–11 and 9:6–37, there are short petitionary prayers in Neh 3:36–37 [4:4–5]; 5:19; 6:14; and 13:14, 22, 29, 31. In comparison, there are hardly any prayer texts in Ezra 1–10. In Ezra 9:6–15, we have the third great penitential prayer, but only the psalm of praise in Ezra 7:27–28 can be named along with it, while in Ezra 1–6, no prayer at all is cited outside the sphere of cultic performance.

The differences in the frequency and the form of integration of the prayer texts in Ezra 1–6, Ezra 7–10, and Neh 1–13, as well as the diversity of the prayers in regard to their length, content, and theology, can be attributed to a multistage genesis of the texts of the books of Ezra and Nehemiah. The originally independent penitential prayer in Neh 9:6–37 was integrated into Neh 8–10 during the shaping of Neh 8–10 as the center of Neh 1–13. The prayer is geared narratively as well as theologically to the conclusion of the contract in Neh 10. Whether Neh 1:5–11 was originally formulated along with the narrative of the building of the wall in Neh 1–7 has been a controversial question.[3] For the short prayers in Nehemiah, most observers assume that they were not inserted secondarily.[4] I assume, along with Titus Reinmuth, that the short prayers in Neh 3:36–37 [4:4–5] and 6:14 belong to the narrative of the building of the wall in Neh 1:1–7:5*, while Neh 5:19; and 13:14, 22, 29, 31 are part of a Nehemiah Memoir in Neh 5:1–19 + Neh 13*, which is different from the narrative of the building of the wall.[5] The penitential prayer in Ezra 9:6–15 was created for the

---

3. Klaus-Dietrich Schunck and Wolfgang Oswald consider the prayer to be a secondary insertion, while according to Christiane Karrer, much speaks in favor "of its original affiliation with Nehemiah's text" (Schunck, *Nehemia*, BKAT 23.2 [Neukirchen-Vluyn: Neukirchener Verlag, 2009], 11–12; Oswald, *Staatstheorie im alten Israel: Der politische Diskurs im Pentateuch und in den Geschichtsbüchern des Alten Testaments* [Stuttgart: Kohlhammer, 2009], 229–30, 240–41; see also Christiane Karrer, *Ringen um die Verfassung Judas: Eine Studie zu den theologisch-politischen Vorstellungen im Esra-Nehemia-Buch*, BZAW 308 [Berlin: de Gruyter, 2001], 135–36).

4. Jacob L. Wright, on the other hand, has a different opinion (*Rebuilding Identity: The Nehemiah-Memoir and Its Earliest Readers*, BZAW 348 [Berlin: de Gruyter 2004], 304).

5. In distinguishing between the narrative of rebuilding the wall and Nehemiah's memoir, I follow Titus Reinmuth, *Der Bericht Nehemias: Zur literarischen Eigenart, traditionsgeschichtlichen Prägung und innerbiblischen Rezeption des Ich-Berichts Nehemias*, OBO 183 (Fribourg: Presses Universitaires, 2002). On the narrative of the building of the wall, see Reinmuth, *Bericht Nehemias*, 183; see also Schunck, *Nehemia*,

narrative in Ezra 9–10.[6] But it also possesses parallels in language, content, and structure with Neh 9:6–37, and individual statements in Ezra 9:6–15 also have reference to Ezra 1–6. These three observations on Ezra 9:6–15 require an explanation of the literary-historical relationships of the individual parts of the books of Ezra and Nehemiah. The lack of prayers in Ezra 1–6 provides an indication that Ezra 1–6 was originally independent before it was integrated into the books of Ezra and Nehemiah.

Which functions fall to the prayers in the books of Ezra and Nehemiah? In order to arrive at answers, it is necessary to investigate their integration into the narrative as well as their linkage with each other and, bearing in mind the diachronic development of the text. According to Samuel Balentine and Barbara Schmitz, the following aspects are important: determining the place, time, actors, and accompanying actions is fundamental for the narrative embedding of a prayer.[7] It is therefore also important to be mindful of a prayer's positioning in relation to other actions, as well as of its dependence on, or independence from, the direct and further narrative context. At the same time, a prayer text possesses a prayer process that does not follow narrative conventions. For this reason, the speech acts of the prayer, as well as the syntactical and semantic elements used therein, must be assessed to determine the intention of the act. In the combination of all these aspects, it is then possible to specify the functions of a prayer text for its narrative context. Expressed quite generally, it can be assumed that a prayer text interrupts the narration. The narrative is structured or periodized through the prayer; turning points or high points are thus marked. The meditative pause in prayer can be used for creating a programmatic overview, for explaining or interpreting actions, for placing theological accents, and, through intertextual links, for introducing theological traditions into the narrative.

403–4; Lester L. Grabbe, *Yehud: A History of the Persian Province of Judah*, vol. 1 of *A History of the Jews an Judaism in the Second Temple Period*, LSTS 47 (London: T&T Clark, 2004), 79–80. H. G. M. Williamson, Jacob L. Wright, and Wolfgang Oswald, on the other hand, are of the opinion that a narrative about rebuilding the wall was transformed into a report about Judah's restoration by the addition of various extensions (Williamson, *Ezra, Nehemiah*, WBC 16 [Waco, TX: Word, 1985], xxvi–xxvii; Wright, *Rebuilding Identity*, 340; Oswald, *Staatstheorie*, 229–30).

6. See below; see also Williamson, *Ezra, Nehemiah*, 128.

7. Samuel E. Balentine, *Prayer in the Hebrew Bible: The Drama of Divine-Human Dialogue*, OBT (Minneapolis: Fortress, 1993); Schmitz, *Gedeutete Geschichte*.

2. Discussions in Research

In "Prayer as Rhetoric in the book of Nehemiah," Mark J. Boda is governed by an interest similar to that of this present chapter.[8] He, however, characterizes the prayers exclusively as speech acts in a narrative context and, for this reason, perceives the prayers as "direct, declarative and dramatic narrative." In this way, though, he is not successful in working out the specific functions of prayers, which are differentiated from other direct speeches, and the linkages of the prayer texts among themselves.

At present, Boda's article and my 2010 article represent the only studies devoted to all the acts of prayer in the books of Ezra and Nehemiah; in other cases either the three "great" penitential prayers in Ezra 9:6–15, Neh 1:5–11, and 9:6–37 or the *zkr*-prayers in the book of Nehemiah are treated.

The texts in in Ezra 9:6–15, Neh 1:5–11, and 9:6–37 have been investigated many times under the title of "postexilic penitential prayers." Here, most articles concentrate either on the determination of the genre penitential prayer, on the question about the *Sitz im Leben*, or on the traditions and texts that are received.[9] Nehemiah 1:5–11 is not considered unanimously to be a penitential prayer.[10] For the question of genre, Dan 9:4–19,

---

8. Mark J. Boda, "Prayer as Rhetoric in the Book of Nehemiah," in *New Perspectives on Ezra-Nehemiah: History and Historiography, Text, Literature, and Interpretation*, ed. Isaac Kalimi (Winona Lake: Eisenbrauns, 2012), 267–84.

9. E.g., Klaus Zastrow, "Die drei großen Bußgebete von Ezra 9, Nehemia 9 und Daniel 9" (PhD diss., University of Heidelberg, 1998); Rodney A. Werline, *Penitential Prayer in Second Temple Judaism: The Development of a Religious Institution*, EJL 13 (Atlanta: Scholars Press, 1998); Mark J. Boda, *Praying the Tradition: The Origin and Use of Tradition in Nehemiah 9*, BZAW 277 (Berlin: de Gruyter, 1999); Michael W. Duggan, *The Covenant Renewal in Ezra-Nehemiah (Neh 7:72b-10:40): An Exegetical, Literary and Theological Study*, SBLDS 164 (Atlanta: Society of Biblical Literature, 2001); Richard J. Bautch, *Developments in Genre between Post-exilic Penitential Prayers and the Psalms of Communal Lament*, AcBib 7 (Atlanta: Society of Biblical Literature, 2003); Mark J. Boda, Daniel K. Falk, and Rodney A. Werline, eds., *The Origins of Penitential Prayer in Second Temple Judaism*, vol. 1 of *Seeking the Favor of God*, ed. Mark J. Boda, Daniel K. Falk, and Rodney A. Werline (Atlanta: Society of Biblical Literature, 2006).

10. Zastrow and Boda classify Neh 1:5–11 as a penitential prayer (Zastrow, "Drei großen Bußgebete," 180–83; Boda, *Praying the Tradition*, 28). Schunck places Neh 1:5–11 in the "transition from the lamentation to the penitential prayer" (*Nehemia*, 13). Karrer and Talstra, on the other hand, do not see the confession of guilt as the central function of the prayer (see below) (Karrer, *Ringen*, 199–207; Eep Talstra, "The

Ps 106, and Ps 136 are used for comparison. The genre of the penitential prayer is contrasted with the genre of communal lament, whereby the origin of the penitential prayer is placed temporally after the communal lament.[11] In contrast to the communal lament, the explicit confession of sin is often considered a characteristic trait of a penitential prayer. The precondition for this is the production of a theological connection between the sinfulness of the previous generation and the confession of sin by the present generation. The prayer itself is understood as an act of penitence. In part, a specific *Sitz im Leben* is postulated for the penitential prayer. Boda, for example, assumes for this a postexilic covenant ceremony.[12]

Since my concern in this essay is the *Sitz* in the literature—that is, the function of the prayers in their literary context—it will be important to examine whether the function of penitence is also displayed by its contextual embedding and is continued in the narrative sphere. Michael W. Duggan, who investigates the literary contexts of the penitential prayers, assesses the three penitential prayers in Ezra and Nehemiah as follows: "The three penitential prayers in Ezra-Nehemiah (Ezra 9:6–15; Neh 1:5–11; Neh 9:6–37) function as keys for interpreting the whole narrative from a theological perspective."[13] Also of interest is the question of which traditions and which texts are received for the three prayers in Ezra 9:6–15, Neh

---

Discourse of Praying: Reading Nehemiah 1," in *Psalms and Prayers: Papers Read at the Joint Meeting of the Society of Old Testament Study and het Oudtestamentisch Werkgezelschap in Nederland en België, Apeldoorn August 2006*, ed. Bob Becking and Eric Peels, OtSt 55 [Leiden: Brill, 2007], 219–36).

11. Bautch compares the penitential prayer, for example, with Isa 63:7–64:11 (*Developments in Genre*). On the centrality of the confession of guilt in the postexilic period, see Erhard Gerstenberger, *Israel in der Perserzeit: 5. und 4. Jahrhundert v. Chr.*, BE 8 (Stuttgart: Kohlhammer, 2005), 192.

12. Boda, *Praying the Tradition*, 32–38, 40–41. Critical of this are Bob Becking, Erhard Gerstenberger, and Othmar Keel, who think rather of an exilic-postexilic supplication and lament ceremony (Becking, "Nehemiah 9 and the Problematic Concept of Context," in *The Changing Face of Form Criticism for the Twenty-First Century*, ed. Marvin A. Sweeney and Ehud Ben Zvi [Grand Rapids: Eerdmans, 2003], 253–65; Gerstenberger, *Israel in der Perserzeit*, 24; Keel, *Die Geschichte Jerusalems und die Entstehung des Monotheismus*, vol. 2 of *Orte und Landschaften der Bibel*, ed. Othmar Keel, Max Küchler, and Christoph Uehlinger [Göttingen: Vandenhoeck & Ruprecht, 2007], 1075).

13. Michael W. Duggan, "Ezra 9:6–15: A Penitential Prayer within its Literary Setting," in Boda, Falk, and Werline, *Origins of Penitential Prayer*, 165; see also Duggan, *Covenant Renewal*, 120.

1:5–11, and 9:6–37. Deuteronomistic terminology and theology, though, is undisputed here. In addition, Boda draws attention to the Ezekiel and priestly traditions, which are verifiable, above all, in Neh 9:6–37.[14]

The short prayers in Neh 3:36–37 [4:4–5]; 5:19; 6:14; and 13:14, 22, 29, 31, which, with the exception of Neh 3:36–37 [4:4–5], are formulated as *zkr*-prayers, are often seen as evidence for the literary unity of the texts in the book of Nehemiah that are formulated in the first-person. They are, in the final analysis, also crucial for the determination of the genre of the book of Nehemiah, or parts of it, as a *memorandum*. The designation Nehemiah Memoir was used for the first time by Sigmund Mowinckel, who sees in the ancient oriental inscriptions for kings and princes the closest literary and tradition-historical parallels to the genre otherwise not represented in the Old Testament.[15] The suggestion by Gerhard von Rad to draw upon the biographical inscriptions on the stelae for Egyptian public officials from the later period in the history of Egypt (the Twenty-Second Dynasty of Egypt until the Roman period) as the closest analogies runs in a similar direction.[16] Kurt Galling and Willy Schottroff, on the other hand, are of the opinion that Nehemiah's self-report is comparable to a foundation inscription like those known from the later Aramaic and Nabataean spheres.[17] None of the suggested extrabiblical genres, however, are completely convincing as a literary model. The formal differences and the differences in the contexts of usage are too great.[18] As already discussed above, a unified memorandum that encompasses all the texts in the book of Nehemiah formulated in the first-person, as well as the short prayers, is no longer postulated today by all researchers as a characteristic trait of the book. If one distinguishes between a narrative about the building of the wall (Neh 1–7) and a "memoir" in the narrow sense (Neh 5 + Neh 13:4–31*), however, then the connectedness of the short prayers in Neh 3:36–37 [4:4–5] and 6:14 with the *zkr*-prayers in Neh 5:19; and 13:14, 22, 29, 31 must be explained in a diachronic sense.

---

14. Boda, *Praying the Tradition*, 186–87.

15. See Sigmund Mowinckel, *Die Nehemia-Denkschrift*, vol. 2 of *Studien zu dem Buche Ezra-Nehemia*, HFK 5 (Oslo: Univeritetsforlaget, 1964), 52–86.

16. See Gerhard von Rad, "Die Nehemia-Denkschrift," *ZAW* 76 (1964): 176–87.

17. See Kurt Galling, *Die Bücher der Chronik, Esra, Nehemia*, ATD 12 (Göttingen: Vandenhoeck & Ruprecht, 1954), 134–42, 227 and 253; Willy Schottroff, *"Gedenken" im Alten Orient und im Alten Testament: Die Wurzel Zākar im semitischen Sprachkreis*, WMANT 15 (Neukirchen-Vluyn: Neukirchener Verlag, 1964), 68–88.

18. See also Karrer, *Ringen*, 142–47.

"So I Prayed to the God of Heaven" (Neh 2:4)   59

Since the short prayers of petition are addressed to God, God also appears as the addressee of the surrounding narrative passages. But, it is seldom the case that the self-report by Nehemiah—whether in the narrow or the broader sense—is classified for this reason as a genuine prayer by an accused person.[19] The short prayers create much more than the fiction that Nehemiah "provides a written account to his God about his conduct and his decisions in Jerusalem.... The personal style and the interposed calls to prayer—apparently are to stand surely for the authenticity of the document."[20]

3. Prayer Is Decisive: A Passage through the Texts

The following section investigates the prayer texts in the books of Ezra and Nehemiah according to their function in each narrative context. The procedure here is oriented toward the kind of interruption of the narrative context. Thus a distinction is drawn between the long prayers in Neh 1:5–11; 9:6–37 and Ezra 9:6–15, on the one hand, and the short psalm of praise text in Ezra 7:27–28 as well as the short petitionary prayers in Neh 3:36–37 [4:4–5]; 5:19; 6:14; and 13:14, 22, 29, 31, on the other. In order to obtain a comprehensive picture of the function of praying or of the prayers, those text passages that speak of praying but do not cite any prayer or only a short call to prayer will also be examined.

3.1. Praying as Narrated Action

As is to be expected, prayer practices are mentioned as a part of ritual-cultic actions. But along with these, there are also prayer practices in the book of Nehemiah without such a framework.

At the celebration described in Ezra 3:10–13 on the occasion of the laying of the foundation of the temple, the participation of the people and their particular joy during the celebration are emphasized. On the other hand, no sacrificial actions are mentioned, although the altar had already been put into use in Ezra 3:3. The joy of the people (רוע *hiphil*, רום *hiphil*) is expressed also in the praise of YHWH (הלל *piel*, ידה *hiphil*), which is supported by music (trumpets and cymbals) and is cited explicitly: כי טוב כי

---

19. E.g., Ulrich Kellermann, *Nehemia: Quellen, Überlieferung und Geschichte*, BZAW 102 (Berlin: de Gruyter, 1967), 82–84; see also Schunck, *Nehemia*, 406.
20. Gerstenberger, *Israel in der Perserzeit*, 81.

לעולם חסדו על ישראל.²¹ According to Christiane Karrer-Grube, the proximity to Jer 33:11 is significant, since the psalm of praise stands in each case in the context of a reconstruction. In the books of Ezra and Nehemiah, the praise text has no parallels, but the celebratory joy points far beyond Ezra 1–6, for it is found also in the double celebration of the reading of the torah with the subsequent Feast of the Tabernacles in Neh 8:9–18 and above all on the occasion of the dedication of the city wall in Neh 12:27–43. With the aid of this celebratory joy, a "great arc is inscribed from the first foundation of the temple to the dedication of the completed city wall."²²

On the occasion of the public reading of the torah, prayer practices precede the actual reading. In Neh 8:6, Ezra speaks a psalm of praise (ברך *piel*) directed to God, which the people confirm. The answer "Amen, Amen!" is accompanied by the gesture of raising the hands (מעל ידים), and there follows a low bow (קדד) and the act of falling face down (חוה *hishtaphal*) on the ground.²³ Striking is the fact that YHWH is mentioned as the object of the veneration, although the action does not take place in the temple or in the forecourt of the temple. It is worth considering here whether YHWH is represented by the book of the torah.²⁴

The dedication of the city wall in Neh 12:27–43 is celebrated with music and song, just as is the laying of the foundation of the temple in Ezra 3:10–13. The purification of the wall by the priests and Levites (Neh 12:30) and the offering of sacrifices (Neh 12:43) also are mentioned briefly. The decisive action, however, falls to two large choirs of thanksgiving or festive processions (תודות גדולות ותהלכות) that consist of singers and musicians (Neh 12:27, 29, 31, 42). They pace off the length of the entire wall and introduce the sacrificial acts with their song and music. The heavily emphasized role of the singers and musicians corresponds to their role in

---

21. Christiane Karrer-Grube, "Scrutinizing the Conceptual Unity of Ezra and Nehemiah," in *Unity and Disunity in Ezra-Nehemiah: Redaction, Rhetoric, and Reader*, ed. Mark J. Boda und Paul L. Redditt, HBM 17 (Sheffield: Sheffield Phoenix, 2008), 136–59; see also Pss 100:5; 103:17; 106:1; 107:1; 118:1, 3, 4. Reference might be made to the celebrations in the books of the Chronicles, which likewise are strongly marked by the joy of celebration: 1 Chr 16:34, 41; 2 Chr 5:13; 7:3, 6; 20:21.

22. Karrer, *Ringen*, 362.

23. Comparable prayer gestures also introduce or frame the two penitential prayers in Ezra 9:6–15 and Neh 9:6–37; in Ezra 9:5; 10:1; and Neh 9:3, 5, it is spoken of as the spreading of the hands, as prostration (on the knees), and as a call for praise (see below).

24. See also Neh 9:3.

the regular temple service as described otherwise in the book of Nehemiah (10:40; 11:17, 23; 12:8, 24, 45–47; 13:10).

Prayer practices are mentioned, though, not only in regard to feasts but also together with other ritual acts. In the edict of Darius in Ezra 6:6–12, Darius decrees the provision of the Jerusalem temple with sacrificial animals paid for from the king's treasury (6:9) in order to ensure the sacrifices for the God of heaven and the prayers (צלה *piel*) for the life of the king and his sons in the temple (6:10).

Fasting, briefly described and justified in Ezra 8:21–23, also belongs to the preparations for Ezra's journey to Jerusalem. The two acts of fasting (צום) (8:21, 23) and the self-deprecating bow (ענה *hithpael*; 8:21) are also found in Isa 58:3 and Neh 9:1–2, where in each case penitential rituals or laments[25] are described. The petition to God (בקש *piel*; Ezra 8:21, 23) for a smooth way (cf. Isa 40:3) is supported in Ezra 8:21 with these actions. The petitionary prayer is not cited; instead, one learns that Ezra has declined the protection of the king in the form of a military escort and has justified this with the protection afforded by God during the journey. This statement to the king is quoted directly in Ezra 8:22: "The hand of our God is gracious to all who seek him, but his power and his wrath are against all who forsake him" (NRSV). This confession expresses a fundamental conviction inherent in all the petitionary prayers, even if it possesses no direct parallels in the Psalms. Ezra 8:23 then also verifies the fact that God has heard the petition (עתר *niphal*). In Ezra 8:31, Ezra is confirmed once again through the first-person narrator. The quoted confession and the narrative thus agree with each other in their statements that God protects those who ask him for protection.

In addition, Ezra 8:21–23 refers back to the psalm of praise in Ezra 7:27–28, which introduces Ezra's preparations for the journey.[26] Ezra 8:21–23 also has a linguistic and factual proximity to the narrative of the building of the wall in Neh 1:1–7:3. Ezra prays and fasts before his journey, just as Nehemiah also prays and fasts (Ezra 7:27–28; Neh 1:4). The problem of protection on the journey is raised in both narratives. In contrast to Nehemiah, Ezra does without the royal protection during his journey (Ezra 8:21–22; Neh 2:7–9). The hand of God is over both of them for good. The idiom כיד אלהים על "because the hand of God was upon" establishes a

---

25. See also Zech 7:1–14 and 8:18–19.
26. See below.

close linguistic connection between Ezra 7–8 and Neh 1:1–7:3 (Ezra 7:6, 9, 28; 8:18, 22, 31; Neh 2:8, 18).[27]

Therewith, we are referred to Nehemiah's narrative of the building of the wall, and the question arises of how prayer is integrated into Neh 1:1–7:3. Praying (פלל hithpael) is spoken of in the narrative passages Neh 2:4–5 and 4:3 [4:9] without this activity taking place in a cultic context and without a prayer being cited. The prayer of Nehemiah in Neh 2:4 precedes Nehemiah's answer to the king's question about what Nehemiah intends to do. Before Nehemiah communicates to the king his intention of wanting to rebuild the city of Jerusalem, he prays to the God of heaven. His prayer lets his intention of building appear as motivated and initiated by God and is in its function comparable to an explicit commission from God. It appears to replace a narrative strategy, which would let God speak and act in the narrative world. In Neh 2:12, Nehemiah then tells the authorities that God has put into his heart what he should do for Jerusalem.[28] Nehemiah's intention, expressed before the king, is known to the readers from Neh 2:5. For this reason, a preceding commission by God can be concealed in the prayer in Neh 2:4. The praying in Neh 2:4 thus marks the beginning of the solution to the problem and leads Nehemiah's initiative back to communication with God, or to God's commandment.[29]

The defense against the planned attacks of the enemies begins in a similar manner in Neh 4:3 [4:9] with the prayers (פלל hithpael) of the builders in Jerusalem. Thus the subsequent defense of the city here, too, is attributed to prayer and therewith indirectly to God's intervention. The scene in Neh 4:9–17 [4:15–23] shows a comparable structure when in Neh 4:9 [4:15] the actions of the enemies, in Neh 4:10 [4:16] the actions of the builders, and between them in Neh 4:9 [4:15] the intervention of God are described. As also in Neh 4:8 [4:14] and Neh 4:14 [4:20], a clear

---

27. See also נתן בלב המלך ("to put it into the king's heart") in Ezra 7:27 and Neh 2:12 (Neh 7:5). Also parallel (even if not literally in agreement) is the fact that Ezra and Nehemiah receive the king's favor (Ezra 7:27, Neh 2:5). The favor before the king is also mentioned in Ezra 9:9, which is part of the prayer Ezra 9:6–15.

28. After the problem of the insufficient population of Jerusalem is mentioned in Neh 7:4, it is recorded before the solution in Neh 7:5 that God has put into Nehemiah's heart the desire to register the population in lists. A reference to Neh 2:12 and the prayers in Neh 2–6 is thereby established.

29. God is also the guarantee for the success of the conversation with the king, as emphasized at the end of the scene in Neh 2:8 and confirmed in Neh 2:18.

reference to the YHWH war traditions is thereby established.[30] God and God's actions are therewith the cause for the defense of the city through the builders, for the frustration of the plans of the enemies, and for salvation in general.[31]

In both cases, the function of the initial action for the solution of the problem falls to prayer in its prominent position. The subsequent references to the action of God that are interwoven into both passages make more than clear the fact that the positive developments reported by Nehemiah are founded in God's intervention. This is true for the intentions put into Nehemiah's heart as well as for the king's consent to these plans, for the frustration of the enemies' agitation, and finally for the successful completion of the project of building the wall. The fact that the building of the city wall goes back to God's initiative is already indicated in Neh 2:20 and finally must be acknowledged in Neh 6:16 even by the enemies.

3.2. Short Prayers and *zkr*-Prayers

The psalm of praise Ezra 7:27–28 marks a threefold boundary. First, after the citation of the Aramaic edict of Artaxerxes in 7:12–26, the language changes to Hebrew with the praise text. Second, a narrative text that is shaped as a self-report by Ezra (7:27–9:6) begins with this prayer, while in 7:1–10 and 10:1–17 (after the prayer in 9:6–15), a report is made about Ezra in the third-person. And, third, the transition from 7:26 to 7:27 is frequently seen in research as a literary-critical seam.[32]

The psalm of praise is not narratively framed; neither the speaker nor the addressees of the prayer are explicitly declared. One assumes a group of speakers at the beginning, in 7:27, since it speaks there of the "God of our ancestors." In 7:28, then, a first-person speaker appears who, by virtue of the fact that the transition from the praise text to Ezra's self-report is not

---

30. See Exod 14:14; Deut 1:30; 3:22; 20:4; Josh 23:10.

31. Karrer provides a very good description of the YHWH war traditions processed in Neh 4 and draws the conclusion that "the building of the wall and the demarcation over against the enemies are interpreted and legitimated religiously in Nehemiah's concept" (*Ringen*, 185–87, my trans.).

32. See Joseph Blenkinsopp, *Ezra-Nehemiah: A Commentary*, OTL (Philadelphia: Westminster, 1988), 159; Karrer, *Ringen*, 239–40; Raik Heckl, *Neuanfang und Kontinuität in Jerusalem: Studien zu den hermeneutischen Strategien im Esra-Nehemia-Buch*, FAT 104 (Tübingen: Mohr Siebeck, 2016), 263–65.

marked, is to be identified with Ezra. I still consider 7:28a to be a part of the praise text, since God is the subject.

Irrespective of the possible theses in regard to the diachronic development of Ezra 7, the psalm of praise consists of elements referring both backward and forward. Thus the statement that the king desires to support the temple in Jerusalem richly refers back to the regulations proclaimed in the previous edict of Artaxerxes, more precisely to Ezra 7:12–24. The law (Ezra 7:14, 25, 26), on the other hand, is not mentioned in the psalm of praise. Since the king is not named explicitly in the praise text either, one can think of Darius's regulations for provisioning the temple as they appear in Ezra 6:9–10. The psalm of praise attributes the instructions of the Persian king to the intervention of God. A configuration is thereby produced that is similar to that in the edict of Cyrus in Ezra 1:2, where Cyrus says that YHWH, the God of heaven, has commissioned him to rebuild the house of God in Jerusalem.

In the psalm of praise, not only the action of the king but also the commissioning of Ezra is attributed to God's intervention. God is the one who brings about the situation wherein Ezra finds grace before the king, his counselors, and his commanders. A similar statement is found already in Ezra 7:6, where it is recorded that the king grants Ezra all his requests thanks to the intervention of God.[33] Both statements thus frame the edict of Artaxerxes. Ezra's travel plans also have a similar framing function. Ezra's decision to go up to Jerusalem in Ezra 7:28 not only picks up on the instruction of the king (Ezra 7:13) but also refers back to Ezra 7:6–9, for it is already said in Ezra 7:6–9 that he went to Jerusalem through God's intervention. The journey to Jerusalem, the support of the temple, and the emphasis on the fact that this is the temple of YHWH, which is in Jerusalem—all of these elements link the psalm of praise in Ezra 7:27–28 with Ezra 1–6. On the other hand, the missing contextual embedding of the psalm of praise and the formulation נתן בלב, "to put into the heart," as well as ביד אלוהים, "thanks to the hand of God," refer to Neh 1–7.[34]

The psalm of praise represents the first action after the royal edict and thereby the initial action on the part of Ezra. With this action, all that is done is attributed to God's intervention. The subsequent travel preparations and the secure journey itself are due to God, who is characterized in

---

33. The naming of the royal officials refers to Ezra 7:14.
34. See above on Ezra 8:21–23.

Ezra 7:27 and 8:28 as "God of our ancestors." God's protection during the journey is once again emphasized especially by means of the prayer in Ezra 8:21–23. The intention of the psalm of praise to attribute all the actions to the working of God is continued in Ezra 7–8 and especially in 8:21–23. Ezra 7–8, however, is not shot through with short prayers, as Neh 1–7, 13 is.

In Neh 1–7, 13, there is a network of *zkr*-prayers (Neh 5:19; 13:14, 22, 29, 31) and short prayers (Neh 3:36–37 [4:4–5]; 6:14) that have the following common aspects. Each of these seven petitionary prayers lacks not only an explicit prayer introduction but also a narrative embedding. The speaker of the prayer can be deduced only from the context. Thus the first-person plural speaking in Neh 3:36–37 [4:4–5] has been the subject since 2:19. It encompasses Nehemiah and the authorities in Jerusalem, who work at building the city wall. In all the other passages, the praying person is identical with the narrating Nehemiah. All the prayers mark a change of scene and, in each case, refer to the previous scene. The prayers also show commonalities in their form and in their lexis. These are always short prayers that begin with an imperative of זכר—except for Neh 3:36 [4:4], which has שמע—and a vocative אלוהי/אלוהינו.

The two short prayers Neh 3:36–37 [4:4–5] and 6:14 stand together with the prayer activities in Neh 2:4 and 4:3 [4:9] in the same literary unit on the building of the wall and connect with the function of prayer described there. They attest to the fact that the punishment of the enemies is also commended to God. In Neh 3:36–37 [4:4–5], there follow imperatives and vetitives that produce a clear reference to the previous narrative context through their pronominal references, their selection of words, and their themes. The term חרפה, "disgrace," in Neh 3:36 [4:4] harks back to Neh 2:17; בוזה, "ridicule," in Neh 3:36 [4:4] refers back to Neh 2:19; and כעס *hiphil*, "to ridicule," in Neh 2:37 refers back to Neh 3:33 [4:1]. This ridiculing on the part of the enemies is qualified as guilt and sin that God should not let remain unpunished. While the actions of the enemies named in the prayer are found again in the previous narrative context, the question of how and where the punishment of the enemies requested of God will be carried out remains unanswered. The petition for punishment in Neh 3:37 [4:5] has its direct literary model in Jer 18:23, a section of text from Jeremiah's confessions. This literary echo from Jeremiah's confessions does not appear to be by chance.[35] Hannes Bezzel thus sees Nehemiah, or the

---

35. The *zkr*-prayers are also close to Jer 15:15.

group of the builders, as "described in the succession of the persecuted prophet.... A saying that the prophet [Jeremiah] utters more or less on his own account here now, in the mouth of a single person, Nehemiah, becomes the concern of a group."[36]

Nehemiah 6:14 likewise expresses a request for the punishment of the enemies Tobiah, Sanballat, and Noadiah. Here, too, a clear reference to the context is produced with the comparison כמאשיו אלה, "according to these his deeds," and with the statement that Noadiah and the other prophets wanted to make Nehemiah afraid, for ירא piel is found also in Neh 6:9, 13, 19. In the preceding narrative context, however, the prophetess Noadiah is not named, whereas Shemaiah, hired by the enemies as a prophet, remains unmentioned in the prayer, so that the prayer stands in a certain tension to the narrative context. This tension must not necessarily be an indication of a secondary addition to the prayer, as Hugh G. M. Williamson assumes.[37] Irmtraud Fischer explains the supposed tension, for example, with the idea that the prophetess Noadiah is present either in or at the temple where Nehemiah is supposed to go because of Shemaiah's saying.[38]

The positioning of both prayers corresponds to the location of the prayer in Neh 4:3 [4:9] and to God's intervention in Neh 4:9 [4:15], both of which likewise stand between the portrayal of the enemies' agitation and the portrayal of the reactions on the part of the builders in Jerusalem. Thus both prayers can be connected with the prayers in the narrative about the building of the wall. God is also seen as the decisive agent/person punishing the guilt of the enemies. The requests in the narrative context are not fulfilled in the narrative but transcend it. Just as the decisive initiative for building the wall, its completion, and the defense against the enemies were already attributed before to God's action, the punishment of the guilty enemies is also commended to God. Praying and the two short prayers are used in this text as a linguistic strategy to connect all decisive impulses back to God.

---

36. Hannes Bezzel, *Die Konfessionen Jeremias: Eine redaktionskritische Arbeit*, BZAW 378 (Berlin: de Gruyter, 2007), 210. Similar petitions to punish guilt are found also in psalms (Ps 137:7; Lam 4:22).

37. Williamson, *Ezra, Nehemiah*, xxvii.

38. See Irmtraud Fischer, *Gotteskünderinnen: Zu einer geschlechterfairen Deutung des Phänomens der Prophetie und der Prophetinnen in der Hebräischen Bibel* (Stuttgart: Kohlhammer, 2002), 262–66.

The *zkr*-prayers in Neh 5:19; 13:14, 22, 29, 31 are, on the other hand, far less related in their content to their surrounding narrative passages than the petitionary prayers in Neh 3:36–37 [4:4–5] and 6:14. They structure Neh 13 into three stanzas (Neh 13:4–14, 23–29; 14:15–22) that are in each case framed by an introductory citation of the exact time and a concluding *zkr*-prayer. Formal relationships with the preceding narrative context in Neh 13:14, 22 are established in each case through cross-referencing pronouns. In addition, the theme of the preceding narrative is taken up in Neh 13:14 with the use of בית אלוהי. On the other hand, Neh 13:29 points far beyond the context and cannot be sufficiently motivated on the basis of the narrative context.[39] The petitionary prayer in Neh 13:31b, together with 13:30, 31, possesses a resultative function and forms the conclusion not only for Neh 13 but also for the entire Nehemiah narrative, for the last word, טובה, "the good," refers not only to Nehemiah's measures, once again enumerated in Neh 13:30, but is also the antithesis in Neh 13 to רעה, "evil/calamity," which appears in each stanza (Neh 13:7, 18, 27). At the same time, טובה and רעה refer back to the beginning of the narrative of the building of the wall, for the situation in Judah and Jerusalem is described with רעה גדולה in Neh 1:3 as well as in 2:10, 17. In Neh 2:10, טובה, the good that Nehemiah will do for the Israelites in Jerusalem, is spoken of at the same time.

In Neh 5, the narrative about Nehemiah's social measures, the prayer 5:19 stands structurally parallel to 5:13, the people's vow and praise. The *zkr*-prayer in 5:19 primarily ends the section 5:14–18 but is at the same time the conclusion of the entire chapter of Neh 5. Striking is the use of טובה, which blends into the conjunction of key words recognized earlier in the section from Neh 2:10 to 13:31. The word טובה thus forms a bracket extending from Neh 2:10, via 5:19, to 13:31. Therewith, the narrative of the building of the wall and the memoir in Neh 5:13 possess a common program in the two lexemes טובה and רעה, both of which are evaluative and occupy a prominent position.[40] The lexeme זכר, so typical of the

---

39. See Christian Frevel, "Mein Bund mit ihm war das Leben und der Friede," in *Für immer verbündet: Studien zur Bundestheologie der Bibel: Festschrift für Frank-Lothar Hossfeld*, ed. Christoph Dohmen and Christian Frevel, SBS 211 (Stuttgart: Katholisches Bibelwerk, 2007), 85–93.

40. Karrer likewise recognizes the significance of the catchwords טובה and רעה but puts the focus on the function of the person Nehemiah in her concluding judgment: "So, the Nehemiah text can be understood as a plea on behalf of the concept of a

zkr-prayers, additionally appears in the prayer in Neh 1:5–11 in a central function. This linkage will be investigated further in the next section.

The lexeme זכר belongs to the typical repertoire of prayer language, whereby, positively formulated, it is a request for the mercy and blessing of God, while, formulated negatively, it belongs to the vocabulary of divine judgment.[41] In the prayers, זכר is used in both senses. Nehemiah hopes to receive from God both the imputation of the good as well as the punishment of the enemies. The *zkr*-prayers and Nehemiah's short prayers therein are similar above all to the confessions of Jeremiah. These are, in addition, comparable in their literary nonembeddedness in the narrative context to the *zkr*-prayers and provide, as already noted above, the literary pre-text for Neh 3:37 [4:5]. If one can take these observations as references to the prophetic book of Jeremiah, then it becomes conspicuous that it is precisely the genre of prayer that is chosen from the prophetic book, while the linguistic strategy of quoting God's direct speech, which is so central for the prophetic book, is lacking in the book of Nehemiah.[42]

3.3. Nehemiah 1:5–11

Read synchronically, the prayer in Neh 1:5–11 possesses in Neh 1:4 a cultic-ritual embedding, for Nehemiah performs rites of mourning as a reaction to the information that Jerusalem is in poor condition: he sits on the ground (ישב), weeps (בכה), mourns (אבל *hithpael*), fasts (צום), and prays (פלל *hithpael*) before the God of heaven. Nehemiah 1:4 does not tell us the location of this action, but we still learn that this mourning lasts for several days.[43]

The prayer in Neh 1:5–11 is structured as follows:[44]

---

governor who in his person unites an Achaemenidic 'official' and the top management of a community and, precisely because of this, is in the position to make 'the best' out of the given situation under Achaemenid rule and to change all of this 'evil' … into 'good'" (*Ringen*, 195, my trans.).

41. Positively: Pss 8:5; 25:6–7; 80:15; 106:4; 115:12; 132:1; negatively: Ps 137:7; Lam 5:1; Jer 14:10; 15:15.

42. This aspect is lacking in Karrer-Grube, "Scrutinizing the Conceptual Unity."

43. Ezra shows similar reactions in Ezra 9:3–5, when he hears of the problem of mixed marriages.

44. See Karrer, *Ringen*, 199.

1. 1:5–7 Opening of the Prayer
   Addressing of YHWH (1:5)
   Introductory request to hear the prayer (1:6)
       (with a qualification of the prayer as an intercessory prayer)
       (with a qualification of the prayer as a confession of sin)
   Citation of the confession of sin (1:7)
2. 1:8–10 Central request to remember (1:8a)
   Object of remembering: Word of promise (1:8–9)
   Justification for the request (1:10)
3. 1:11 Concluding request to hear the prayer (1:11)
       (with the concrete request for success in the following scene)

Verses 5–7 are to be seen as the opening of the prayer that, along with the confession to God as the one who preserves the covenant and the good (v. 5), comprises the introductory request for hearing the prayer. That God is qualified here as the one who preserves the covenant and the good points ahead to the words of promise in verses 8–10.[45] Verses 6–7 determine the prayer to be Nehemiah's intercessory prayer for the children of Israel, the servants of God, and as a confession of sin that encompasses the sins of the generation before and of the present one. The sins here are concretized as noncompliance with the commandments, the laws, and the ordinances that God gave to Moses.[46] In the asyndetic concluding verse 8, however, it is not the request for acceptance of this confession of sin that follows, but rather the request that God might remember the word that he gave to Moses.[47] This word does not have to do with commandments and instructions, but rather with the promise that God will gather his people and his servants at the place that God himself has chosen when they follow his instructions. [48] The central request of God to remember thus aims at the promise that God might think of the pledge given by him to Moses

---

45. See Deut 7:9, 12; 1 Kgs 8:23.

46. The assumed pre-texts were convincingly gathered by Klaus Baltzer or Eep Talstra and are not repeated here. See Baltzer, "Moses Servant of God and the Servants: Text and Tradition in the Prayer of Nehemiah (Neh 1:5–11)," in *The Future of Early Christianity: Essays in Honour of Helmut Koester*, ed. Birger A. Pearson (Minneapolis: Fortress Press, 1991), 121–30, Talstra, "Discourse of Praying," 219–36.

47. For this reason, according to Talstra, Neh 1:5–11 is in no case to be classified as a penitential prayer ("Discourse of Praying," 234–35).

48. Talstra, "Discourse of Praying," 226–27.

and the people. When the people will observe the commandments, he will gather them at the place he himself has chosen.[49] With verse 10, the prayer extends the arc into the present and hopes for the fulfillment in the present of the promise given to Moses in the past. God's pledge is also valid now, in the period of Nehemiah, since "these people," that is, the present generation under Nehemiah, are identified with the people of God, with his servants.[50] Verse 11 closes the prayer with a second request for hearing the prayer. The request is concretized as one for success in Nehemiah's negotiations with the Persian king, which is narrated subsequently and thus leads into the narrative context. Nehemiah consciously places his request for the goodwill of the king in the context of the promise of God and so interprets his success as a fulfillment of God's covenantal promises in the narrative present. For this reason, Eep Talstra characterizes Neh 1:5–11 as follows: "This art of praying is neither something ritual, nor an individual meditation. Rather it is *communication*, based on a long tradition of texts about God, his people and their common history.... [The prayer] wants the common history to continue."[51]

In the context of the narrative, the prayer thus does not possess the function of illustrating the mourning described in verse 4. The prayer is not to be understood as a reaction to the bad news from Jerusalem. Rather, it prepares Nehemiah's next act in Neh 2. By calling to mind God's covenantal promise given to Moses and the people, it connects to theological traditions and, with God's promise in the covenant, outlines the framework for the legitimation of Nehemiah's initiatives. Christiane Karrer thus correctly points out the fact that, through the prayer,

> Nehemiah's work should be understood as a realization of the covenantal promise in Deut 30:4.... The governor Nehemiah, according to this concept, is the one who takes care that, through the observance of the commandments and the demarcation over against the peoples, the positive promises of God's covenant can become reality for the Judeans, promises that make them a strong people "gathered at the place chosen by God for them."[52]

---

49. The pre-text here certainly must be Deut 30:1–4; see also Jer 23:3; 29:14; 32:37; Ezek 11:17; 20:34, 41; 28:25; 29:13.

50. Neh 1:10 can be considered as a modified part of the covenantal formula; see Deut 7:8; 9:26.

51. Talstra, "Discourse of Praying," 235.

52. Karrer, *Ringen*, 206–7, my trans.

"So I Prayed to the God of Heaven" (Neh 2:4)   71

Therewith, this prayer, which stands at a prominent position before Nehemiah's initiative, is given the same function as that given to the narrated prayer activities in Neh 2:4 and 4:3 [4:9]. They can be interpreted for this reason on the synchronic level as references back to the theological legitimation of Nehemiah's actions contained in his opening prayer. On the basis of the contextual incorporation of the prayer in Neh 1:5–11, the fact that the prayer was not inserted secondarily but was rather created for and with the narrative of the building of the wall seems to suggest itself from the literary-critical perspective.

The request to remember in Neh 1:8, standing in the center of the prayer and directed to God with זכר, creates at the same time a lexemic bridge to the *zkr*-prayers or short prayers of Nehemiah. In the short petitions, זכר means the imputation of the good and the punishment of the enemies by God. In Neh 1:8, on the other hand, God is reminded of his commitment in the covenant. Thus although the content that God is intended to remember is different, the statements therein correspond to the fact that God's remembrance is the precondition for the well-being of the people. God's promise in the covenant is the basis for this well-being. It refers, at the same time, to the concluding of the covenant in Neh 10 and Ezra 9, which in each case is preceded by prayers (Neh 9:6–37 and Ezra 9:6–15).

3.4. Nehemiah 9:6–37

The prayer in Neh 9:6–37 is integrated into religious-cultic actions that, however, hardly correspond to a genuine liturgical plan: The children of Israel gather themselves on the twenty-fourth day of the seventh month for a fast (9:1).[53] The "seed of Israel" (זרע ישראל) separate themselves from all that is alien, confess their sins (9:2), and read from the book of the torah of YHWH for a fourth of the day, while they confess their sins and prostrate themselves before God for a further fourth of the day. Finally, eight Levites mentioned by name rise up and lament or call with a loud voice to God (9:4). Eight further (?) Levites call for the praise of God (9:5a), which is cited in 9:5b.[54] The prayer in Neh 9:6–37 then connects with this directly

---

53. The dating produces a linkage with the reading of the torah in Neh 8:2 (day one of the seventh month) and with the celebration of the Feast of Tabernacles in Neh 8:13–14 (day two of the seventh month).

54. On the structure here, see Duggan, *Covenant Renewal*, 139–49.

without further introduction so that it appears to be introduced by a praise text that itself is not a part of the prayer.[55] It is unclear how the speech acts of the confession of sin, of the loud lament, of the praise, and of the cited prayer are related to each other. The end of the penitential prayer is likewise not marked on the surface of the text, since the first-person plural of the prayer is continued in Neh 10:1–40.

Nehemiah 9–10 reports about the conclusion of a contract that is prepared through fasting, the confession of sin, reading from the book of the torah, and the prayer in Neh 9:6–37. The prayer itself is characterized by a consciousness of the guilt of the people in the past and in the present. Unmistakable in Neh 9:6–31 is the Deuteronomistic scheme of the guilt of the people, the punishment by God resulting from this, the plea for help uttered by the people, and the answer of mercy from God.[56] "Israel cries for help and is pardoned, has a relapse and is amnestied—an almost endless chain of falling away and restoration."[57] Nehemiah 9:32–37 devotes itself to the present, which is described as a situation of distress. In this situation, too, the praying people cry to God and hope in God's mercy. They intend to use the singular request of God in Neh 9:32, and the observation at the end of the prayer that they are in great distress, to make God aware of the present emergency situation. In terms of functional intention, the prayer expresses the hope in God's mercy, in the salvific care by God in the present situation of distress. This hope is grounded in the retrospection into the past, in which God's mercy was experienced.

In the context of Neh 9–10, though, the essential performative act of the prayer is not the confession of sin or the call in the midst of distress but rather the reminiscent listening to the word of God. The prayer shows God to be one who acts in history, and it evokes the central formative elements found therein.[58] The sequence of the events that are called to mind corresponds to the narrative thread from Genesis, beginning with Abraham and extending to the book of Judges. The gift of the Sinai torah (Neh 9:13, 14) is the essential formative element; listening to the torah is

---

55. See Duggan, *Covenant Renewal*, 155.
56. See the citation from Exod 34:6; the further text references will not be discussed in detail here. On this, see Duggan, *Covenant Renewal*, 157–233; Boda, *Praying the Tradition*, 75–187.
57. Gerstenberger, *Israel in der Perserzeit*, 191.
58. See Anja Klein, *Geschichte und Gebet: Die Rezeption der biblischen Geschichte in den Psalmen des Alten Testaments*, FAT 94 (Tübingen: Mohr Siebeck, 2014).

deemed to be central. The noncompliance with the torah and with its commandments is identified as a renunciation of God or as a transgression on the part of the people. The prayer, which calls to mind the gift of the torah and other central formative elements of history, is for this reason less a penitential or petitionary prayer than it is torah in the sense of current instruction constitutive for the conclusion of the contract in Neh 10.

Neh 9–10 on the whole resembles the Sinai pericope. After the listening to the word (Exod 20–23; 24:3; Neh 9:1–40), there follows the recording of the covenantal/contractual content (Exod 24:4; Neh 10:1), the commitment to keep the covenant/contract (Exod 24:4–8; Neh 10:30), and the public reading, or citation, of the covenantal/contractual content (Exod 24:7; Neh 10:31–40). The current text of the contract is thus to be interpreted as a covenantal document, which is lacking in the remembrance of the Sinai pericope. Nehemiah 9–10 can thus be understood as an imitation—or, more exactly, as a realization—of the events on Sinai when, after the listening of God's word (above all in the form of the prayer Neh 9:6–37), there then follows the conclusion of the covenant.

3.5. Ezra 9:6–15

Ezra 9–10 describes the solution to the problem of mixed marriages in compliance with the torah. The explicitly declared conformity with the torah (Ezra 10:3) does not mean that there must be corresponding instructions in the Pentateuch.[59] It rather means that the commitment to a common act (conclusion of the covenant) is preceded by instruction. For this reason, Karrer speaks, in regard to Ezra 9–10, of the "minutes of the

---

59. Sara Japhet drew attention to the tensions existing between the explicitly declared conformity with the torah and the lack of corresponding instructions in the Pentateuch. She comes to the following conclusion that "the details of the legislation respond to actual historical situations, prevalent customs, legal traditions and norms, and religious concepts. At the same time, and with no sensation of incoherence, the people of the Restoration regard themselves as acting according to the written book" (Japhet, "Law and 'The Law' in Ezra-Nehemiah," in *Proceedings of the Ninth World Congress of Jewish Studies: Jerusalem 1985: Panel Sessions; Hebrew and Aramaic*, ed. Moshe Bar-Asher [Jerusalem: Magnes, 1988], 115). Japhet correctly sees the resolution as grounded in the concrete historical situation. But, she cannot dissipate the tension with this statement. This can be dissipated only when the torah is not identified with a written text but rather is understood as a notion of a communication process.

proceedings."[60] Ezra acts here as a (priestly)[61] intermediary figure whose function Karrer describes as follows: "The relationship of the community to God is expressed in the figure of Ezra, his actions, and his words.... The priestly intermediary figure in the 'center' of the population here guarantees that the content of the decisions corresponds to the will of God."[62] The prayer in Ezra 9:6–15, which is preceded by cultic-religious acts of self-diminution and repentance (Ezra 9:3–5), functions as a resolution to the problem of mixed marriages comparable to the function of the prayer in Neh 9:6–37 for the conclusion of the contract in Neh 10, for in the prayer Ezra expresses the community's relationship to God as well as the will of God. Its structure can be described as follows:

1. 9:6 Opening of the prayer
   Addressing of God
   Shame in turning to God
   Reason: extent of collective guilt
2. 9:7–9 Memory of their own guilt and abandonment and of God's renewed mercy in the past
   God referred to in the third-person
   Collective guilt to the present (9:7)
   Punishment by the sword, captivity, plundering, and shame to the present (9:7)
   But the mercy of God in the most recent past: life of the escaped remnant in Judah and Jerusalem (9:8, 9)
3. 9:10–14 Confession of renewed guilt in the present
   Addressing of God (9:10a, 13b)
   Beginning of the confession of sin: forsaking of the commandments (9:10)
   Citation of the commandments of the prophets while taking possession of the land (9:11–12)
   Pollution of the land through the previous inhabitants (9:11)
   Mutual prohibition of exogamy (9:12)
   Situation of the confession of sin: renewed life in the land (9:13)
   Explicit confession of sin: breaking of the commandments, intermarriage with the peoples (9:14)

---

60. See Karrer, *Ringen*, 242.
61. Ezra 10:10, 16.
62. Karrer, *Ringen*, 255, 261, my trans.

Feared reaction on the part of God: renewed abandonment (9:14)
4. 9:15 Devotion to God
   Addressing of God
   Confession of God's righteousness (expression of trust)
   Renewed confession of collective guilt

The structure and content of the prayer are in accordance with the two functions mentioned above. The people stand before God as guilty and dependent upon God's mercy. Before the concrete guilt in the present is named, the sequence of guilt and punishment (here abandonment) and likewise the mercy of God are called to mind as an introduction. The mercy of God makes it possible for the escaped remnant of the present to live in Judah and Jerusalem, if also in servitude (9:6–9). The will of God, on which action is to be oriented, is proclaimed before the real confession of guilt (9:14–15) in the form of a prophetic word that prominently and explicitly cites the commandments of God against which the people have transgressed (9:12).

The fact that, in the prayer, a request of God to hear the prayer or for the forgiveness of sins is lacking is due to these two functions of the prayer. The prayer thus works only in a limited sense as a penitential or petitionary prayer; it works much more as torah, as current instruction, by citing the word of God and God's commandments.

The prayer is in accordance linguistically with the narrative context. It is to be identified with torah, God's word, and Ezra's counsel, and it forms the foundation for the resolution of the problem in Ezra 10, for the words of God (in 9:4) and the commandments of God (in 10:3), before which one trembles, are the subjects of speech. In Ezra 10:3, in addition, the counsel of Ezra and the torah, according to which it is intended to proceed, are mentioned in parallel. The prayer references the present situation three times: guilt, abandonment, and mercy persist to the present day (9:7, 15). The cited prophetic word (9:11–12) makes reference to the narrative in Ezra 9–10 as well as to other pre-texts. Thus 9:1, 11, and 14 speak about the peoples of the lands and about their abominations (תועבה) and in 9:2 and 12 about the taking of daughters for their sons (נשא).[63] The prophetic word cannot be attributed to any prophetic text known to us, but rather it is supplied from Lev 18:24–30 and Deut

---

63. Duggan, "Ezra 9:6–15," 171–72.

7:1–4.⁶⁴ In Deut 7:1–4, however, the prohibition on mixed marriages serves to keep Israel apart from illegitimate cultic practices. Ezra 9:12, on the other hand, demands a fundamental separation from the "peoples of the abomination" through a prohibition of mixed marriages.⁶⁵ In the retrospective portion (9:7), guilt and abandonment are formulated stereotypically according to the Deuteronomistic model.⁶⁶ The description of God's mercy (9: 8–9) makes clear reference to Ezra 1–6, especially to the edict of Cyrus, as well as to the edict of Artaxerxes in Ezra 7 (see also 8:28), for these texts describe the benevolent actions of the Persian kings that leads to the erection of the temple and to living in Judah and Jerusalem. When Ezra 9:8, 15 speaks of the "escaped remnant," this calls to mind Neh 1:2, and the present status of the people as slaves (Ezra 9:9) refers to Neh 9:32.

The prayer is thus in accordance not only with the narrative context of Ezra 9–10, but it also takes up Ezra 1–6 and Neh 1–13 linguistically and thematically.⁶⁷

4. Prayer as the Key to the Theology of Ezra 7–Nehemiah 13

The analyses show that in the book of Nehemiah prayer possesses a key function, while in Ezra 1–6 prayer plays no role as a form of action. In its use of prayers, Ezra 7–10 remains oddly unclear and appears to stand between the two other text units.

In the book of Nehemiah, prayer has the essential function of bringing God into the narrative as an actor. Other narrative strategies for letting God appear as an actor apparently are not available. All the decisive initiatives, actions, and responsibilities are thus attributed to God via prayer— whether or not the prayer itself is explicitly given.

---

64. Above and beyond this, Ezra 9:10–12 is reminiscent of other texts, especially because of the terms תועבה and נדה, which are used in Priestly and Deuteronomistic contexts for the condemnation of illegitimate cultic practices.

65. This calls to mind Deut 1:38–39; 6:11; 11:8; 23:7. See Rothenbusch, "...*Abgesondert zur Tora Gottes hin*," 162: "The taking or the possession of the land is linked there [in the Deuteronomic/Deuteronomistic literature] many times with the observance of the commandment" (my trans).

66. See Ezek 20; Neh 9:6–30.

67. Duggan likewise verifies the proximity to Ezra 1–6 and to the prayer in Neh 9:6–37 ("Ezra 9:6–15," 175–79).

The prayer in Neh 1:5–11, therefore, proves to be a central key in the book of Nehemiah when observed synchronically, for Neh 1:5–11 contains all the aspects that prayer or the prayers subsequently unfold. Nehemiah 1:5–11 is inserted before Nehemiah's actions so that all Nehemiah's activities appear to be initiated and legitimated by God. The following references to prayer in Neh 2:4 and 4:3 [4:9] confirm this function. In addition, the short prayers in Neh 3:36–37 [4:4–5] and 6:14, as well as the *zkr*-prayers, all expect retribution from God. The *zkr*-prayers are thereby linked via the key word זכר with the prayer in Neh 1:5–11. God's remembering is fundamental for the well-being of the people. This well-being is expressed with the term טובה.

The prayer in Neh 9:6–37 is also linked with the other prayers in the book of Nehemiah via the key words "remembering" and טובה. The term טובה is found five times in Neh 9:6–37 (vv. 13, 20, 25, 35, 36), and the opposing term, צרה גדולה, which is reminiscent of Neh 1:3, is used in Neh 9:37. The term טובה refers to the good deeds of God in history and makes remembering a reality that clarifies the most important positions in Israel's history with God. Although the theme word זכר is not used, one still can speak of a prayer method for which remembering is central.

The two long prayers in Neh 1:5–11 and 9:6–37 show further commonalities that go beyond the specific characteristics of the genre. In Neh 1:5 and 9:32, God bears a nearly identical title: He is great/strong and awesome, but at the same time he is the one who preserves the covenant and the good. Both prayers bring God's positive action in the past into their theological argumentation. In Neh 1:5–11, God is reminded explicitly of his promise and his acceptance of the covenant in the past. In Neh 9:6–37, the past serves as the guarantee for the fact that God will see the distress of the people and show mercy to them in the present, too. Nehemiah 1:5–11 calls to mind God's acceptance of the covenant; a central memory in Neh 9:6–37 is the gift of the torah on Sinai. The prayer in Neh 9:6–37, as instruction evoking memory, is itself torah (of God) and the foundation of the conclusion of the contract (the covenant) in Neh 10. God thereby appears in the prayer as agent, while he is lacking in this capacity in the process of concluding the contract. In a similar way, the prayer in Neh 1:5–11 replaces Nehemiah's commissioning by God, a commissioning known from the prophetic books, and thus avoids God's direct speech. Thus both praying and specific prayers appear in the book of Nehemiah to be the literary means that replaces direct divine speech and God's appearance.

If one compares the function of praying in Neh 1–13 with that in Ezra 7–10, it quickly becomes clear that praying does not have the central significance in Ezra 7–10 that it has in Neh 1–13. In Ezra 7–10, fewer prayers on the whole are woven into the text. The function of initiating action hardly exists for Ezra 7:27, 28a. This passage has an absolutely pallid effect, above all when compared with Neh 1:5–11. The prayer, of course, is inserted at a similar position in the narrative and attributes all the initiative to God. But the fact that the hand of God has an effect is seen already in Ezra 7:6, 9, and the edict of Artaxerxes that directly precedes this and is cited in detail likewise has a function of initiating action. In Ezra 7–8, in addition to this, there is only one more report about prayer activities, in Ezra 8:21–23. The function of the prayer in Ezra 9:6–15 in the resolution of the problem of mixed marriages in Ezra 9–10 is, on the other hand, comparable with the function of Neh 9:6–37 for the conclusion of the contract in Neh 10. In both situations, each prayer functions as torah, as current instruction. Ezra 9:6–15 is thereby more clearly in accordance with the context of Ezra 9–10, but at the same it time makes linguistic reference to Ezra 1–6 and Neh 1–13.

On the whole, it can be established that all the prayers and prayer activities in Ezra 7–10 show connections in language, content, and structure with the book of Nehemiah as well as with Ezra 1–6. These connections cannot be explained without citing dependencies of a literary-historical character. Since the prayers in Ezra 7–10 have a connection with Ezra 1–6 as well as with the book of Nehemiah, the assumption that Ezra 7–10 was shaped in the knowledge of the other texts, or as a bridge text between Ezra 1–6 and the book of Nehemiah, appears very probable, for the connections are to be found not only in the prayers but also in other text passages in Ezra 7–10. If this dependency, which cannot be substantiated here in detail, is true, then the more minor significance of Ezra 7:27–28 can be explained by the fact that the explicit and detailed commissioning of Ezra by a Persian king was imported in the form of an edict from Ezra 1–6, and that this edict thus comes to stand in rivalry with the prayer in Ezra 7:27–28. The function of praying in Ezra 8:21–23 becomes more understandable when one recognizes that therewith more divine trust is intended to be attributed to the scribe Ezra than to Nehemiah in Neh 2. The function of distinguishing Ezra as a particular figure is also present in Ezra 7–10, for Ezra functions as a mediatory figure that gives torah in the prayer in Ezra 9:6–15 and, therewith, prepares the resolution in Ezra 10 of the mixed marriage problem. In comparison with this, the action in

Neh 9–10 is borne by all the participants; there is no prominent mediatory figure here, although Neh 9–10 realizes the events on Sinai in the present. The prayers in Ezra 7–10 can thus be best explained with the fact that Nehemiah's praying in Neh 1–7, which initiates action, and the torah-giving prayer in Neh 9–10, which is borne there by the community, are united in the Ezra figure of Ezra 7–10. This Ezra is intended to be depicted in Ezra 7–10 as an outstanding and exemplary figure.

Bibliography

Balentine, Samuel E. *Prayer in the Hebrew Bible: The Drama of Divine-Human Dialogue*. OBT. Minneapolis: Fortress, 1993.

Baltzer, Klaus. "Moses Servant of God and the Servants: Text and Tradition in the Prayer of Nehemiah (Neh 1:5–11)." Pages 121–30 in *The Future of Early Christianity: Essays in Honour of Helmut Koester*. Edited by Birger A. Pearson. Minneapolis: Fortress, 1991.

Bautch, Richard J. *Developments in Genre between Post-exilic Penitential Prayers and the Psalms of Communal Lament*. AcBib 7. Atlanta: Society of Biblical Literature, 2003.

Becking, Bob. "Nehemiah 9 and the Problematic Concept of Context." Pages 253–65 in *The Changing Face of Form Criticism for the Twenty-First Century*. Edited by Marvin A. Sweeney and Ehud Ben Zvi. Grand Rapids: Eerdmans, 2003.

Bezzel, Hannes. *Die Konfessionen Jeremias: Eine redaktionskritische Arbeit*. BZAW 378. Berlin: de Gruyter, 2007.

Blenkinsopp, Joseph. *Ezra-Nehemiah: A Commentary*. OTL. Philadelphia: Westminster, 1988.

Boda, Mark J. "Prayer as Rhetoric in the book of Nehemiah." Pages 267–84 in *New Perspectives on Ezra-Nehemiah: History and Historiography, Text, Literature, and Interpretation*. Edited by Isaac Kalimi. Winona Lake: Eisenbrauns, 2012.

———. *Praying the Tradition: The Origin and Use of Tradition in Nehemiah 9*. BZAW 277. Berlin: de Gruyter, 1999.

Boda, Mark J., Daniel K. Falk, and Rodney A. Werline, eds. *The Origins of Penitential Prayer in Second Temple Judaism*. Vol. 1 of *Seeking the Favor of God*. Atlanta: Society of Biblical Literature, 2006.

Duggan, Michael W. *The Covenant Renewal in Ezra-Nehemiah (Neh 7:72b–10:40): An Exegetical, Literary, and Theological Study*. SBLDS 164. Atlanta: Society of Biblical Literature, 2001.

———. "Ezra 9:6–15: A Penitential Prayer within its Literary Setting." Pages 165–80 in *The Origins of Penitential Prayer in Second Temple Judaism*. Vol. 1 of *Seeking the Favor of God*. Edited by Mark J. Boda, Daniel K. Falk, and Rodney A. Werline. Atlanta: Society of Biblical Literature, 2006.

Gerstenberger, Erhard. *Israel in der Perserzeit 5. und 4. Jahrhundert v. Chr.* BE 8. Stuttgart: Kohlhammer, 2005.

Fischer, Irmtraud. *Gotteskünderinnen: Zu einer geschlechterfairen Deutung des Phänomens der Prophetie und der Prophetinnen in der Hebräischen Bibel*. Stuttgart: Kohlhammer, 2002.

Frevel, Christian. "Mein Bund mit ihm war das Leben und der Friede." Pages 85–93 in *Für immer verbündet: Studien zur Bundestheologie der Bibel; Festschrift für Frank-Lothar Hossfeld*. SBS 211. Edited by Christoph Dohmen and Christian Frevel. Stuttgart: Katholisches Bibelwerk, 2007.

Galling, Kurt. *Die Bücher der Chronik, Esra, Nehemia*. ATD 12. Göttingen: Vandenhoeck & Ruprecht, 1954.

Grabbe, Lester L. *Yehud: A History of the Persian Province of Judah*. Vol. 1 of *A History of the Jews and Judaism in the Second Temple Period*. LSTS 47. London: T&T Clark, 2004.

Häusl, Maria. "'Ich betete zum Gott des Himmels' (Neh 2:4): Zur kontextuellen Einbettung der Gebete in Neh 1–13." Pages 47–64 in *Studien zu Psalmen und Propheten: Festschrift für Hubert Irsigler*. Edited by Carmen Diller. HBS 64. Freiburg im Breisgau: Herder, 2010.

Heckl, Raik. *Neuanfang und Kontinuität in Jerusalem: Studien zu den hermeneutischen Strategien im Esra-Nehemia-Buch*. FAT 104. Tübingen: Mohr Siebeck, 2016.

Japhet, Sara. "Law and 'The Law' in Ezra-Nehemiah." Pages 99–115 in *Proceedings of the Ninth World Congress of Jewish Studies: Jerusalem 1985; Panel Sessions, Hebrew and Aramaic*. Edited by Moshe Bar-Asher. Jerusalem: Magnes, 1988.

Karrer, Christiane. *Ringen um die Verfassung Judas: Eine Studie zu den theologisch-politischen Vorstellungen im Esra-Nehemia-Buch*. BZAW 308. Berlin: de Gruyter, 2001.

Karrer-Grube, Christiane. "Scrutinizing the Conceptual Unity of Ezra and Nehemiah." Pages 136–59 in *Unity and Disunity in Ezra-Nehemiah: Redaction, Rhetoric, and Reader*. Edited by Mark J. Boda and Paul L. Redditt. HBM 17. Sheffield: Sheffield Phoenix, 2008.

Keel Othmar. *Die Geschichte Jerusalems und die Entstehung des Monotheismus*. Vol. 2 of *Orte und Landschaften der Bibel*. Edited by Othmar Keel, Max Küchler, and Christoph Uehlinger. Göttingen: Vandenhoeck & Ruprecht, 2007.

Kellermann, Ulrich. *Nehemia: Quellen, Überlieferung und Geschichte*. BZAW 102. Berlin: de Gruyter, 1967.

Klein, Anja. *Geschichte und Gebet: Die Rezeption der biblischen Geschichte in den Psalmen des Alten Testaments*. FAT 94. Tübingen: Mohr Siebeck, 2014.

Mowinckel, Sigmund. *Die Nehemia-Denkschrift*. Vol. 2 of *Studien zu dem Buche Ezra-Nehemia*. HFK 5. Oslo: Univeritetsforlaget, 1964.

Oswald, Wolfgang. *Staatstheorie im alten Israel: Der politische Diskurs im Pentateuch und in den Geschichtsbüchern des Alten Testaments*. Stuttgart: Kohlhammer, 2009.

Rad, Gerhard von. "Die Nehemia-Denkschrift." *ZAW* 76 (1964): 176–87.

Rautenberg, Johanna. *Verlässlichkeit des Wortes: Gemeinschaftskonzepte in den Reden des Buches Tobit und ihre Legitimierung*. BBB 176. Göttingen: Vandenhoeck & Ruprecht, 2015.

Reinmuth, Titus. *Der Bericht Nehemias: Zur literarischen Eigenart, traditionsgeschichtlichen Prägung und innerbiblischen Rezeption des Ich-Berichts Nehemias*. OBO 183. Freiburg: Universitätsverlag, 2002.

Rothenbusch, Ralf. *"...Abgesondert zur Tora Gottes hin": Ethnisch-religiöse Identitäten im Esra/Nehemiabuch*. HBS 70. Freiburg: Herder, 2012.

Schmitz, Barbara. *Gedeutete Geschichte: Die Funktion der Reden und Gebete im Buch Judith*. HBS 40. Freiburg im Breisgau: Herder, 2004.

Schottroff, Willy. *"Gedenken" im Alten Orient und im Alten Testament: Die Wurzel Zākar im semitischen Sprachkreis*. WMANT 15. Neukirchen-Vluyn: Neukirchener Verlag, 1964.

Schunck, Klaus-Dietrich. *Nehemia*. BKAT 23.2. Neukirchen-Vluyn: Neukirchener Verlag, 2009.

Talstra, Eep. "The Discourse of Praying: Reading Nehemiah 1." Pages 219–36 in *Psalms and Prayers: Papers Read at the Joint Meeting of the Society of Old Testament Study and het Oudtestamentisch Werkgezelschap in Nederland en België, Apeldoorn August 2006*. Edited by Bob Becking and Eric Peels. OtSt 55. Leiden: Brill, 2007.

Werline, Rodney A. *Penitential Prayer in Second Temple Judaism: The Development of a Religious Institution*. EJL 13. Atlanta: Scholars Press, 1998.

Williamson, Hugh G. M. *Ezra, Nehemiah*. WBC 16. Waco, TX: Word, 1985.

Wright, Jacob L. *Rebuilding Identity: The Nehemiah-Memoir and Its Earliest Readers*. BZAW 348. Berlin: de Gruyter 2004.

Zastrow, Klaus. "Die drei großen Bußgebete von Ezra 9, Nehemia 9 und Daniel 9." PhD diss., University of Heidelberg, 1998.

Identity and Social Justice in Postexilic Yehud: Reading Nehemiah 9 in an African Liberationist Perspective

Ndikho Mtshiselwa

1. Introduction

As Pieter M. Venter proposed, the formation of the biblical canon was enacted on different interactive levels in which an authoritative status was conferred to ancient texts.[1] This proposal is partly based on Michael A. Fishbane's argument that "the final process of canon formation, which meant the solidification of the biblical *traditum* and the onset of the postbiblical *traditio*, was thus a culmination of several related processes," wherein "each transmission of received traditions utilized materials which were or became authoritative in this very process; and each interpretation and explication was made in the context of an authoritative *traditum*."[2] The penitential prayer of Neh 9 therefore became authoritative by using already-authoritative texts and traditions. In each transmission of received

---

This essay is a continuation of my work on the penitential prayer of Neh 9:6–37 as well as on the African reading of biblical texts. See Ndikho Mtshiselwa, "Re-reading the Israelite Jubilee in Leviticus 25:8–55 in the Context of Land Redistribution and Socio-economic Justice in South Africa: An African Liberationist Perspective" (PhD diss., University of South Africa, 2015); Mtshiselwa, "Remembering and Constructing Israelite Identity in Postexilic Yehud: Some Remarks on the Penitential Prayer of Nehemiah 9:6–37," *VetE* 37.1 (2016): 1–6.

1. See Pieter M. Venter, "The Connection between Wisdom Literature, Apocalypses, and Canon," *OTE* 15 (2002): 470–88.

2. Michael A. Fishbane, *Biblical Interpretation in Ancient Israel* (Oxford: Clarendon, 1985), 18.

traditions, the authors and redactors of the text under investigation used materials that were authoritative.

This essay is not meant to investigate the literary transmission of the penitential prayer of Neh 9:6–37 in its oral stage. Nor does it intend to focus on how the transmission of the prayer under consideration took its form from the written stage in the postexilic period to the present-day version. Nor does it aim to substantially discuss the way that the penitential prayer of Neh 9 received an authoritative status. There is a place for all that. This essay does, however, attempt to offer some remarks on the written stage of the transmission of Neh 9:6–37. It will be argued that Neh 9:6–37 was composed and transmitted with a view to remembering and constructing the identity of the Judeans in postexilic Yehud as well as to addressing issues of social justice in the text. The process of revision, addition, compilation, and editing of the selected literature was thus in reaction to different social factors—the sociohistorical context.[3] This essay concludes that the retelling of the story of Israel in Neh 9:6–37 and the way the penitential prayer of Neh 9:6–37 unfolds and shapes the identity of the Judeans in postexilic Yehud addressed concerns for social justice. With respect to the retelling of the story of Israel, this essay will focus on selected prophetic undertones, which include prophecies of doom and deliverance, reference to the work of the prophets and to the prophets themselves, and allusions to Moses, who is partly viewed as a prophet. Furthermore, an African liberationist approach to ancient biblical texts shapes the reading of Neh 9 in the way this essay teases out ideals and concerns for social justice in the Hebrew Bible and highlights the oppressive ideologies of the dominant social class at the time of the production and transmission of the prayer of Neh 9:6–37. By teasing out concerns for social justices, we will hopefully arrive at a liberative reading of the penitential prayer of Neh 9.

2. An African Liberationist Paradigm

That the reading of the Hebrew Bible in African biblical scholarship has been shaped by the historical-critical method and the interests of western biblical scholarship is indisputable.[4] Importantly, in this essay, I am

---

3. See Venter, "Connection between Wisdom Literature, Apocalypses, and Canon," 485.

4. See Gerald O. West, "Indigenous Exegesis: Exploring the Interface between

sympathetic to the view that it is unwise and unhelpful to reject western Old Testament scholarship in the reading of the Hebrew Bible in South Africa.⁵ The meaning of the ancient biblical text is partly uncovered through the so-called western Old Testament scholarship. In order for the methodology to be relevant to the South African context, the historical-critical approach may be used within the theoretical and methodological framework of an African liberationist paradigm. This approach of reading the Hebrew Bible draws on Itumeleng J. Mosala's black biblical hermeneutics of liberation. It equally departs from his approach, however, in the manner in which it places emphasis on African philosophy, culture, and epistemology.⁶ Contextual readings of the Hebrew Bible in South Africa, by and large, stand in continuity with Mosala's liberationist reading of the Hebrew Bible. Similar to Latino/a biblical criticism, the black biblical hermeneutic of liberation grew out of liberation theologies from the Catholic Church in South America; especially on the southern hemisphere, it was also greatly influenced by Marxist theories and concerns and by prevailing inequality and economic conditions in countries under dictatorships.⁷ Mosala's black biblical hermeneutics of liberation, in particular, emerged from James H. Cone's liberation theology, which partly grew out of the North American theology of black power as well as Marx's theory on liberation.⁸ An African liberationist approach to ancient biblical texts is therefore applicable to the South African context,

---

Missionary Methods and the Rhetorical Rhythms of Africa; Locating Local Reading Resources in the Academy," *Neot* 36 (2002): 150–51.

5. See Jurie H. Le Roux, "Africa and the Future of Our Scholarly Past," in *African and European Readers of the Bible in Dialogue: In Quest of a Shared Meaning*, ed. Hans De Wit and Gerald O. West, SRA 32 (Leiden: Brill, 2008), 307–8.

6. Mtshiselwa, "Re-reading the Israelite Jubilee," 17, 261–63.

7. See Fernando F. Segovia, "Introduction: Approaching Latino/a Biblical Criticism; A Trajectory of Visions and Missions," in *Latino/a Biblical Hermeneutics: Problematics, Objectives, Strategies*, ed. Francisco Lozada Jr. and Fernando F. Segovia (Atlanta: SBL Press, 2014), 17–20; Alejandro F. Botta, "What Does It Mean to Be a Latino Biblical Critic? A Brief Essay," in Lozada and Segovia, *Latino/a Biblical Hermeneutics*, 109; Ahida Calderón Pilarski, "A Latina Biblical Critic and Intellectual: At the Intersection of Ethnicity, Gender, Hermeneutics, and Faith," in Lozada and Segovia, *Latino/a Biblical Hermeneutics*, 233.

8. See James H. Cone, *A Black Theology of Liberation* (Maryknoll, NY: Orbis Books, 1990), 30.

especially the Christian context that not only contains both Catholicism and Protestantism but also prevailing conditions of economic inequality.

Mosala proposes a critical reading of the Hebrew Bible concerning the contributions of the political elites who created the indebtedness of the poor in the story of Israel.[9] His proposal is impressive, as it requires a modern reader of the Hebrew Bible to tease out instances in which the poor experienced oppression in the world of the text's production. Furthermore, Mosala's hermeneutic insists that a socially engaged reader of the Hebrew Bible uncovers cases in which the composers and redactors of the ancient texts showed bias toward the poor.[10] An African liberationist reading of Neh 9, one that stands in continuity with Mosala's liberationist reading of the Hebrew Bible, will thus highlight the ideological contestations in the text. Mosala also draws on Norman K. Gottwald's liberationist approach to the Bible, which adds a curious dimension to his hermeneutic. For instance, based on "the reality that economic systems cannot be 'imported' from the Bible to meet our needs," Gottwald argues that "the ethical force of the Bible on issues of economics will have to be perspectival and motivational rather than prescriptive and technical."[11] Thus from Gottwald's argument and Mosala's hermeneutic, I submit that in order for an African liberationist reading of Neh 9 to be liberative, it ought to adopt a hermeneutic suitable for a socioeconomic discourse. This approach enables one to reread the given text in a way that is relevant in the South African context. Gottwald, however, cautions us about easily discerning liberative lessons from not-so-liberative texts, specifically with regard to the economic relief laws of the Bible, as they were a project of the kings and priests.[12] Thus an African liberationist reading of the penitential prayer of Neh 9 will take Gottwald's warning seriously as we inquire in whose interests Neh 9 was composed and redacted.

---

9. See Itumeleng J. Mosala, "The Politics of Debt and the Liberation of the Scripture," in *Tracking "The Tribes of Yahweh": On the Trial of a Classic*, ed. Ronald Boer (Sheffield: Sheffield Academic, 2002), 84.

10. See Mtshiselwa, "Re-reading the Israelite Jubilee," 18.

11. Norman K. Gottwald, "How Does Social Scientific Criticism Shape Our Understanding of the Bible as a Resource for Economic Ethics?," in *The Hebrew Bible in Its Social World and in Ours*, SemeiaSt 25 (Atlanta: Scholars Press, 1993), 345.

12. See Norman K. Gottwald, *The Tribes of Yahweh: A Sociology of the Religion of Liberated Israel 1250–1050 BCE*, BibSem 66 (Sheffield: Sheffield Academic, 1999), 35.

An African liberationist reading of Neh 9 in the present essay therefore teases out ideals and concerns for social justice in the Hebrew Bible. In other words, this essay investigates the possibility that the text of Neh 9 was intended to address the concerns for social justice in postexilic Yehud. Importantly, an African liberationist reading is critical of the ideological contestations embedded in ancient texts. Teasing out both the oppressive and liberating ideologies of the authors and redactors of ancient texts therefore becomes important for an African liberationist critic. In other words, an African liberationist critic of the Hebrew Bible highlights the oppressive ideologies of the dominant social class at the time of the production of ancient texts. Thus one may argue that an attempt at highlighting the oppressive tendencies of the community of Yehud constitutes a positive step toward a liberative reading of the text of Neh 9.

3. Retelling the Story of Israel in the Postexilic Context

As Judith H. Newman observed, a fundamental element of the "scripturalization" of the penitential prayers in ancient Israel is its representation of Israel's past.[13] If the concept of scripturalization is related to the process of conferring an authoritative status to ancient stories of Israel, as I am inclined to believe, it may thus be argued that the penitential prayer of Neh 9:6–37 received an authoritative status because it retold the story of Israel. Drawing on written traditions therefore became the means by which the past of ancient Israel was not only recalled but also used to shape the identity of the Judeans in postexilic Yehud.[14] A discussion of the way in which the author and redactor of Neh 9:6–37 used older traditions and texts is thus required.

3.1. Confession of Sins

The combination of *Gattungen* of a historical review presents the prayer of Neh 9:6–37 as the confession of sins by the Judeans.[15] From a form-

---

13. See Judith H. Newman, "Nehemiah 9 and the Scripturalization of Prayer in the Second Temple Period," in *The Function of Scripture in Early Jewish and Christian Tradition*, ed. Craig A. Evans and James A. Sanders, JSNTSup 154 / SSEJC 6 (Sheffield: Sheffield Academic, 1998), 113.

14. See Judith H. Newman, *Praying by the Book: The Scripturalization of Prayer in Second Temple Judaism*, EJL 14 (Atlanta: Scholars Press, 1999), 61.

15. See Mark A. Throntveit, *Ezra-Nehemiah*, IBC (Louisville: Westminster John

critical point of view, Neh 9:6–37 consists of "a direct address to God in which an individual, a group, or an individual on behalf of a group confesses sins and petitions for forgiveness as an act of repentance."[16] The penitential prayer of Neh 9:6–37 thus condemns the sins of the ancestors.[17] In terms of the intertextuality of the preceding text, Rodney A. Werline has convincingly submitted that Neh 9:6–37 has its roots in earlier texts, specifically, Deut 4:29–30 and 30:1–10.[18] Making a similar point as Werline, Samuel E. Balentine argues that the Deuteronomistic "politics of penitence" adopted by the author of Neh 9:6–37 aimed to articulate a confession of the ancestors' sins as also manifested in the abuse of power during the period of the monarchy that imposed exile on the people.[19] The integration of the confession of sins into the prayer sought to restore the covenantal relationship that the people enjoyed with YHWH and that the injustices committed in the postexilic period had adversely affected. The behavior of the Judeans caused YHWH's anger. Because of the tendency of those in positions of authority to abuse power, particularly the agents of the Persian Empire, the Deuteronomistic politics of penitence seem to have been relevant in postexilic Yehud. On this point, the idea that the sins of the ancestors are condemned in Neh 9:6–37 appears to be an appealing view. It is also worth pointing out the view that certain texts of the Deuteronomistic Deuteronomy, having partly emerged in the sixth

---

Knox, 1992), 100; Pieter M. Venter, "Canon, Intertextuality and History in Nehemiah 7:72b–10:40," *HTS* 65 (2009): 5.

16. Venter, "Canon, Intertextuality and History," 5; see Rodney A. Werline, "Defining Penitential Prayer," in *The Origins of Penitential Prayer in Second Temple Judaism*, vol. 1 of *Seeking the Favor of God*, ed. Mark J. Boda, Daniel K. Falk, and Rodney A. Werline, EJL 21 (Atlanta: Society of Biblical Literature, 2006), xv.

17. See Samuel E. Balentine, "I Was Ready to Be Sought Out by Those Who Did Not Ask," in Boda, Falk, and Werline, *Origins of Penitential Prayer*, 17.

18. See Rodney A. Werline, *Penitential Prayer in Second Temple Judaism: The Development of a Religious Institution*, EJL 13 (Atlanta: Scholars Press, 1998), 62–64; see Daniel K. Falk, "Scriptural Inspiration for Penitential Prayer in the Dead Sea Scrolls," in *The Development of Penitential Prayer in Second Temple Judaism*, vol. 2 of *Seeking the Favor of God*, ed. Mark J. Boda, Daniel K. Falk, and Rodney A. Werline, EJL 22 (Atlanta: Society of Biblical Literature, 2007), 133–34; Donald P. Moffat, *Ezra's Social Drama: Identity Formation, Marriage and Social Conflict in Ezra 9 and 10*, LHBOTS 579 (New York: Bloomsbury, 2013), 91.

19. See Balentine, "I Was Ready," 17; see Edward W. Said, *Reflections on Exile and Other Essays*, Convergences (Cambridge: Harvard University Press, 2000), 184.

century during the exilic period, were reused in the postexilic period (cf. Deut 4:29–30 and 30:1–10).[20]

Although it is generally accepted that the author of Neh 9:6–37 draws on Deut 4:29–30 and 29:21–30:10, the connections between these texts need to be teased out. Worthy of note is the relation particularly in terms of the theological outlook of these texts. On the issue of exclusively serving YHWH, Neh 9:6 recognizes YHWH as the only deity existing, while Deut 29:26 alludes to how the people worshiped other gods and Deut 4:28 refers to a specific instance in which they worshiped other gods. It certainly seems that Neh 9:6 is responding to the texts of both Deut 29:26 and 4:28 by contesting the worship of other gods. Furthermore, both Deut 29:23 and 4:25 express the way YHWH is angry toward the sins of the Judeans. Surprisingly, however, Neh 9:17 articulates the manner in which YHWH is slow to anger. Although at first glance one may see a contradiction, in the end it seems that the text of Nehemiah is providing a response to sins in which YHWH is slow in anger. Thus it becomes clear that Neh 9:6–37 is a direct reaction to both the texts of Deut 29:23 and 4:25. The result, however, of YWHW's anger—namely, the scattering of the Judeans among other nations, as evident in both Deut 29:28 and 4:27—is not mentioned in Neh 9:6–37, thus revealing a contrast between the penitential prayer of Neh 9 and the Deuteronomistic texts. Furthermore, on the point of Judeans being instructed to return to the torah and subsequently YHWH, Neh 9:29 is related to Deut 4:30 and 30:10.

The prophetic motifs in the book of Deuteronomy, specifically in Deut 4, 29–30, and 34, add an interesting aspect to the relation of Neh 9:6–37 to Deut 4:29–30 and 29:21–30:10.[21] In the postexilic period of the fourth and fifth centuries, the figure of Moses was reinterpreted in prophetic terms because there would never again be a prophet like Moses (see Deut 34:10–12).[22] Unlike Christophe Nihan, Eckart Otto argues that Moses acted as a prophet announcing the catastrophe of Israel and deliverance (see Deut 4:29–30).[23] In the text of Deut 29 and 30, Moses is portrayed

---

20. See Eckart Otto, "Torah and Prophecy: A Debate of Changing Identities," *VetE* 34.2 (2013): 2.
21. See Christophe Nihan, "Moses and the Prophets: Deuteronomy 18 and the Emergence of the Pentateuch as Torah," *SEÅ* 75 (2010): 21–55; Otto, "Torah and Prophecy," 1–5.
22. See Nihan, "Moses and the Prophets," 23.
23. See Otto, "Torah and Prophecy," 2.

as articulating a prophecy of doom in exile and deliverance. Not only do those prophecies presuppose the end of exile, they equally suggest that the postexilic redactor of the Pentateuch found it necessary to reiterate YHWH's position on sin.[24] The use of Moses's prophecies in Deut 4:29–30 and 29:21–30:10 by the author of Neh 9:6–37 adds a prophetic dimension to the penitential prayer. Nehemiah 9 captures the prophecy of doom and deliverance in verses 26–30 when the author states that the Judeans were warned against awful blasphemies (sins) but did not listen to the prophets. YHWH continued, however, to deliver the Judeans, enabling a reading prophecy of both doom and deliverance in some strata of Neh 9:6–37. Thus the view that the penitential prayer of Neh 9:6–37 served to offer a prophetic imagination of a liberated (or delivered) community in the postexilic period may hold true, for the idea of deliverance is articulated in 9:9–15, 27. That Neh 9:37 reads "Its rich yield goes to the kings whom you have set over us because of our sins; they have power also over our bodies and over our livestock at their pleasure, and we are in great distress" supports the idea that the penitential prayer under consideration suggests the persistence of sin. Drawing on Deut 4:29–30 and 29:21–30:10, the author of Neh 9:6–37 speaks against the sins of the Judeans in postexilic Yehud and, even more purposefully, refers to the torah.

The idea of Neh 9:6 is responding to the texts of both Deut 29:26 and 4:28 by contesting the worship of other gods, and Neh 9 manifests the abuse of power during the monarchic period that imposed exile on the people and draws to mind the story of Ahab, Naboth, and Jezebel. Moreover, Neh 9:37's allusion to the power that the political elites had over the people and their livestock points in a similar direction. The story of Ahab, Naboth, and Jezebel caricatures the abuse of power by the Assyrian Empire and contests the worship of other gods, namely, Baal. As I have written elsewhere, "1 Kings 16:29–31 gives explicit evidence of negative judgements directed at Ahab," mainly "because of his marriage … to Jezebel of Sidon."[25] The point here is that "King Ahab receives a negative judgment because of his adaptation of a foreign god, Baal, who was imported

---

24. See Otto, "Torah and Prophecy," 2.

25. Quotes from, respectively, Ndikho Mtshiselwa, "Narratology and Orality in African Biblical Hermeneutics: Reading the Story of Naboth's Vineyard and Jehu's Revolution in Light of *Intsomi YamaXhosa*," *VetE* 37.1 (2016): 6; and Konrad Schmid, *The Old Testament: A Literary History*, trans. Linda M. Maloney (Minneapolis: Fortress, 2012), 76.

from Phoenicia together with Jezebel."²⁶ Furthermore, the story of Ahab, Naboth, and Jezebel presents a depiction in which the means of productions, the productive land, were often confiscated from the less privileged by those in power. Moreover, the economic system during the Assyrian regime caused the poverty of many, as taxation led to indebtedness, which resulted in the loss of land. In addition, the Israelites were encouraged to worship Baal. Inspired by an African liberationist paradigm, it is worth noting that the poor and the middle-class people were oppressed by those in power, especially by the Assyrians. It may thus be observed that the Israelites who were in a position of power—namely, the royal families and the military—played a role in oppressing the poor and the middle class. Wolff argues that the oppressed people in the epoch of the Assyrians were also "men from the Shephelah who were forced to labor in Jerusalem." Hence, "it becomes intelligible why Micah especially takes the side of the women and children in his homeland."²⁷ Interestingly, the abuse of power and the exploitation of the poor in the epoch of Assyrian imperialism seem to have been a reality during the Persian administration in postexilic Yehud. We will return to this point shortly. We turn now, however, to the discussion of Judeans being instructed in Neh 9 to return to the torah and subsequently YHWH.

3.2. The Rise of the Torah

In his critique of the formation of the Pentateuch, particularly with regard to Deut 34:4 and 34:10–12, a text often linked to Neh 9:6–37, Konrad Schmid holds that the process of "theologizing" Moses is best explained by the desire to confer authoritative status to the torah (for which "Moses" stands). Moses is placed in close connection to God, so that the torah can lay claim to equivalent authority.²⁸ Put differently, not only does the theologizing of Moses give the torah an authoritative status, it also suggests that

---

26. Mtshiselwa, "Narratology and Orality," 6.

27. Hans W. Wolff, *Micah: A Commentary*, trans. Gary Stansell (Minneapolis: Augsburg Fortress, 1990), 75; see Daniel L. Smith-Christopher, *Micah: A Commentary*, OTL (Louisville, Kentucky: Westminster John Knox, 2015), 103.

28. See Konrad Schmid, "The Late Persian Formation of the Torah: Observations on Deuteronomy 34," in *Judah and the Judeans in the Fourth Century BCE*, ed. Oded Lipschitz, Gary N. Knoppers, and Rainer Albertz (Winona Lake, IN: Eisenbrauns, 2007), 242.

ancient texts linking the torah to Moses received an authoritative status. On this point, Moses is a "normative character and teacher who vouches for the authority of the corpus of the Torah."[29] It therefore made sense to foreground the identity of the Judeans on the torah, since it enjoyed an authoritative status. Prior to the consideration of the allusions made to the torah in Neh 9:6–37, we should consider the interpretation of the torah in Neh 8. Not only does the reference to the torah in Neh 8 restore the dignity of the Judeans; it equally confers authority to the text.[30] Some scholars also argue that Neh 8 introduces a unit in which Ezra's reading of the torah (see Neh 8:1–12, 13–14; 9:3) is followed by a confession of sin (see Neh 9:6–37) and concluded by "the firm agreement" of Neh 10.[31] An interesting point, though, is that the torah in Neh 8–10 "becomes the directive of the people's actions."[32] Following the assertion that the torah became a directive of the Judeans' behavior, it is reasonable to argue that the incorporation of the torah in the penitential prayer of Neh 9 enabled the prayer to have moral ground to shape their identity. The Judeans may therefore be identified as people who are living according to the torah. With respect to the penitential prayer of Neh 9:6–37, it must be noted that YHWH is presented as the giver of the torah (9:13–14). Here YHWH is portrayed as a speaker and the lawgiver, enabling the notion of divine law. In this case, the rise of the torah in Neh 9:6–37 (though not limited to this section) conferred an authoritative status to the penitential prayer under consideration because it provided a directive to the people's actions and expressed the identity of the Judeans.

Interestingly, Nehemiah mentions Mount Sinai alongside the torah (see Neh 9:13, 14). In this case, the storyteller of Neh 9 directly links Israel's disobedience to the revealed torah. Both Tamara Cohn Eskenazi and Mark A. Throntveit agree that Mount Sinai is mentioned in the penitential prayer, but they differ on the reasons for its insertion in the prayer,

---

29. Walter Brueggemann, *An Introduction to the Old Testament: The Canon and Christian Imagination* (Louisville: Westminster John Knox, 2003), 16.

30. See Brueggemann, *Introduction to the Old Testament*, 367–68.

31. See David J. A. Clines, "The Force of the Text: A Response to Tamara C. Eskenazi's 'Ezra-Nehemiah: From Text to Actuality,'" in *Signs and Wonders: Biblical Texts in Literary Focus*, ed. J. Cheryl. Exum, SemeiaSt 18 (Atlanta: Scholars Press, 1989), 202; Ralph W. Klein, "A Response," in *Revisiting the Composition of Ezra-Nehemiah: In Conversation with Jacob Wright's Rebuilding Identity; The Nehemiah Memoir and its Earliest Readers*, ed. Gary N. Knoppers, BZAW 348 (Berlin: de Gruyter, 2004), 22.

32. Clines, "Force of the Text," 202.

especially concerning the idea of the covenant and Abraham. Eskenazi suggest that Neh 9:13–14 does not reference the covenant because the Abrahamic covenant is still intact.[33] Throntveit, however, views Neh 9 "as a return to the faithfulness of Abraham."[34] The latter view makes more sense. The link between Israel's disobedience to the torah revealed at Mount Sinai (see Neh 9:13–14) and the mention of the covenant and Abraham's faithfulness (see Neh 9:8) supports Throntveit's argument. The proposed identity and the conduct of the Judeans in the postexilic period is linked not only to the torah but also to the faithfulness of Abraham to the covenant made with YHWH. On a level of identity, the Judeans therefore become the people who are associated with the Abrahamic covenant and whose actions are directed by the torah.

3.3. Second Exodus

Based on an African liberationist paradigm, the allusion to the first "captivity" of the Israelites in Egypt made in Neh 9:9–11 becomes intriguing, as it presupposes the oppression of some Judeans. This allusion has led Throntveit to propose a theme of a "second exodus."[35] If one reads the retelling of the story of YHWH's deliverance of his people from Egypt (9:9–15, 21) in the light of the portrayal of slavery—oppression—of the Judeans in postexilic Yehud (9:36–37), one may appreciate the theme of a second exodus.[36] The theme stands in continuity with the Exodus tradition. Regarding Neh 9:9, the suffering of the Israelites in Egypt (see Exod 3:7; Deut 26:7) is linked to the crisis at the Red Sea (see Exod 14:10, 15a) to describe YHWH's response to the predicament of the people.[37] The response of YHWH may be viewed as a call for the liberation of the oppressed Judeans.

Furthermore, the prophetic undertones of Neh 9:10 add an interesting dimension to the use of the exodus tradition in the penitential prayer

---

33. See Tamara Cohn Eskenazi, "Nehemiah 9–10: Structure and Significance," *JHebS* 3 (2001): 3.3.

34. Throntveit, *Ezra-Nehemiah*, 108.

35. See Throntveit, *Ezra-Nehemiah*, 99.

36. See H. G. M. Williamson, *Studies in Persian Period History and Historiography*, FAT 38 (Tübingen: Mohr Siebeck, 2004), 286.

37. See Mark J. Boda, *Praying the Tradition: The Origin and Use of Tradition in Nehemiah 9*, BZAW 277 (Berlin: de Gruyter, 1999), 117.

under consideration. The statement ותתן אתת ומפתים "You performed signs and wonders" (9:10) carries prophetic undertones. In the context of the Pentateuch, the reference to signs and wonders in Neh 9:10 shows that the author of Neh 9:6–37 probably borrowed the theme of exodus from Exod 7:3, 9 and Deut 6:22. Furthermore, in the context of the prophetic literature, a sign was given by a prophet to support the word of YHWH (see Joel 3:3; Ezek 12:6; Isa 8:18).[38] With respect to Neh 9:11, however, Mark J. Boda has argued that "9:11b reveals the influence of the Song of Moses in Exod 15, while incorporating other poetic descriptions connected with sea imagery. Of these images, the only one connected to the exodus tradition was that found in Deutero-Isaiah."[39] The phrase במצולת כמו־אבן, "depths like a stone," is used in both Exod 15:5 and Neh 9:11. In addition, the reference to במים עזים, "mighty waters," in Neh 9:11 relies on Exod 15:10. The author of Neh 9:11 based the retelling of the Israel story on the Song of Moses in Exod 15.[40] On this point, the author of Neh 9:11 first depicts the deliverance from the pharaoh and then makes reference to the Song of Moses. Furthermore, the phrase במים עזים, "mighty waters" (Isa 43:16), marks an allusion to the crossing of the Red Sea, which is equally evident in Neh 9:11. The allusion of the penitential prayer to the prophetic literature allows one to view Neh 9:6–37 as inspiring a hopeful and prophetic imagination of a liberated community in postexilic Yehud.

Thus it seems reasonably certain that Neh 9:6–37 includes a reference to the suffering of the Israelites in Egypt (see Exod 3:7; Deut 26:7), an allusion to the crisis at the Red Sea (see Exod 14:10, 15a), a reference to the "performed signs and wonders" (see Exod 7:3, 9; Deut 6:22; Neh 9:10), and an allusion to the Song of Moses (see Exod 15; Isa 43:16). That all these references and allusions seem to be made in the postexilic context supports the view that the penitential prayer drew on authoritative texts to retell a story articulating a statement of hope to the oppressed Judeans. As will be argued below, it must first be said that the Judeans in the postexilic period were the slaves of the Persian authorities; they do not, however, seem to have been enslaved in the usual sense of the word but rather became exploited peasants.[41] Although Neh 9:6–37 presents a

---

38. See Boda, *Praying the Tradition*, 118.
39. Boda, *Praying the Tradition*, 124.
40. See Boda, *Praying the Tradition*, 122–23.
41. See Walter Brueggemann, *Great Prayers of the Old Testament* (Louisville: Westminster John Knox, 2008), 109.

retelling of a story, it also seems to be aimed at shaping the identity of the Judeans in postexilic Yehud.

4. Judean Identity and Social Justice in Postexilic Yehud

African theologians and philosophers have made a remarkable contribution to the topic of identity formation. For his part, John S. Mbiti remarks: "In traditional life, the individual does not and cannot exist alone except corporately. He [She] owes this existence to other people, including those of past generations and his [her] contemporaries. He [She] is simply part of the whole. The community must therefore make, create, or produce the individual; for the individual depends on the corporate group."[42] The point made here is that a reliable portrait of an individual's identity is mirrored by the image and experiences of the community as a whole. The norms, values, and experiences that are embedded in the stories of African people constitute a critical role in the formation of the identity of individuals. As such, one is reminded of the contribution made by Louis Jonker and Pieter M. Venter on the topic of identity formation, who in turn argued that both the social environment and the narratives of Israel's history shed light on the identity formation of the Judeans in postexilic Yehud.[43] Two issues are critical in the discussion of identity formation in postexilic Yehud: narratives and social-justice issues.

4.1. Narratives and Identity Formation of the Judean Community

Balentine addresses the issue of the institutionalization of penitential prayer in the postexilic period.[44] He draws on Werline's argument that the generalized and accepted use of motifs that defines a community's identity in terms of its origins and distinguishes the Jewish community from other

---

42. John S. Mbiti, *African Religions and Philosophy* (London: Heinemann, 1969), 108; see Mogobe B. Ramose, *African Philosophy through Ubuntu* (Harare: Mond Books, 1999), 79. Bracketed text is my insertion.
43. See Louis Jonker, "Textual Identities in the Books of Chronicles: The Case of Jehoram's History," in *Community Identity in Judean Historiography: Biblical and Comparative Perspectives*, ed. Gary N. Knoppers and Kenneth A. Ristau (Winona Lake, IN: Eisenbrauns, 2009), 201–6; Venter, "Canon, Intertextuality and History," 5.
44. See Balentine, "I Was Ready," 14.

communities indicates a process of institutionalizing penitential prayers.[45] Said differently, the theological motifs embedded in the penitential prayer of Neh 9 shaped the identity of the Judeans in postexilic Yehud. Walter Brueggemann has decisively argued that Neh 9:6–37 functioned "to recall the community to its singular identity, unmixed and uncompromised, committed to the one who is the source of identity and the only possible giver of 'new life' in the future."[46]

The identity of the Judeans as nuanced in Neh 9:6–37 appears to be linked to the patriarch Abraham (9:7–8); to the liberation of the Israelites from Pharaoh (9:9–15, 21); to the possession of the Promised Land (9:22–25); to the caution about the consequence of disobedience to YHWH, the exile (9:16–21, 26–30); and to the end of the Babylonian exile (9:31–37).

Nehemiah 9:2 suggests that "those of Israelite descent" separated themselves from all foreigners and stood and confessed their sins and the iniquities of their ancestors.[47] It is interesting to note that those of Israelite descent are called the exiles.[48] This identification is linked to the figure of Abraham who is chosen by YHWH based on his faithfulness—a sense of sacredness (see Neh 9:8). The image of sacredness expressed by the image of purity and exclusiveness in Lev 19:19 and Deut 30:6, as well as in Ezra-Nehemiah (Ezra 9:2 even calls it "holy seed"; cf. Neh 9:2, 8), presupposes that Ezra attempts to construct a Jewish national identity in Neh 9:6–37.[49] The idea of a holy people supports the view that what we have in Ezra 9:2, 8 is an articulation of the identity of the Judeans (probably the Babylonian exilic returnees) in postexilic Yehud. No doubt, the penitential prayer of Neh 9:6–37, and more specifically the reference to the figure of Abraham, identifies the Judeans as a sacral community (see Neh 8:13–18; 10).[50]

---

45. See Werline, "Penitential Prayer," 3–4.

46. Brueggemann, *Great Prayers*, 98; see also Venter, "Canon, Intertextuality and History," 7.

47. See Ntozakhe Cezula, "Identity Formation and Community Solidarity: Second Temple Historiographies in Discourse with (South) African Theologies of Reconstruction" (PhD diss, University of Stellenbosch, 2013), 127.

48. See Fishbane, *Biblical Interpretation*, 114.

49. See Mark G. Brett, "National Identity as Commentary and as Metacommentary," in *Historiography and Identity (Re)formulation in Second Temple Historiographical Literature*, ed. Louis Jonker, LHBOTS 534 (New York: T&T Clark, 2010), 34.

50. See Mark Leuchter, "Coming to Terms with Ezra's Many Identities in Ezra-Nehemiah," in Jonker, *Historiography and Identity (Re)formulation*, 56.

At first glance, it appears that the existential problems of identity in postexilic Yehud are linked to the loss of king, temple, land, and independence, to a point where the idea of the torah is given a prominence in Neh 9:6–37 that displaces the ideas of land, king, and temple, while a text later than Neh 9, Dan 9:4–19, returns to the focus on the land, king, and temple. The issue of the land, however, is not entirely replaced by the torah in the penitential prayer of Neh 9:6–37, as the reference to the promised land is made in the text. The land is mentioned seven times in the prayer and four times in conjunction to the land promise made to the patriarchs (cf. 9:8, 15, 22, 23, 24, 25, 35).[51] The reference to land in Neh 9 is made probably because the promise made to the patriarchs was still not fulfilled for some Judeans, as they were landless and some had lost land to the wealthy elites.[52] Based on the rise of the torah and the authority given to texts upholding the torah, as and based on the emphasis on land, it seems clear that the torah became a symbol of identity for the Judeans in the postexilic period, which also applies to the promise of the land made to the patriarch Abraham.

Regarding the motif of exile embedded in Neh 9:6–37, there seems to be no consensus among the Ezra-Nehemiah commentators. For instance, H. G. M. Williamson rejects the idea that a reference to the Babylonian exile is made in Neh 9:6–37, while Venter supports the idea.[53] Williamson based his argument on the observation that the captivity, exile, and return receive no mention in Neh 9. This observation has also led him to argue that the addressees of the penitential prayer are the Judeans who remained in the land, the so-called people of the land (9:30). Although the view that the captivity, exile, and return are not mentioned in Neh 9 is indisputable, there are, however, instances in the text where the Babylonian exile is presupposed. First, an allusion to being handed to the enemies as a result of sin fits in the situation of exile (see 9:27–28). Second, the idea that people

---

51. See Newman, "Nehemiah 9," 113.

52. See Ndikho Mtshiselwa, "Who Possessed the Promised Land? Scribal Scholarship in the Formation of Patriarchal Narrative(s) and the Holiness Code," *Sem* 58 (2016): 65–66; see Ehud Ben Zvi, "The Memory of Abraham in Late Persian/Early Hellenistic Yehud/Judah," in *Remembering Biblical Figures in the Late Persian and Early Hellenistic Periods*, ed. Diana V. Edelman and Ehud Ben Zvi (Oxford: Oxford University Press, 2013), 13–14.

53. See Williamson, *Persian Period History*, 292–93; Venter, "Canon, Intertextuality and History," 5.

being handed over to the "people of the lands" in Neh 9:30 suggests the Babylonian exilic returnees were handed over to those who remained in the land. In that case, an exilic situation is presupposed. Thus on this point I would argue that although the exile is not explicitly mentioned in Neh 9:6–37, the situation of exile is presupposed. The idea of exile forms part of the identity of the Judeans in postexilic Yehud.

4.2. Identity Formation and Social-Justice Issues

With respect to recital of the penitential prayer of Neh 9 in the postexilic epoch, Eskenazi notes that "like all public liturgy, such a recital aims at community building by cementing a common story and identity."[54] In other words, the *Gattung* of penitential prayer in Neh 9 presents a theology simultaneously accounting for the postexilic circumstances and advancing faith as well as an identity that is grounded in YHWH. As mentioned earlier, a critical issue in the discourse of identity formation in postexilic Yehud is the impact that the social realities—postexilic circumstances—alluded to in ancient texts had on the formation of the identity of the Judeans. The view that ancient texts participated in the discourse on identity is appealing.[55] Worthy of note is Jonker's argument that "the close relationship between the social environment within which a group exists, the textual resources that are available in the given culture, and the role that renewed textual construction plays in the process of identity formation" are critical in the discourse of identity construction in postexilic Yehud.[56] This means that the *Sitz im Leben*, old traditions, and the inner-biblical exegesis of ancient texts, as participants, were incorporated into Neh 9 to shape the identity of the Judeans in the postexilic context. Put differently, "for both exiles and Judean inhabitants, kinship and traditions of the past, along with imperialism and resistance to imperializing forces, influenced the identities they forged."[57] This statement further confirms the influence that the context from which Neh 9:6–37 emerged had on the formation of the identity of the Judeans in postexilic Yehud. As mentioned previously, the context of Neh 9 included, among other issues,

---

54. Eskenazi, "Nehemiah 9–10," 2.6.
55. See Moffat, *Ezra's Social Drama*, 23.
56. See Jonker, "Textual Identities," 201–6.
57. Moffat, *Ezra's Social Drama*, 28.

persistent sin, awful blasphemies, abuse of power, and the oppression of some Judeans in the form of slavery (socioeconomic injustice).

The argument that the addressees of Neh 9:6–37 experienced socioeconomic injustice that widened the gap between the poor and the wealthy sheds light on the identity of the Judeans. As a collective, the addressees of the Judeans in postexilic Yehud were an unequal community divided on economic and class lines. That there was disproportional benefit from land ownership confirms this impression. Furthermore, the addressees of Neh 9:6–37 may be identified as a community working the farms under harsh realities and subsequently not receiving what was rightfully due to them. The text regards such a community as slaves. For instance, Brueggemann argues that the Judeans who were treated as slaves in Babylonia were likewise treated as slaves by the Persian authorities in the postexilic period.[58] Based on 9:33, he explains Ezra's action in the following manner: "He describes for God the exploited status of the Judeans in Jerusalem at the hands of the Persians.... For all of the generosity and support of Artaxerxes for Nehemiah, the Persians are effective tax collectors. They exploited the colony of Yehud so vigorously that Ezra can say, 'we are slaves…' The Jews are back at work in the homeland, but are exploited peasants."[59]

Based on this explanation and on the textual evidence of Neh 9:6–37—and, more specifically, based on the statement אנחנו עבדים, "we are slaves" (9:36)—there is no doubt that the Judeans considered themselves to be slaves during the postexilic period. Intriguingly, the reference to slavery in Neh 9 recalls the issue of indentured servants and debt-slaves suggested by Neh 5. That the historical review of Neh 5 partly nuances the social background of the penitential prayer of Neh 9 presents an inspiring idea. In addition to the noticeable reference to slavery in both these texts, however, it is necessary to observe additional links. The consensus that a significant portion of the book of Nehemiah is made up of an account written by Nehemiah himself, the Nehemiah memoir, suggests that the texts of Neh 5

---

58. See Brueggemann, *Great Prayers*, 109; see also Walter Brueggemann, *Cadences of Home: Preaching among Exiles* (Louisville: Westminster John Knox, 1997), 115; Emmanuel O. Usue, "Restoration or Desperation in Ezra and Nehemiah? Implications for Africa," *OTE* 20 (2007): 843; Temba Rugwiji, "Appropriating Judean Post-exilic Literature in a Postcolonial Discourse: A Case for Zimbabwe" (PhD diss., University of South Africa, 2013), 46.

59. Brueggemann, *Great Prayers*, 109; see also Cezula, "Identity Formation," 91; Moffat, *Ezra's Social Drama*, 49.

and 9 have a similar date.[60] If credence is given to the view that the stories of these texts are told by a single person—namely, Nehemiah—it is reasonable to argue that they have a similar social background. Furthermore, the dating of the book of Nehemiah to betwee 433 and 400 BCE suggests that Neh 5 and 9 emerged from a similar period and context.[61] Nehemiah 5 and 9 also contain related themes and ideas. An allusion to the payment of tribute to the kings appears in both these texts (see 5:4; 9:37). Nehemiah 5:5 and 9:37 allude to the powerlessness of the Judeans. Nehemiah 5:7 and 9:34 mention the misconduct of the officials—political elites. In addition, both Neh 5 and 9 allude to the experience of hardship—slavery (see 5:5; 9:17, 36).

A case in point in the relations between Neh 9 and 5, especially from an African liberationist perspective, is the suggestion of the extraction of labor in ancient Israel. An allusion to indentured slaves who worked on the estate of other wealthy Judeans in Neh 5:5, 8, as well as the reference to the feasting of the elite in 5:17–18, provides a clue about the extraction of labor. On the manner in which monarchs ruled, 1 Sam 8 shows that often in ancient Israel not only did the elites take the yield of the people's crops and the flocks, but they also took their children to work in their fields and kitchens.[62] In that case, the extraction of labor is noticeable. In keeping with the prophet's warning, Solomon designed a system of heavy taxation in order to provide for the table of the elites (see 1 Kgs 5:7–8)."[63] Similar to the case of 1 Sam 8, among others, Neh 5 shows the extraction of labor that sought to provide for needs of the elites.

In 5:17, Nehemiah boasts that the large number of guests (150 people), Judeans and officials, besides those who came from the nations around, enjoyed hospitality in his house. Verse 18 gives details of what was prepared on a daily basis: one ox, six choice sheep, and poultry; at ten-day intervals, wine of every kind was offered in abundance to Nehemiah's

---

60. See Lester L. Grabbe, *Yehud: A History of the Persian Province of Judah*, vol. 1 of *A History of the Jews and Judaism in the Second Temple Period*, LSTS 47 (London: T&T Clark, 2004), 78.

61. See Lester L. Grabbe, *Ezra-Nehemiah*, OTR (London: Routledge, 1998), 24; see also Cezula, "Identity Formation," 83.

62. See Jacob L. Wright and Michael J. Chan, "Feasting: From Kings to Communities," in *Oxford Encyclopedia of the Bible and Archaeology*, edited by Daniel M. Master et al. (Oxford: Oxford University Press, 2013), 11.

63. See Wright and Chan, "From Kings to Communities," 11.

guests. Importantly, "feasting similar to that described by Nehemiah is encountered throughout the ancient world, where it played a central role in displaying power, forming social bonds, and fortifying political alliances."[64] As Jacob L. Wright observes, within the satrapal administration of the Achaemenid empire, "Satraps often mimicked the great-king in material culture, court life and behaviour." Based on this observation, he compares what is known about the satraps to Nehemiah's statements regarding his house (see Neh 2:8), bodyguards (see Neh 2:9), and financial reforms (see Neh 5), as well as the personal wealth and benefaction he displays at his table (see Neh 5).[65] Nehemiah's boasts of providing wide assortments of meat, poultry, and wine may be compared to the ostentation that characterized satrapal tables in ancient Israel.[66] As Jacob L. Wright and Meredith E. Hollman argued, "The tables of the satraps and governors were modeled on that of the king; thus Nehemiah in Judah not only boasts of his hospitality but also refers to taxation as 'eating the bread of the governor.'"[67] Artaxerxes showing extraordinary favor to the Spartan Antalcidas by honoring him publicly after a meal supports Wright and Hollman's argument.[68] Provisions for the king's daily meals were a huge expense paid from both the private estates of the palace, which were located in Persia and throughout the empire, and gifts from the provinces.[69] More importantly, satrapal (royal) tables in ancient Israel were an expense borne by the laborers.

Various issues may be raised regarding Nehemiah's feast, including whether the text refers to regular (daily) commensality or a single occasion, as in the case of triumphal banqueting.[70] Another issue could be the probable exaggeration of the amount of meat consumption.[71] The primary

---

64. Jacob L. Wright, "Commensal Politics in Ancient Western Asia: The Background to Nehemiah's Feasting (Part I)," *ZAW* 122 (2010): 212.
65. Jacob L. Wright, "Commensal Politics in Ancient Western Asia: The Background to Nehemiah's Feasting (continued, Part II)," *ZAW* 123 (2010): 349–50.
66. See Wright, "Commensal Politics (Part II)," 349–50.
67. Jacob L. Wright and Meredith Elliot Hollman, "Society and Politics: Banquet and Gift Exchange," in *A Companion to the Achaemenid Persian Empire*, ed. Bruno Jacobs and Robert Rollinger, BCAW (London: Wiley-Blackwell, 2012), 3–4; see also Neh 5:14–18.
68. See Wright and Hollman, "Society and Politics," 3–4.
69. See Wright and Hollman, "Society and Politics," 3–4.
70. See Wright, "Commensal Politics (Part II)," 348.
71. See Wright, "Commensal Politics (Part II)," 349–50.

concern here, however, is the extraction of labor, particularly under Nehemiah's administration. As is now widely accepted, "securing labor was a much greater concern than owning real estate in the economy of ancient Israel."[72]

Of significance to the issue of Nehemiah's feasts and the extraction of labor is Gale Yee's contribution on "Royal Feasts and Rural Extraction." Drawing on the Deuteronomistic historiography, Yee argues that labor extracted from the village communes was responsible for providing and processing food, especially for royal feasts.[73] The daily meals of the royal courts contributed to the extraction of labor (1 Kgs 4:22–24). In addition, labor was forcefully extracted for feasts on special occasions (1 Kgs 3:15; 8:65; 10:5)."[74] In the case of the oppressed female laborers who prepared flour, Yee remarks that ancient Near Eastern texts "revealed that the expected labor performance for these millers was probably beyond the abilities of the normal worker, given their overall workload. There were no incentives to produce more, since their compensation was no more than the minimum amount of grain and clothing to keep them able to produce."[75]

Based on the preceding remark, the oppression of younger women in particular is not shocking (see Neh 5:5). The verb כבש, "to subdue, make subservient," in Neh 5:5 captures the manner in which young women and men were made to be subservient in the regime of Nehemiah. Food also had to be prepared for Nehemiah's feast by the labor from the village communes. The feast in Neh 5 thus stands in continuity with the royal feasts for which the extraction of labor is presupposed. Nehemiah 9:36–37 also makes a point that "rich yield"—produce—accrued from farming that was

---

72. Gale Yee, "'He Will Take the Best of Your Fields': Royal Feasts and Rural Extraction," paper presented at the Annual Meeting of the Society of Biblical Literature, Atlanta, 2015, 6; Roland Boer, *The Sacred Economy of Ancient Israel*, LAI (Louisville: Westminster John Knox, 2015), 70, 228–29; Gershon Galil, *The Lower Stratum Families in the Neo-Assyrian Period*, CHANE 27 (Leiden: Brill, 2007), 348–50; Mario Liverani, "The Near East: The Bronze Age," in *The Ancient Economy: Evidence and Models*, ed. Joseph G. Manning and Ian Morris, SSH (Stanford, CA: Stanford University Press, 2005), 50–1; Carol Meyer, *Rediscovering Eve: Ancient Israelite Women in Context* (New York: Oxford University Press, 2013), 97–102.

73. See Yee, "Royal Feasts," 3.

74. Yee, "Royal Feasts," 13.

75. Yee, "Royal Feasts," 17; see also Robert K. Englund, "Hard Work—Where Will It Get You? Labor Management in Ur III Mesapotamia," *JNES* 50 (1991): 255–80.

channeled to the elites, that is, the kings, came from the hardship of the Judeans. The extraction of labor that Neh 9:36–37 sees as slavery was to the benefits of the kings.

At issue in the great cry—distress—of the people seems to be the extraction of labor. Why? Various scholars have argued that "because labor shortage was a persistent issue, the primary tax on the village communities was the levy of human bodies rather than their quota of crops or flocks." It comes as no surprise that Nehemiah charges the elites with transferring as many subsistence workers as possible into the estate system and keeping them there as indentured servants and debt-slaves (see Neh 5:5, 6–8). Conflicts, and most importantly the cry of the people in Neh 5—and, by abstraction, in Neh 9—occurred when the ruling classes extracted more labor from the villages and subsequently placed intense strain upon the agriculture of the villages.[76] From the time when the Assyrians imposed their own demands for tribute upon the royal courts of Israel and Juda to Nehemiah's context, class conflicts became exacerbated.

Notably, the extraction of laborers in the text under investigation is exemplified in Marx's alienation of the workers. Nehemiah 5:3–5 suggests loss of land. The laborers from the village communes were therefore alienated from the means of production by the Israelite economic system under Nehemiah's administration. On the issue of being alienated from means of production, Yee highlights an interesting factor. She argues that "since the grinding stones (mortars, querns), cooking vessels (griddles, trays, pots), and ovens (*tabun* and *tannur*) belonged to the estate," the female laborer in particular was "alienated from bread, the product of her labor, in that she toiled not for herself or her family, but for rations for other servile workers like her and the conspicuous consumption of bread for the elite."[77] Nehemiah 5 therefore shows the oppression of laborers in the way they were alienated from the means of production as well as from the production itself.

It becomes clear that the penitential prayer of Neh 9:6–37 shaped the identity of the Judeans and raised concerns for social justice in postexilic Yehud. Worthy of note are some of the issues embedded in the prayer:

---

76. Yee, "Royal Feasts," 9; see also Norman K. Gottwald, "Sociology (Ancient Israel)," *ABD* 6:84; Boer, *Sacred Economy*, 118–21, 149–55, 158–63; Peter R. Bedford, "The Economy of the Near East in the First Millennium BC," in Manning and Morris, *Ancient Economy*, 76.

77. Yee, "Royal Feasts," 18.

first, the memory of the patriarch Abraham (9:7–8); second, an allusion to the liberation of the Israelites from Pharaoh under the leadership of Moses (9:9–15, 21); third, the idea of the possession of the Promised Land (9:22–25); and fourth, caution about the consequence of disobedience to YHWH—the exile (9:16–21, 26–30). Interestingly, the expression of the identity of the Judeans and concerns of social justice in Neh 9 are enveloped in the preceding issues. However, a cardinal question to pose is: Why are the identity of the Judeans and the concerns of social justice presented in the form of a prayer in Neh 9?

5. The Use of *Gattungen* in Creating Nehemiah 9

That "the *Gattungen* of historical review and penitential prayer are combined into a new composition" in Neh 9 is indisputable.[78] My interest, however, lies in the use of the *Gattung* of the penitential prayer. Notably, the *Gattung* of the penitential prayer was employed "on purpose because it was the most suitable form available to the author(s) to present Israel's unique theology formulated in both positive and negative terms."[79] Interestingly, Throntveit calls the penitential prayer of Neh 9 a "doxology of judgement."[80] This means that Neh 9 may be viewed as an expression of "God's mercy not only in terms of what God did for his people in the past, but also in terms of Israel's disobedience and their total demeritorious receiving of God's care throughout history."[81] The confession of sin (see Neh 9:6–37) and the petition for mercy (9:32–37), as well as "the firm agreement" of Neh 10, suggest that the *Gattung* of the penitential prayer was used to lead the Judeans to the ceremonial commitment to the torah.

As in Dan 9:17–19, YHWH is requested in Neh 9 to change the circumstances of the Judeans. As Eskenazi observed, however, the penitential prayer of Neh 9 diverges from the other confessions of penitence (see Dan 9).[82] Nehemiah 9 recites transgressions of earlier generations in order not only to explain why their catastrophes came about but also to chal-

---

78. Venter, "Canon, Intertextuality and History," 5.
79. Venter, "Canon, Intertextuality and History," 6; see also Hans-Peter Mathys, *Dichter und Beter: Theologen aus spätalttestamentlicher Zeit*, OBO 132 (Fribourg: Universitätsverlag, 1994), 4.
80. Throntveit, *Ezra-Nehemiah*, 106.
81. Venter, "Canon, Intertextuality and History," 6.
82. See Eskenazi, "Nehemiah 9–10," 2.9.

lenge the postexilic community to adopt an ethical behavior grounded in the torah. Confession of sins, repentance, and living according to the torah would lead to YHWH's intervention and redress of the postexilic distresses. "According to the Deuteronomistic scheme of history, change always takes place when Israel repents and they confess their sin."[83] The theme of penitence, and, more importantly, the *Gattung* of penitential prayer, is employed to articulate YHWH's sovereignty, mercy and justice in a context of injustices. Thus I concur with Patrick D. Miller that the theological heart and rationale of the penitential prayer of Neh 9 lies at the "juxtaposition of a clear acknowledgement of the justice and rightness of God's judgment with an appeal to the mercy of God."[84] The use of the form of a penitential prayer made sense in the postexilic community, especially one that not only sought to rebuild the temple but also was searching for its identity as a people of YHWH. The articulation of the identity of the Judeans and the concerns of social justice in the form of a prayer stood a chance of being well received by the Judeans in a cultic setting. Reciting the prayer of such a nature in a context of worship meant that it would bear a positive impact on the identity formation of the Judeans as well as on their attempts to live according to the torah.

6. Conclusion

In conclusion, this essay submits that the penitential prayer of Neh 9:6–37 presented a retelling of the story of Israel that in turn shaped the identity of the Judeans and addressed concerns of social justice. It has been argued here that Neh 9:6–37 was set to cast a hopeful and prophetic imagination of a liberated community in postexilic Yehud, especially in a context where the concern for social justice was also at issue. Put differently, the penitential prayer of Neh 9:6–37 drew on authoritative texts and traditions to articulate a statement of hope to the oppressed Judeans in postexilic Yehud. In addition, because the penitential prayer of Neh 9:6–37 challenged the sins of the addressees and drew on traditions that had prophetic undertones, the prayer may be viewed as set to offer a prophetic imagination of a liberated (delivered) community in the postexilic period. Importantly, not only has an African liberationist reading of Neh 9 teased out ideals

---

83. Venter, "Canon, Intertextuality and History," 6.
84. Patrick D. Miller, *They Cried to the Lord: The Form and Theology of Biblical Prayer* (Minneapolis: Fortress, 1994), 257.

and concerns for social justice, it has equally highlighted the oppressive ideologies of the dominant social class at the time of the production and transmission of the prayer in this text.

Bibliography

Balentine, Samuel E. "I Was Ready to Be Sought Out by Those Who Did Not Ask." Pages 1–20 in *The Origins of Penitential Prayer in Second Temple Judaism*. Vol. 1 of *Seeking the Favor of God*. Edited by Mark J. Boda, Daniel K. Falk, and Rodney A. Werline. EJL 21. Atlanta: Society of Biblical Literature, 2006.

Bedford, Peter R. "The Economy of the Near East in the First Millennium BC." Pages 58–83 in *The Ancient Economy: Evidence and Models*. Edited by Joseph G. Manning and Ian Morris. SSH. Stanford: Stanford University Press, 2005.

Ben Zvi, Ehud. "The Memory of Abraham in Late Persian/Early Hellenistic Yehud/Judah." Pages 7–22 in *Remembering Biblical Figures in the Late Persian and Early Hellenistic Periods*. Edited by Diana V. Edelman and Ehud Ben Zvi. Oxford: Oxford University Press, 2013.

Boda, Mark J. *Praying the Tradition: The Origin and Use of Tradition in Nehemiah 9*. BZAW 277. Berlin: de Gruyter, 1999.

Boer, Roland. *The Sacred Economy of Ancient Israel*. LAI. Louisville: Westminster John Knox, 2015.

Botta, Alejandro F. "What Does It Mean to Be a Latino Biblical Critic? A Brief Essay." Pages 107–20 in *Latino/a Biblical Hermeneutics: Problematics, Objectives, Strategies*. Edited by Francisco Lozada Jr. and Fernando F. Segovia. Atlanta: SBL Press, 2014.

Brett, Mark G. "National Identity as Commentary and as Metacommentary." Pages 29–40 in *Historiography and Identity (Re)formulation in Second Temple Historiographical Literature*. Edited by Louis Jonker. LHBOTS 534. New York: T&T Clark, 2010.

Brueggemann, Walter. *Cadences of Home: Preaching among Exiles*. Louisville: Westminster John Knox, 1997.

———. *Great Prayers of the Old Testament*. Louisville: Westminster John Knox, 2008.

———. *An Introduction to the Old Testament: The Canon and Christian Imagination*. Louisville: Westminster John Knox, 2003.

Cezula, Ntozakhe. "Identity Formation and Community Solidarity: Second Temple Historiographies in Discourse with (South) African

Theologies of Reconstruction." PhD diss., University of Stellenbosch, 2013.

Clines, David J. A. "The Force of the Text: A Response to Tamara C. Eskenazi's 'Ezra-Nehemiah; From Text to Actuality.'" Pages 199–216 in *Signs and Wonders: Biblical Texts in Literary Focus*. Edited by J. Cheryl Exum. SemeiaSt 18. Atlanta: Scholars Press, 1989.

Cone, James H. *A Black Theology of Liberation*. Maryknoll, NY: Orbis Books, 1990.

Englund, Robert K. "Hard Work—Where Will It Get You? Labor Management in Ur III Mesapotamia." *JNES* 50 (1991): 255–80.

Eskenazi, Tamara Cohn. "Nehemiah 9–10: Structure and Significance." *JHebS* 3 (2001): 1.1–4.3.

Falk, Daniel K. "Scriptural Inspiration for Penitential Prayer in the Dead Sea Scrolls." Pages 127–57 in *The Development of Penitential Prayer in Second Temple Judaism*. Vol. 2 of Seeking the Favor of God. Edited by Mark J. Boda, Daniel K. Falk, and Rodney A. Werline. EJL 22. Atlanta: Society of Biblical Literature, 2007.

Fishbane, Michael A. *Biblical Interpretation in Ancient Israel*. Oxford: Clarendon, 1985.

Galil, Gershon. *The Lower Stratum Families in the Neo-Assyrian Period*. CHANE 27. Leiden: Brill, 2007.

Gottwald, Norman K. "How Does Social Scientific Criticism Shape Our Understanding of the Bible as a Resource for Economic Ethics?" Pages 341–47 in *The Hebrew Bible in Its Social World and in Ours*. SemeiaSt 25. Atlanta: Scholars Press, 1993.

———. "Sociology (Ancient Israel)." *ABD* 6:79–89.

———. *The Tribes of Yahweh: A Sociology of the Religion of Liberated Israel 1250–1050 BCE* BibSem 66. Sheffield: Sheffield Academic, 1999.

Grabbe, Lester L. *Ezra-Nehemiah*. OTR. London: Routledge, 1998.

———. *Yehud: A History of the Persian Province of Judah*. Vol. 1 of History of the Jews and Judaism in the Second Temple Period. LSTS 47. London: T&T Clark, 2004.

Jonker, Louis. "Textual Identities in the Books of Chronicles: The Case of Jehoram's History." Pages 197–217 in *Community Identity in Judean Historiography: Biblical and Comparative Perspectives*. Edited by Gary N. Knoppers and Kenneth A. Ristau. Winona Lake, IN: Eisenbrauns, 2009.

Klein, Ralph W. "A Response." Pages 21–27 in *Revisiting the Composition of Ezra-Nehemiah: In Conversation with Jacob Wright's Rebuilding Iden-*

tity; *The Nehemiah Memoir and Its Earliest Readers*. Edited by Gary N. Knoppers. BZAW 348. Berlin: de Gruyter, 2004.

Le Roux, Jurie H. "Africa and the Future of Our Scholarly Past." Pages 307–23 in *African and European Readers of the Bible in Dialogue: In Quest of a Shared Meaning*. Edited by Hans De Wit and Gerald O. West. SRA 32. Leiden: Brill, 2008.

Leuchter, Mark. "Coming to Terms with Ezra's Many Identities in Ezra-Nehemiah ." Pages 41–64 in *Historiography and Identity (Re)formulation in Second Temple Historiographical Literature*. Edited by Louis Jonker. LHBOTS 534. New York: T&T Clark, 2010.

Liverani, Mario. "The Near East: The Bronze Age." Pages 47–57 in *The Ancient Economy: Evidence and Models*. Edited by Joseph G. Manning and Ian Morris. SSH. Stanford, CA: Stanford University Press, 2005.

Mathys, Hans-Peter. *Dichter und Beter: Theologen aus spätalttestamentlicher Zeit*. OBO 132. Freiburg: Universitätsverlag, 1994.

Mbiti, John S. *African Religions and Philosophy*. London: Heinemann, 1969.

Meyer, Carol. *Rediscovering Eve: Ancient Israelite Women in Context*. New York: Oxford University Press, 2013

Miller, Patrick D. *They Cried to the Lord: The Form and Theology of Biblical Prayer*. Minneapolis: Fortress, 1994.

Moffat, Donald P. *Ezra's Social Drama: Identity Formation, Marriage and Social Conflict in Ezra 9 and 10*. LHBOTS 579. New York: Bloomsbury, 2013.

Mosala, Itumeleng J. "The Politics of Debt and the Liberation of the Scripture." Pages 77–84 in *Tracking "The Tribes of Yahweh": On the Trial of a Classic*. Edited by Ronald Boer. Sheffield: Sheffield Academic, 2002.

Mtshiselwa, Ndikho. "Narratology and Orality in African Biblical Hermeneutics: Reading the Story of Naboth's Vineyard and Jehu's Revolution in Light of *Intsomi YamaXhosa*." *VetE* 37.1 (2016): 1–10. http://www.scielo.org.za/pdf/vee/v37n1/48.pdf.

———. "Remembering and Constructing Israelite Identity in Postexilic Yehud: Some Remarks on the Penitential Prayer of Nehemiah 9:6–37." *VetE* 37.1 (2016): 1–6. http://www.scielo.org.za/pdf/vee/v37n1/03.pdf.

———. "Re-reading the Israelite Jubilee in Leviticus 25:8–55 in the Context of Land Redistribution and Socio-economic Justice in South Africa: An African Liberationist Perspective." PhD diss., University of South Africa, 2015.

———. "Who Possessed the Promised Land? Scribal Scholarship in the Formation of Patriarchal Narrative(s) and the Holiness Code." *Sem* 58 (2016): 63–78.

Newman, Judith H. "Nehemiah 9 and the Scripturalization of Prayer in the Second Temple Period." Pages 112–23 in *The Function of Scripture in Early Jewish and Christian Tradition*. Edited by Craig A. Evans and James A. Sanders. JSNTSup 154. SSEJC 6. Sheffield: Sheffield Academic, 1998.

———. *Praying by the Book: The Scripturalization of Prayer in Second Temple Judaism*. EJL 14. Atlanta: Scholars Press, 1999.

Nihan, Christophe. "Moses and the Prophets: Deuteronomy 18 and the Emergence of the Pentateuch as Torah." *SEÅ* 75 (2010): 21–55.

Otto, Eckart. "Torah and Prophecy: A Debate of Changing Identities." *VetE* 34.2 (2013): 1–5.

Pilarski, Ahida Calderón. "A Latina Biblical Critic and Intellectual: At the Intersection of Ethnicity, Gender, Hermeneutics, and Faith." Pages 231–48 in *Latino/a Biblical Hermeneutics: Problematics, Objectives, Strategies*. Edited by Francisco Lozada Jr. and Fernando F. Segovia. Atlanta: SBL Press, 2014.

Ramose, Mogobe B. *African Philosophy through Ubuntu*. Harare: Mond Books, 1999.

Rugwiji, Temba. "Appropriating Judean Post-exilic Literature in a Postcolonial Discourse: A Case for Zimbabwe." PhD diss., University of South Africa, 2013.

Said, Edward W. *Reflections on Exile and Other Essays*. Convergences. Cambridge: Harvard University Press, 2000.

Schmid, Konrad. "The Late Persian Formation of the Torah: Observations on Deuteronomy 34." Pages 236–45 in *Judah and the Judeans in the Fourth Century BCE*. Edited by Oded Lipschitz, Gary N. Knoppers, and Rainer Albertz. Winona Lake, IN: Eisenbrauns, 2007.

———. *The Old Testament: A Literary History*. Translated by Linda M. Meloney. Minneapolis: Fortress, 2012.

Segovia, Fernando F. "Introduction: Approaching Latino/a Biblical Criticism: A Trajectory of Visions and Missions." Pages 1–39 in *Latino/a Biblical Hermeneutics: Problematics, Objectives, Strategies*. Edited by Francisco Lozada Jr. and Fernando F. Segovia. Atlanta: SBL Press, 2014.

Smith-Christopher, Daniel L. *Micah: A Commentary*. OTL. Louisville: Westminster John Knox, 2015.

Throntveit, Mark A. *Ezra-Nehemiah*. IBC. Louisville: Westminster John Knox, 1992.

Usue, Emmanuel O. "Restoration or Desperation in Ezra and Nehemiah? Implications for Africa." *OTE* 20 (2007): 830–46.

Venter, Pieter M. "Canon, Intertextuality and History in Nehemiah 7:72b–10:40." *HTS* 65 (2009): 1–8.

———. "The Connection between Wisdom Literature, Apocalypses, and Canon." *OTE* 15 (2002): 470–88.

Werline, Rodney A. "Defining Penitential Prayer." Pages xiii–xvii in *The Origins of Penitential Prayer in Second Temple Judaism*. Vol. 1 of *Seeking the Favor of God*. Edited by Mark J. Boda, Daniel K. Falk, and Rodney A. Werline. EJL 21. Atlanta: Society of Biblical Literature, 2006.

———. *Penitential Prayer in Second Temple Judaism: The Development of a Religious Institution*. EJL 13. Atlanta: Scholars Press, 1998.

West, Gerald O. "Indigenous Exegesis: Exploring the Interface between Missionary Methods and the Rhetorical Rhythms of Africa; Locating Local Reading Resources in the Academy." *Neot* 36 (2002): 147–62.

Williamson, H. G. M. *Studies in Persian Period History and Historiography*. FAT 38. Tübingen: Mohr Siebeck, 2004.

Wolff, Hans W. *Micah: A Commentary*. Translated by Gary Stansell. Minneapolis: Augsburg Fortress, 1990.

Wright, Jacob L. "Commensal Politics in Ancient Western Asia: The Background to Nehemiah's Feasting (Continued, Part II)." *ZAW* 122 (2010): 333–52.

———. "Commensal Politics in Ancient Western Asia: The Background to Nehemiah's Feasting (Part I)." *ZAW* 122 (2010): 212–33.

Wright, Jacob L., and Michael J. Chan. "Feasting: From Kings to Communities." Pages 1–14 in *Oxford Encyclopedia of the Bible and Archaeology*. Edited by Daniel M. Master et al. Oxford: Oxford University Press, 2013.

Wright, Jacob L., and Meredith E. Hollman. "Society and Politics: Banquet and Gift Exchange." Pages 1–17 in *A Companion to the Achaemenid Persian Empire*. Edited by Bruno Jacobs and Robert Rollinger. BCAW. London: Wiley-Blackwell, 2012.

Yee, Gale. "'He Will Take the Best of Your Fields': Royal Feasts and Rural Extraction." Paper presented at the Annual Meeting of the Society of Biblical Literature, Atlanta, 2015.

(Re)modeling Biblical Figures through Prayers

Testing Tales: Genesis 22 and Daniel 3 and 6

Christo Lombaard

1. Three Testing Tales

The proposal put forward in this chapter is a simple one, concerning the theological possibility that God would test the faith of believers. The question to which an answer is sought is: When would this theological possibility that God would explicitly test one's faith have occurred prominently, at least as it is attested to by the Hebrew Bible texts? It seems, as will be argued below, that this is a late development in the history of the religion of Israel, probably emerging under Hellenistic influence, introduced as a reaction to aspects of the dominating culture at that time.[1] Even if the kernel of

---

Presentation at the "Israel and the Production and Reception of Authoritative Books in the Persian and Hellenistic Period" group's session, "Prayers: Remembering and Constructing Israelite identity, 2," European Association for Biblical Studies Annual Meeting in Córdoba, Spain, July 12–15, 2015. The paper has been published in a shorter version in the *Pharos Journal of Theology* 97 (2016) (https://tinyurl.com/SBL2633b) and is republished here with the permission of the editors. I dedicate this contribution to St. John Vianney Seminary in Pretoria, South Africa, in sincere gratitude for the possibility afforded me during 2013 as a guest lecturer to teach some Old Testament classes. It was during my preparation for those classes that the insight that led to the proposal put forward in this contribution dawned on me. My thanks to colleague Hans van Deventer for much-valued comments on the postconference version of this article.

1. The problematic content of the concept "Israel" indicated by Philip R. Davies and others is not meant to be overlooked here (see Davies, *In Search of 'Ancient Israel,'* JSOTSup 148 [Sheffield: JSOT Press, 2006]). Rather, I follow the habit among scholars of employing the term as a matter of shorthand, all the while acknowledging just how complex a construct this is, as the people represented by it over time underwent changes in identity, composition, and location.

the idea that God would test had existed earlier, with this kernel occuring a few times earlier in the Hebrew Bible, the idea became narrativized—that is, more prominent and in a way culturally and theologically institutionalized—only later in the religious history of Israel—at least, as far as the texts give evidence of the development of this theological possibility.

This lateness, however, should not be construed as therefore being an inauthentic or syncretistic form of religion. Neither newness/lateness nor intercultural influence imply either lesser or greater legitimacy, as is at times assumed within Hebrew Bible scholarship—for various reasons—with respect to texts, traditions, or developments. The theological coherence of the possibility of a testing God was, moreover, affirmed in the three narratives in view by the juxtaposition of this possibility with different kinds of prayer material. The religious intimacy of prayer is accepted as a theological given. Legitimacy was therefore conferred on the possibility of a testing God. By associating such divine testing with prayer in these texts, further credence had been given to the experienced validity of this aspect of faith. This, I propose, occurred relatively late in Israel's faith history within the period of the development of the biblical texts.

2. The God Who Tests

The idea that YHWH would test those who believe in him is not a dominant theme in the Old Testament. By employing the verb נסה, "to test," a mere mention of this idea is, for instance, found in the following verses: Ps 26:2 ("Probe me, YHWH, examine me, Test my heart and my mind in the fire"; see 2 Chr 32:31), Exod 20:20 ("Moses said to the people, 'Do not be afraid; God has come to test you, so that your fear of him, being always in your mind, may keep you from sinning'"), and Deut 8:2 ("Remember the long road by which YHWH your God led you for forty years in the desert, to humble you, to test you and know your inmost heart—whether you would keep his commandments or not").[2]

The synonymous בחן occurs, for instance, in Job 23:10 ("And yet he knows every step I take! Let him test me in the crucible: I shall come out pure gold"), Zech 13:9a ("I shall pass this third through the fire, refine them as silver is refined, test them as gold is tested"), and Ps 17:3 ("You probe my heart, examine me at night, you test me by fire and find no evil").

---

2. All translations are from the NJB.

These are instances of the rare occurrence of the simple, unexplored idea that God would test.

In more narratival formats, the idea of God putting people to the test comes to the fore in somewhat expanded form, yet really still only in something of a précis, in texts such as Judg 2 (as a summary of typical Deuteronomistic theology; see specifically 2:22), in the book of Job (in philosophical format, as a question of theodicy rather than of adherence to God in the face of other religions), in Gen 2–3 (especially 2:16–17 with chapter 3, on the tree of knowledge of good and evil), and, in a way, in the Joseph account.

In the three "short short stories" to be discussed below, however, the understanding of God testing people's faith stands explicitly in the foreground.[3] The merest mention or the briefest summary is here expanded into a full tale, thrice, with all the narrative elements inherent to a developed piece of literature. As an act of loyalty, in Daniel, amidst the presence of other religious orientations, narrativized expressions are found of what has in these accounts clearly become a demonstrable, maturely unfolded theological position. Obstacles to faith are in these accounts set, in each instance, both as an experience in itself and as a means to an end: to refine faith. For this reason, Gen 22 and Dan 3 and 6 may be called "testing tales"; the dominant theme of these three legends of loyalty is an unwavering commitment to YHWH. The communicative intent of such accounts is clearly to encourage commitment to faith on the part of the intended audience, most probably—if an allusion to a popular modern song would be pardoned—when they found themselves in times of trouble.

2.1. The Genesis 22 Text

The Akedah is not a text without its difficulties; the main problems may be summarized as follows: (1) What is the most appropriate exegetical methodology: namely, historical or narratological?[4] (2) What are the possible

---

3. The expression "short short stories" was first related to such accounts in Christo Lombaard, "Isaac in the Old Testament: A New Interpretation from Genesis 22, Based on Hermeneutical-Methodological and Exegetical Investigations" (DD diss., University of Pretoria, 2009), 100.

4. On this matter, see also Elizabeth Boase, "Life in the Shadows: The Role and Function of Isaac in Genesis—Synchronic and Diachronic Readings," VT 51 (2001): 312–35.

historical explanations for the origination of the text during its main stages of composition? (3) What are the theological-ethical considerations raised by a Bible narrative on divine instruction to commit child sacrifice? (4) How should verses 1 and 15–18 be treated? The last of these four aspects is the most important for the argumentation presented here.

With rare exceptions (which include, most prominently, the objections by George W. Coats and John Van Seters), Gen 22:1b and 15–18 are held to be insertions within an already-existing account that we now have in the composite text Gen 22:1–19.[5] The earlier text, *sans* 22:1b and 15–18, narrated an event in which the patriarch Abraham was instructed by God to take his son Isaac to Moriah as a burnt offering. That constituted the whole account, without any added editorial interpolations.

The historical aspects of this account's meaning—possibly related to a protest against human sacrifice, to etiology, to theodicy, or to internecine power relations (which are the historical explanations attested in the scholarly literature)—are not of prime concern here; most important to note for the sake of the argument here are the editorial additions. Accurately dubbed by R. Walter Moberley "the earliest commentary on the Akedah," these few verses, particularly the framing insertion of 22:1b, "(and/that) God tested Abraham," altered the popular and much of the academic (usually based on methods such as close reading or narratological analysis) reception of Gen 22 for more than two millennia.[6] From that point on, the meaning of this text would predominantly be understood as "God tests Abraham."[7]

The *theological* turn implied by the insertions of 22:1b and 15–18 should not escape us. Especially verse 1b alters a text with cultic-protest, etiological, philosophical, or power-play intentions into an account of exemplary religious piety. God sets a test; Abraham passes the test. The account now becomes one of how the father of all believers treated a rather dramatic examination of his personal fidelity. The result of this success story is, explicitly, reward: progeny, protection, and influence/

---

5. George W. Coats, "Abraham's Sacrifice of Faith: A Form-Critical Study of Genesis 22," *Int* 28 (1973): 389–412; John Van Seters, *Abraham in History and Tradition* (New Haven: Yale University Press, 1975), 229.

6. R. Walter Moberly, "The Earliest Commentary on the Akedah," *VT* 38 (1988): 302–23.

7. H. A. J. Kruger, "God Tests Abraham: The Command to Sacrifice Isaac," *NGTT* 32 (1991): 187–200.

honor. Verses 15–18 therefore go on to expand the kernel of 1b: obedience and unquestioning religious loyalty are compensated with very concrete blessings (namely, progeny and international power, in 22:17 and 18). The implied encouragement intended by such a positive (now, *with* 22:1b and 15–18) testing tale is this: the addressed audience should follow this example of blind trust in all circumstances, even in incomprehensible and reprehensible situations.

The dating ascribed to this textual and hence theological insertion has consistently been late; my own work has led me, albeit hesitantly, to propose the period of the first half of the third century BCE.[8] Given what follows below on the Daniel texts, the theological parallels that come to the fore seem to offer increased intertextual linkage evidencing such a dating.

2.2. The Daniel Texts

The composition history of the book of Daniel is a principal issue of scholarly debate. I follow here the research trajectory of Johan D. Michaelis and James A. Montgomery via Rainer Albertz and then Hans J. M. Van Deventer.[9] The Hebrew chapters 8–12 are regarded as the oldest textual collection in the book of Daniel, with the Aramaic chapters 4–7 added roughly a decade later (that is, the mid-second century BCE), to which the Aramaic chapter 3 was subsequently appended. After this, the opening and closing chapters were added to this loose collection of "Märchen- und Legendenmotive" (Jan-Wim Wesselius employs the imaginative term "dossier on Daniel") at different stages, with the deuterocanonical Greek prayer and narrative sections appended even later.[10]

---

8. See Lombaard, "Isaac Multiplex: Genesis 22 in a New Historical Representation," *HvTSt* 64 (2008): 915–17, doi.org/10.4102/hts.v64i2.49.

9. Johann D. Michaelis, *Ezechiel und Daniel*, part 10 of *Johann David Michaelis deutsche Übersetzung des Alten Testaments, mit Anmerkungen für Ungelehrte* (Göttingen: Dieterich, 1781); James A. Montgomery, *A Critical and Exegetical Commentary on the Book of Daniel*, ICC (Edinburgh: T&T Clark, 1979); Rainer Albertz, *Der Gott des Daniel: Untersuchungen zu Daniel 4–6 in der Septuagintafassung sowie zu Komposition und Theologie des aramäischen Danielbuches*, SBS 131 (Stuttgart: Katholisches Bibelwerk, 1988); Hans J. M. Van Deventer, "Another Look at the Redaction History of the Book of Daniel: or, Reading Daniel from Left to Right," *JSOT* 38 (2013): 239–60.

10. Hans-Peter Müller, "Märchen, Legende und Enderwartung: Zum Verständnis des Buches Daniel," *VT* 26 (1976): 340; Jan-Wim Wesselius, "The Writing of Daniel," in *The Book of Daniel: Composition and Reception*, vol. 2 of *Formation and Interpreta-*

Given the seemingly deferred addition of Dan 3, a brief description of the Dan 6 text sets the initial, earlier context here. Daniel 6 deals with the possibility of sociopolitical challenges to the faith of an individual. During succession politics, machinations by court officials render Daniel's personal piety *religio non grata*; Daniel, however, miraculously survives the resultant death sentence in the famous lion's pit. This leads to two outcomes, rhetorically meant to encourage the addressed readers during testing times: royal recognition of an "act of God" (here meant in a positive, redemptive sense, rather than in the modern negative sense akin to the expression *force majeure*), and a state of acceptance of the Jewish faith.

This "success story" is expanded in Dan 3. In a world of high politics—an emperor, a bevy of powerful officials, international relations, and orchestrated religion—this time a group of people are threatened for religious reasons. Associated with Daniel by means of the renaming scene inserted in the Hebrew chapter 1 (specifically Dan 1:7), Shadrach, Meshach and Abed-Nego in Dan 3 find themselves an assembly on the receiving end of, successively, imperial fury, a fiery death sentence, divine protection, and, again, royal affirmation and state sanction.[11] This affirmation of overtly recognized loyalty to God forms a kind of *mantra* throughout the Daniel stories, clearly meant as lessons of encouragement to the intended audience.

In both these testing tales within Daniel, despite their differences, the relative passivity of the main characters begs attention. It is not through their own activity that these characters find themselves protected and their fidelity vindicated; their saving grace is divine, and the resulting confession is at one and the same time both official and heathen, both aspects that are notably beyond the sphere of influence of the Jewish characters.

The communicative intent is evidently to place the events outside of the hands of the faithful adherents: threatening circumstances develop outside their control (the persecution by Antiochus Epiphanes); divine protection coincides with fidelity, more so than humans would expect (the extent of divine benevolence remains surprising); and a restoration of religious peace occurs in superlative forms. The placement of these tales at the imperial court increases the intended audience's sense of identifica

---

tion of Old Testament Literature, ed. John J. Collins and Peter W. Flint, VTSup 83.2 (Leiden: Brill, 2001), 296.

11. Dan 1:7: "The chief eunuch gave them other names, calling Daniel Belteshazzar, Hananiah Shadrach, Mishael Meshach, and Azariah Abed-Nego."

with leadership (hence, also, the connection of the three with Daniel in 1:7) and adds in this way a universalizing scope to these events. In this emancipating theology, when God allows for testing times, redemption is dramatic and at once wide-ranging and personally representative.

3. In God We Trust: The Three Testing Tales Taken Together

It should be clear by now that the idea of historical reliability subscribed to in this contribution is not the kind in which it is assumed that historical veracity about the figures referred to in these narratives—principally Abraham, Isaac, Daniel, and the three men of Dan 3—is a goal.[12] Rather, the kind of historical understanding that may be deduced from the texts is restricted to the community in which these ancient writings were developed and/or accepted. The idea-logical context—that is, the theology and mores of the acceptance community—can be inferred. This idea-logical context may be described in broad outline only, given the difficulties of all historical reconstruction. Such broad insight, however, is already enough to grasp at least some dimensions of the religious sensibilities of an acceptance community.

Drawing upon the testing tales above, then, with their respective editorial histories and dating possibilities as outlined above, the argument can be made that it was only late in the history of Israel's religion that the theological possibility of God testing heroes of faith became more fully developed.

The concept does occur throughout the Hebrew Bible, in passing references and in précis texts, which together indicate that the idea of a testing God was alive within ancient Israel's faith conception. The divine assessment of the quality of the commitment on the part of believers, however, is given great prominence in the accounts discussed above through narrative expansion that illustrates the idea more fully and encourages the intended audience to persevere in their faith commitment, even (or perhaps especially) in trying times. This happened late:

- The editorial insertions within the narrative of Gen 22:1–19, verses 1b and 15–18, transform the original account into a

---

12. See Christo Lombaard, "Getting Texts to Talk: A Critical Analysis of Attempts at Eliciting Contemporary Messages from Ancient Holy Books as Exercises in Religious Communication," *NGTT* 55 (2014): 210–16.

testing tale. In the earlier third century, the already-venerated patriarch Abraham now becomes a hero of fidelity to all who take this text seriously.

- About a century later, Dan 6 and then the Dan 3 narrative additions expand this idea, initially relating to the individual but then democratizing this message by also relating the same idea to a group.[13]

In these accounts, the core idea is thus *unfolded*, in fully construed narratives, that God has at times examined the faith of important figures. The intended implication is apparent: those who read/hear these texts and hold them as religiously important should emulate these examples.

Apart from the dating of the pertinent verses and chapters to Hellenistic times, it seems also that aspects of the Hellenistic culture provide milieus that best fit these testing tales. This placement is not simply part of the trend (again recently indicated by Christoph Levin) of understanding by far the greater part of the Hebrew Bible to be late; as Niels Peter Lemche warns, "The Old Testament may be a Jewish collection of literature dating to the Hellenistic and Roman Period, but it is definitely not a Greek or Roman book."[14] I do not propose the Hellenistic background to these testing tales simply for the sake of such a late dating trend. In the two Daniel accounts discussed here, the influence of the politics of Antiochus Epiphanes is foundational to understanding them. In the Gen 22 additions, parallels from Hellenistic mythology such as the testing of Jason by Hera may well have provided additional impulses for expanding an existing idea into a fuller theological construct and then for relating that idea of divine examination to some of the basic foundations of Israel's theology, namely, blessing in its various forms.

The thematically relatively tightly-knit nature of the Gen 22 additions and these two Daniel stories, discussed above, could be further explored.

---

13. See Van Deventer, "Another Look at the Redaction History," 257, drawing on Gabriele Boccaccini, *Roots of Rabbinic Judaism: An Intellectual History, from Ezekiel to Daniel* (Grand Rapids: Eerdmans, 2002), 164.

14. Niels Peter Lemche, "Does the Idea of the Old Testament as a Hellenistic Book Prevent Source Criticism of the Pentateuch?," *JSOT* 25 (2011): 92; see also Christoph Levin, "Die Entstehung des Judentums als Gegenstand der alttestamentlichen Wissenschaft," in *Congress Volume Munich 2013*, edited by Christl M. Maier, VTSup 163 (Leiden: Brill, 2014), 1–17.

Similarities in terminology may, for instance, be indicated by pointing to the appearance of the angel of God motif in all three accounts. Given the methodological uncertainties related to linguistic links, however, thematic association provides for a broader frame of reference here. The occurrence of prayer in all three of these texts provide a good case in point.

This relates at the same time also to the issue of the perceived legitimacy of a theology about a God who tests, rather than a God who either remains unremittingly true regardless of the actions of the human party (as is generally the case with respect to the patriarchs of ancient Israel) or who would omnisciently know the result before a test would be set (as in ancient Greek mythology). Such theological questions are not argued in these texts. Clearly, however, this testing theology has no difficulty functioning alongside one of the most intimate acts of experienced and expressed religiosity: prayer.

In Gen 22, the interaction between Abraham and God is constituted by the former's response, in word and deed, to the divine initiative. In Dan 6, it is the faith of the hero's daily devotions that is the trigger of the events set up to play out the way they then do. In Dan 3, the Greek prayers (3:24–90 LXX, the so-called Prayer of Azariah and Song of the Three Holy Children) are often disregarded in academic discussions.[15] Yet they show a continued acceptance, and perhaps even expansion, of the theological notion of a testing God.[16] That such affirmation could be expressed by means of an inserted prayer is not an unknown phenomenon in the Hebrew Bible, with the underwater prayer in Jon 2:2–10 as a well-known example.

Such prayer shows that the theological context in which it appears is experienced as valid and authentic. Prayers display a unique kind of religious intimacy, with canonized prayer carrying the additional implication of accepted theological soundness.

With additional legitimacy therefore added to the possibility of a testing God, precisely by associating a testing God in these texts with prayer, greater credence had been given to the experienced authenticity of this aspect of faith. A God who tests thus is not, as could perhaps be assumed, on the prey; rather, the figures affected pray. The emphasis here is not on a God who creates hurdles or temptations; the emphasis is on the act of human-divine communication. This, too, was most probably

---

15. See Albertz, *Gott des Daniel*, 9.
16. The better-known prayer in Daniel is in chapter 9, with its strong Deuteronomistic influences.

intended to direct and/or reflect the experience of the intended audiences of these texts.

4. Addendum: On a Wing and a …

Perhaps the proposal made in this contribution is couched too comfortably in my own theological history, in which the notion of *sola gratia* has been foundational. From such an existential vantage point, the idea that God would test believers does not fit well. This introspective theological self-placement does not mechanistically invalidate the proposal set forth here—that the three Old Testament testing tales discussed above are late developments in Israel under Hellenistic influence. Such a dating is not understood here as a corrupting influence on the texts, though it was possibly a somewhat syncretistic development—which is, however, regarded here not as something negative but as a fully natural part of all expressions of religiosity. (The implications of this for contextualizing more thoroughly the testing of Job should be thought through further.)

My own contextual position as an investigator, along with all the historiographical vagaries involved in reconstructing a part of the history of the religion of ancient Israel, is another aspect that should lead to intellectual modesty; this interpretative possibility is here only proposed, rather than put forward firmly. When theology and history intersect, the result is as much a case of faith seeking understanding as it is a case of seeking to understand an aspect of ancient Israel's faith.

Bibliography

Albertz, Rainer. *Der Gott des Daniel: Untersuchungen zu Daniel 4–6 in der Septuagintafassung sowie zu Komposition und Theologie des aramäischen Danielbuches*. SBS 131. Stuttgart: Katholisches Bibelwerk, 1988.

Boase, Elizabeth. "Life in the Shadows: The Role and Function of Isaac in Genesis—Synchronic and Diachronic Readings." *VT* 51 (2001): 312–35.

Boccaccini, Gabriele. *Roots of Rabbinic Judaism: An Intellectual History, from Ezekiel to Daniel*. Grand Rapids: Eerdmans, 2002.

Coats, George W. "Abraham's Sacrifice of Faith: A Form-Critical Study of Genesis 22." *Int* 28 (1973): 389–412.

Davies, Philip R. I*n Search of 'Ancient Israel'*. JSOTSup 148. Sheffield: JSOT Press, 2006.
Kruger, H. A. J. "God Tests Abraham: The Command to Sacrifice Isaac." *NGTT* 32 (1991): 187–200.
Lemche, Niels Peter. "Does the Idea of the Old Testament as a Hellenistic Book Prevent Source Criticism of the Pentateuch?" *JSOT* 25 (2011): 75–92.
Levin, Christoph. "Die Entstehung des Judentums als Gegenstand der alttestamentlichen Wissenschaft." Pages 1–17 in *Congress Volume Munich 2013*. Edited by Christl M. Maier. VTSup 163. Leiden; Boston: Brill, 2014.
Lombaard, Christo. "Getting Texts to Talk: A Critical Analysis of Attempts at Eliciting Contemporary Messages from Ancient Holy Books as Exercises in Religious Communication." *NGTT* 55 (2014): 205–25.
———. "Isaac in the Old Testament: A New Interpretation from Genesis 22, Based on Hermeneutical-Methodological and Exegetical Investigations." DD diss., University of Pretoria, 2009.
———. "Isaac Multiplex: Genesis 22 in a New Historical Representation." *HvTSt* 64 (2008): 907–19. doi.org/10.4102/hts.v64i2.49.
Michaelis, Johann D. *Ezechiel und Daniel*. Part 10 of *Johann David Michaelis deutsche Übersetzung des Alten Testaments, mit Anmerkungen für Ungelehrte*. Göttingen: Johann Christian Dieterich, 1781.
Moberly, R. Walter. "The Earliest Commentary on the Akedah." *VT* 38 (1988): 302–23.
Montgomery, James A. *A Critical and Exegetical Commentary on the Book of Daniel*. ICC. Edinburgh: T&T Clark, 1979.
Müller, Hans-Peter. "Märchen, Legende und Enderwartung: Zum Verständnis des Buches Daniel." *VT* 26 (1976): 338–50.
Van Deventer, Hans J. M. "Another Look at the Redaction History of the Book of Daniel: or, Reading Daniel from Left to Right." *JSOT* 38 (2013): 239–60.
Van Seters, John. *Abraham in History and Tradition*. New Haven: Yale University Press, 1975.
Wesselius, Jan-Wim. "The Writing of Daniel." Pages 291–310 of *The Book of Daniel: Composition and Reception*. Vol. 2 of *Formation and Interpretation of Old Testament Literature*. Edited by John J. Collins and Peter W. Flint. VTSup 83.2. Leiden: Brill, 2001.

Glory and Remorse:
Transitions in Solomon's Prayer (1 Kgs 8)

Susanne Gillmayr-Bucher

1. Introduction[1]

The stories in the first book of Kings present Solomon as one of the most successful kings in the Bible. He is a most wise and rich ruler, establishing justice, maintaining peace, and he also builds the first temple for YHWH in Jerusalem. Visits and homages from kings all over the world further emphasize Solomon's glory. This dominant image of King Solomon is, however, contradicted at the beginning and ending of the story. The executions that guarantee Solomon's succession to the throne (1 Kgs 2), Solomon's apostasy (1 Kgs 11), and the oppression of opponents tarnish the king's reputation.

The story of Solomon primarily unfolds as a narration about this king: the narrating voice presents Solomon and his actions, allowing the readers to follow the literary figure of the king, while hardly providing any insight into his perspective. Thus Solomon's inner world of ideas, his wishes, intentions, or emotions, are not revealed, and the readers are only allowed an external view of this figure.

Two of the rare exceptions, where the narration presents Solomon's words in some detail, are Solomon's oneiric dialogue with God in Gibeon (1 Kgs 3) and his prayer of dedication for the temple (1 Kgs 8). These texts allow the readers to perceive Solomon's thoughts, hopes, beliefs, and knowledge. Through Solomon's own words, the image of the wise and mighty king presented by the narrative voice is modified and complemented. In contrast to the well-established king that the narrative voice

---

[1] This essay is is part of the research project "Ruler, Lover, Sage and Sceptic: Receptions of King Solomon," funded by the Austrian Science Fund.

shows in 1 Kgs 2, Solomon's self-presentation in the following chapter reveals a young man who still has to learn how to be king. He is not yet the wise king but rather wisdom's apprentice. In Solomon's prayer of dedication for the temple, the king's image changes again. While the narration depicts a most splendid consecration ceremony with Solomon as its main protagonist, the prayer evokes a rather different picture, showing him as a prudent, praying man, speaking of sin and asking for forgiveness for his people. The king and builder of the temple is thereby introduced as a farsighted advocate for his people.

The inner world of this figure therefore reveals a much more differentiated image of the king than the narration of his deeds. On the one hand, the narration's positive image is enhanced, and he is presented as a knowledgeable man, well acquainted with Israel's traditions, which he intends to continue.[1] On the other hand, however, Solomon's prayers in 1 Kgs 8 do not create a unanimous portrait but rather show diverse aspects of Solomon's self-concept. Furthermore, the long prayers in 1 Kgs 8 develop a quite different view on the role of the monarchy and the significance of the temple. The world Solomon constructs in his prayers and the world created by the narrating voice are not congruent and thus offer a counterdiscourse.[2] In this essay, I will focus on how the prayers modify and transform the image of the king[3] and the temple and examine how the new images offer links to postexilic issues and challenges.

---

1. This image is strengthened by several allusions to Priestly and Deuteronomistic traditions from the Pentateuch. Judith H. Newman has shown that such an approach is typical for prayers at the time of the Second Temple. These prayers frequently refer to Israel's history and thereby reinterpret single events or familiar characters. See Newman, *Praying by the Book: The Scripturalization of Prayer in Second Temple Judaism*, EJL 14 (Atlanta: Scholars Press, 1999), 1–2.

2. A counterdiscourse problematizes "something that the dominant discourse takes for granted. Although counter-discourse may be polemical, often its relationship is not directly oppositional. It is, however, always interruptive or disruptive. It disturbs the smooth flow of what everyone takes for granted and in so doing calls attention to itself and gains a measure of cultural power by doing so. Whatever its particular strategy, counterdiscourse presupposes and depends upon the existence of the dominant discourse in order to articulate itself" (Carol A. Newsom, *The Self as Symbolic Space: Constructing Identity and Community at Qumran*, STDJ 52 [Leiden: Brill, 2004], 18).

3. When dealing with Solomon's prayer, most studies focus on the transformation of the prayer and/or the text's historical origins, while the transformation of the figure of Solomon has been widely neglected. See Michael Avioz, "The Characterization

2. The Structure of the Text 1 Kings 8

The description of the dedication of the new temple begins and ends with narrative statements. It starts with a description of the people's assembly at the temple (8:1–2) and the transfer of the ark and the liturgical items to the temple (8:3–9), which is accompanied by sacrifices (8:5). The description ends with a short reference to the huge amount of further sacrifices offered by Solomon (8:62–64) and a summary of the seven-day festival (8:65–66). The largest part of the text, however, reports Solomon's words to the assembly and to God. The king starts by announcing to the people and to God that he has built the temple (8:12–13). He then blesses the assembly (8:14) and recounts Israel's history from the exodus until the building of the temple (8:15–21). Later on in the text, the narrating voice explicitly mentions that Solomon stands before the altar in the presence of the assembly (8:22) offering an extensive prayer. In this prayer, he first emphasizes God's steadfast love and loyalty to Israel and David and then urges God in seven petitions to listen to Israel's cry for help in possible future situations of distress (8:31–53). At the end of his address, Solomon once more blesses the assembly and reminds the people to keep God's commandments (8:54–61). God's answer to Solomon's prayer is not included in the description of the festive dedication of the temple but only reported later in 1 Kgs 9:1–9.

Solomon's prayers are clearly emphasized by this depiction of the festive events. While the narrative voice presents the sacrifices (8:5; 62–64) as a summary, Solomon's prayer explicitly lays out the history and the intended or hoped-for role of the temple.

3. Forming and Transforming the Image of the King

The discrepancy between Solomon's image as a powerful and determined king, whose reign is already firmly established, and the praying king, who is still trying to establish legitimacy and stability and who can only offer hope for Israel's future in his intercessory pleas, opens a discourse on different concepts of kingship and, likewise, different expectations connected

---

of Solomon in Solomon's Prayer (1 Kings 8)," *BN* 126 (2005): 19. Unlike Avioz, I do not regard the critical tones of the prayer as an ironic deconstruction of Solomon but rather a deliberate reflection of the wise king that presents the figure of Solomon in a positive way. See Avioz, "Solomon," 26.

to a sovereign. In this way, Solomon's "inner worlds" reveal diverging constructions of the king. References to well-known figures of Israel's past help to shape the portrait of Solomon.

3.1. Solomon and David

In Solomon's praise of God following his first blessing of the assembly, as well as in the introduction to the petitions, Solomon puts the building of the temple into the context of Israel's history. The short retrospect into Israel's history with its God focuses only on David. Solomon points out that from the beginning God had chosen David but not a city for his temple (8:16). Furthermore, David is not allowed to build a temple, but he is assured that one of his sons might carry out this project in the future. With this summary, Solomon refers to 2 Sam 7 and recalls the connection between the divine election of King David and a future temple, thus emphasizing the outstanding task of building the temple. In 1 Kgs 8:20, Solomon skillfully applies this unspecific prediction, that one of David's sons will build the temple (2 Sam 7:13), to himself and takes on the role of David's chosen successor. Solomon thereby declares his reign and the building of the temple to be the fulfillment of the divine promise to David. Consequently, Solomon's legitimacy as king and his mission to build the temple are confirmed.[4] The reporting of these considerations as a prayer adds special significance. In Solomon's prayer, the retrospective view on history is not just presented, but the events mentioned are integrated into a praise of God and his great deeds. The slightly biased retrospect thus becomes a laudable reality, while the authenticity of the selection process and decision-making is no longer questioned.

The introduction to the most elaborate part of Solomon's prayer (1 Kgs 8:22–30) once more refers to the theme of royal succession and legitimation. Although the main theme remains the same, the focus and its expression are markedly different. Now, the continuation of God's

---

4. Gary N. Knoppers points out that "a concern with dynastic legitimacy is found in a number of ancient Near Eastern royal dedicatory inscriptions and prayers. The successful completion of the temple effects a bond between king and deity, confirming the king's right to rule" (Knoppers, "Prayer and Propaganda: Solomon's Dedication of the Temple and the Deuteronomist's Program," *CBQ* 57 [1995]: 243). In Solomon's case, however, the erection of the temple and the right to rule each require a separate legitimization.

support for the king is the main topic: formulated as a request in prayer, Solomon does not take God's continuous support for granted but asks for it (8:25–26). The promise David received in 2 Sam 7 is again alluded to. This divine commitment is repeatedly referenced and forms an important basis for the legitimacy of Solomon's reign throughout 1 Kgs 2–10. It is mentioned in connection with the legitimacy of Solomon's succession to the throne (see 1 Kgs 2:24; 3:6, 7) and Solomon's divine mission to build the temple (see 1 Kgs 5:17, 19; 8:17, 18, 20). Furthermore, the reference to God's promise to David is also used to highlight Solomon's obligation to follow the divine commandments. When Solomon steps into this promise as the one (chosen) son, this is enhanced further, as the moderate penalty of 2 Sam 7:14–16 is tightened: at stake is not a castigation with rods but the loss of the kingship, and with it the end of the Davidic dynasty (1 Kgs 3:14; 6:12–13; see also 9:4–5). Simultaneously, David becomes the role model for Solomon, who is instructed to follow God's commandments like his father David before him (see 1 Kgs 2:2–4). Nonetheless, as Michael D. Matlock correctly points out, the references in Solomon's prayer (1 Kgs 8:23–26) shift the focus from Solomon's obligations to God's promise.[5] Although Solomon mentions the need of obedience and even refers to the more demanding form (8:23–26), still the divine promises are at the center of his interest.[6] His plea stresses the hope that God will fulfill the promise given to David (2 Sam 7:13) guaranteeing an everlasting dynasty.

Solomon's prayer is again used to modify a retrospect, and with it David's legacy. King Solomon is presented as a humble man, accepting God's reinforced conditions without complaint, but also as a self-confident king and a demanding petitioner. Applying the promises David received for his sons exclusively to himself is an important precondition for the following petitions. Solomon needs to ascertain God's benevolent

---

5. Michael D. Matlock argues that Solomon downplays obedience and the conditional character of the covenant (Matlock, "Prayer Changes Things or Things Change Prayer: Innovations of Solomon's Temple Prayer in Early Jewish Literature," in *The Letters and Liturgical Traditions*, vol. 2 of *"What Does the Scripture Say?" Studies in the Function of Scripture in Early Judaism and Christianity*, ed. Craig A. Evans and H. Daniel Zacharias, LNTS 470, SSEJC 18 [London: T&T Clark, 2012], 163).

6. This emphasis points to an exilic/postexilic reflection on God's covenant. As in Lev 26 or Deut 4, the covenant is not abandoned due to the unfaithfulness of the people, but God, in his mercy, still holds on to his promises. See Walter Groß, *Zukunft für Israel: Alttestamentliche Bundeskonzepte und die aktuelle Debatte um den Neuen Bund*, SBS 176 (Stuttgart: Katholisches Bibelwerk, 1998), 71–84.

attitude toward himself and the Davidic dynasty before he can state his daring requests.

3.2. Solomon and Moses

In addition to mentions of David, references to Moses play an important role in 1 Kgs 8. The first allusion to the time of Moses already occurs in the description of a cloud filling the sanctuary and prohibiting the priests' ministry (8:10–11). With this link to Exod 40:34–35, the narrating voice confirms that God is present and has accepted Solomon's temple. The ceremony thus draws a parallel between Solomon and his building of the temple on the one hand and Moses and the tent of meeting on the other. Solomon's attitude as an intercessor for his people before God establishes another analogy between Moses and Solomon. Like Moses, Solomon is concerned for the people, knows their weaknesses, and understands the resulting consequences.

Solomon's prayer, however, does not continue this line of thought but rather emphasizes instruction and execution, as well as promise and fulfillment. Building the temple is not only the fulfillment of a divine promise to David but also of the divine command to build a central sanctuary (Deut 12:10–11).[7] Furthermore, the temple alludes to the rest promised to Israel in Deut 12:10, consequently characterizing Solomon's reign as a time of rest and safety. Once more, Solomon justifies his rule as based on God's promise by claiming that his actions agree completely with divine providence. In his second blessing, Solomon refers to Israel's rest again (1 Kgs 8:56), but now it appears as part of a praise. In this way, Solomon connects his own perspective on his reign to the future Moses envisioned and declares it as a God-given, laudable fact.

Following from Solomon's conviction that the completion of the temple is a symbol for God's care, it is only natural that once Solomon has finished the building he asks God to hear the prayers and supplications offered at the temple.[8] Even in utmost distress, when Israel's disloyalty leads to its scattering among the nations, the temple, as the place chosen by YHWH to make his name dwell there, should remain a place of hope that God will still remember his people, as Moses had promised (see Deut 30:2–4; also

---

7. See Knoppers, "Prayer and Propaganda," 250.
8. See Knoppers, "Prayer and Propaganda," 245.

Deut 4:29–31; Lev 26:39–42; Neh 1:8–9). In the last petition, Solomon also refers to Moses but uses yet another line of argumentation. He explicitly reminds God to remember Israel, whom he brought out of Egypt, and asks him to acknowledge this special role by answering all the people's pleas (1 Kgs 8:51–53). In this way, Solomon combines God's choosing of Israel as his heritage with God's constant attention to Israel's needs, thus pointing out and specifying the divine obligation.

To sum it up, on the one hand, Solomon interprets the temple as a place of hope, where the divine promises given to Moses and David come true. On the other hand, the newly established temple should help Israel refocus on following the divine commands.[9] Thus Solomon asks God to incline the hearts of the assembled people toward him, "to walk in all his ways, and to hear his commandments and his statutes and his rulings, which he commanded our fathers" (1 Kgs 8:58).[10] By referring to Moses and David, Solomon interprets the building of the temple as an implementation of Moses's commandments and a fulfillment of David's wish. By building the temple, Solomon ties up loose ends and marks the start of a new era. Solomon thus presents his reign and his building of the temple as the crowning point of the history of Israel's relationship with God. It is the last element in a long line of divine choices, reaching from Moses, the exodus, and the people to David and, finally, Solomon himself.

3.3. Solomon, the Exemplary Praying King

The insight into Solomon's thoughts that this prayer offers transforms the image of the glorious king who spares no expense to build a magnificent temple. The praying Solomon knows the limitations of his efforts and his achievements and is aware of the endangered future of his people. At the height of his reign, Solomon is depicted as a humble king, who uses his position—which is granted to him by a divine promise—to secure the future of his people by acting as their advocate before God (see Exod 32). The focus lies on the welfare of the people and their relationship to God: Solomon exclusively refers to Israel as God's people, not to the glory of the king. Instead, Solomon is portrayed as the loyal, God-fearing king pleading for his people.

---

9. See Knoppers, "Prayer and Propaganda," 250.
10. Unless otherwise indicated, all biblical translations are mine.

The composition of the prayer, which includes various sources and combines different theological discourses, shows Solomon as a king with comprehensive knowledge regarding Israel's traditions and the ability to uphold a sophisticated perspective.[11] In addition to the references to Moses and David or the images of God's presence, the petitions also refer to God's commandments (see Lev 26:22–45; Deut 4:26–31; 28; 30). In this way, Israel's history, but also its future, is linked with the king and the temple.[12]

Although Solomon's prayer is not offered in any actual situation of distress, in the nucleus of his prayer, the seven petitions, he anticipates events to come. He considers possible conflicts and attempts to establish a solution.[13]

The crisis situations mentioned cover all kinds of disaster: from a lawsuit to drought, famine, vermin, sickness, or enemies. Several times the petitions even include a combination of all possible situations. Some of the situations depicted resemble the promises and punishments announced in Lev 26 and Deut 28.[14] Because these texts deal explicitly with the obligation to follow divine commandments and the corresponding reward or

---

11. The question of whether Solomon's prayer is preexilic or exilic has been a matter of controversy. While today most exegetes assume an exilic context, some assume that the prayer requires an intact sanctuary and date it to the late exilic period (e.g., Hermann-Josef Stipp, "Die sechste und siebte Fürbitte des Tempelweihegebets [1 Kön 8, 44–51] in der Diskussion um das Deuteronomistische Geschichtswerk," *JNSL* 24 (1998): 205; see also Knoppers, "Prayer and Propaganda," 252.) It is more likely, however, that "events such as the Temple dedication function as magnets, attracting multiple texts and causing great reflection, redaction, and re-redaction. These reflections would increase in the exile, when theologians grappled with the relationship between prayer, exile, the Temple site, the holy city and Eretz Israel" (Marc Zvi Brettler, "Interpretation and Prayer: Notes on the Composition of 1 Kings 8.15–53," in *Minḥah le-Naḥum: Biblical and Other Studies Presented to Nahum M. Sarna in Honour of His 70th Birthday*, ed. Marc Zvi Brettler and Michael Fishbane, JSOTSup 154 [Sheffield: JSOT Press, 1993], 34).

12. Judith Newman has shown that it is typical for Second Temple-period prayers to reflect earlier scripture. They refer to history and reinterpret single events or familiar characters in a typological way (see Newman, *Praying by the Book*, 1–2). Thus Solomon's prayer fits this description.

13. In this way, Solomon's prayer can be seen as a model for all later penitential prayers. For example, 1 Kgs 8:47 is quoted in Dan 9:5 and Ps 106:6.

14. See, e.g., 1 Kgs 8:33 (Deut 28:25; Lev 26:17); 1 Kgs 8:35 (Deut 28:23–24); 1 Kgs 8:37 (Deut 28:21, 22, 27, 35, 38, 39, 42, 59–61; Lev 26:25); 1 Kgs 8:46 (Deut 28:36, 64; Lev 26:33).

punishment, references to them enhance the aspect of wrongdoing and guilt mentioned in Solomon's petitions. In 1 Kgs 8, however, these situations are not presented as punishment but as situations to come. Similar to Moses in the book of Deuteronomy, Solomon is able to see as far as the catastrophe of exile and to raise hope for this time (see Deut 4:25–31; 30:1–10).[15] Solomon's role in the prayer parallels that of a prophet representing the people before God.[16] Solomon does not, however, share the hope expressed in Deut 4 or 30—namely, that the people will make the right decision and follow God's commandments. Rather, he assumes that the people will sin (this is made explicit in the seventh petition: "There is no person who does not sin" [1 Kgs 8:46]) and that these events will occur.[17] The king is no exception, and thus this statement, as Linville points out, casts a shadow on the glorious king as well.[18] Rather, he hopes for God's forgiveness (8:30, 34, 36, 39, 50) if the people pray (חנן, פלל) to God, repent of their sins (1 Kgs 8:47), and return to God.[19] As in Lev 26 and Deut 4:29–30; 30:2–3, Solomon imagines the people's repentance, which in turn will cause God to have mercy and to remember his covenant with their fathers (Lev 26:42, 44–45).[20] Nevertheless, Solomon's petitions do not take this

---

15. See Ehud Ben Zvi, "What Is New in Yehud? Some Considerations," in *Yahwism after the Exile: Perspectives on Israelite Religion in the Persian Era*, ed. Rainer Albertz and Bob Becking, STR 5 (Assen: Van Gorcum, 2003), 38.

16. See William M. Schniedewind, *The Word of God in Transition: From Prophet to Exegete in the Second Temple Period*, JSOTSup 197 (Sheffield: JSOT Press, 1995), 189–93.

17. In contrast to later penitential prayers, Solomon's prayer does not link the present generation of the prayers with the past generation of guilt. See Mark J. Boda, "Confession as Theological Expression: Ideological Origins of Penitential Prayer," in *The Origins of Penitential Prayer in Second Temple Judaism*, vol. 1 of *Seeking the Favor of God*, ed. Mark J. Boda, Daniel K. Falk, and Rodney A. Werline, EJL 21 (Atlanta: Society of Biblical Literature, 2006), 38. Sinfulness does not appear as a repeated aspect of Israel's history but rather as a constitutive element of human nature.

18. James R. Linville, *Israel in the Book of Kings: The Past as a Project of Social Identity*, JSOTSup 272 (Sheffield: Sheffield Academic, 1998), 136.

19. Not only does Solomon plead with God to hear his prayer (1 Kgs 8:28, 29, 59), but he also envisions the people's prayers (8:30, 33, 35, 42, 44, 48).

20. 1 Kgs 8 picks up elements from the Deuteronomic tradition, especially its concern for a return to the observance of torah, but also the Priestly tradition, with its concern over sin and the demand of penitential prayer. See Boda, "Confession," 34; see also Daniel K. Falk, "Scriptural Inspiration for Penitential Prayer in the Dead Sea Scrolls," in *The Development of Penitential Prayer in Second Temple Judaism*, vol. 2 of

connection for granted (see Jer 15:1) but rather ask for God's forgiveness and help.[21] Solomon's prayer thus combines the different traditions, picks up a well-known list of punishments, and anticipates their execution. For these cases, Solomon tries to establish a solution so that God might turn to his people once more and rescue them.

The petitions are composed according to a common pattern: the situation is outlined, mentioning the petitioners, who with one exception are Israelites, depicting the situation of crisis and anticipating the people's actions—namely, to turn away from sin, to repent,[22] and to offer a prayer in or toward the temple.[23] In this way, "Solomon's seven petitions actively promote the temple as a site of popular prayer.... Solomon's prayer becomes a unifying symbol in Israel's worship."[24] This description is followed by a supplication asking God to hear the prayers and to act, to forgive, or to uphold their cause (1 Kgs 8:32, 34, 36, 39, 43, 49). Thus the hoped-for divine reaction always includes God's attention and the restoration of the people. "The temple in Solomon's strategy is envisioned as God's visual reminder of his covenant and promises to David. Prayers toward Solomon's temple can become the basis for God to remit even the most inconceivable punishment, exile, if the guilty confess and repent of their sin."[25] Petitions 4 and 5 also mention what the effect of God's intervention will be: fear of God, knowing his name, remembering this God, and hope that this God remembers his people and their mutual history.

Seeking the Favor of God, ed. Mark J. Boda, Daniel K. Falk, and Rodney A. Werline, EJL 22 (Atlanta: Society of Biblical Literature, 2007), 138.

21. In contrast, Deut 28 does not foresee that the threatening penalties will not be revoked.

22. The short descriptions offered by Solomon are only elaborated in v. 47, when a (hypothetical) confession is cited: "We have sinned, and we did wrong, we acted wickedly." Newman (*Praying by the Book*, 51) suggests that "the use of a standard confessional form had developed by the time this prayer was written."

23. In the fifth petition, the petitioners are foreigners. Thus it becomes clear that God is accessible to all humans, whether they are Israelites or not, whether they are at the temple or far away, and regardless of what they are praying for—God will listen from heaven. See Volker Haarmann, *JHWH-Verehrer der Völker: Die Hinwendung von Nichtisraeliten zum Gott Israels in alttestamentlichen Überlieferungen*, ATANT 91 (Zürich: TVZ, 2008), 197–98.

24. Knoppers, "Prayer and Propaganda," 246.

25. Michael D. Matlock, *Discovering the Traditions of Prose Prayers in Early Jewish Literature*, LSTS 81 (London: T&T Clark, 2012), 22.

Solomon's petitions modify the royal image by foreseeing a situation when Israel must accept the fact that it is not in the land or of no political importance (see Neh 9). It envisions a transition from monarchy to a period without a king, and it suggests that such a transition is already inherent in the concept of the temple. In this way, it opens a counterdiscourse, interrupting the dominant image of stability and duration presented by the narration. The hopes for help and rescue that are tied to the temple also anticipate a possible end of the monarchy. This concept of the temple thus transcends the concept of monarchy.

Yet another shift occurs as the center of attention moves from the king to the people. Solomon asks God to acknowledge the temple and to remember his people. The future prayers Solomon envisions, however, are not an act reserved for royalty, or even for Israel, but an opportunity for anyone at any time.[26] Furthermore, "these petitions imagine the temple to be a place where Israelites and non-Israelites alike gather to offer their prayers to God."[27] In this way, Solomon abandons the role and importance of the king in this respect. The only recently established dynasty—in which Solomon was so eager to secure a place for himself—is already depicted in its transience. In this way, the dominant discourse of establishing the monarchy through the building of the temple is interrupted. Nevertheless, despite the deconstruction of the royal image, the king is still presented as an authoritative figure, establishing an interpretation of the world for times to come. The idea he emphasizes is a concept of repentance and forgiveness obtained by prayer.[28] Thus world-defining qualities are attributed to Solomon, which, in turn, allude to Solomon's image of the exemplary wise man and king. In this way, Solomon's prayer

---

26. See Daniel F. O'Kennedy, "Prayer of Solomon (1 Ki 8:22–53): Paradigm for the Understanding of Forgiveness in the Old Testament," *OTE* 13 (2000): 78.

27. Leslie J. Hoppe, "The Afterlife of a Text: The Case of Solomon's Prayer in 1 Kings 8," *LASBF* 51 (2001): 19.

28. Werline points out, that 1 Kgs 8 "is not a penitential prayer per se, but it does instruct Israel about repentance and encourages God to respond in an expected way, with forgiveness and restoration, all of this in the form of a prayer" ("Defining Penitential Prayer," in Boda, Falk, and Werline, *Origins of Penitential Prayer*, xvi). Texts like 1 Kgs 8 represent a later phase of reflection, reinterpreting "the Deuteronomic agenda to include prayer as an essential component of this repentance" (Boda, "Confession," 27). See also Rodney A. Werline, *Penitential Prayer in Second Temple Judaism: The Development of a Religious Institution*, EJL 13 (Atlanta: Scholars Press, 1998), 28.

is more than just a prayer; rather, it is a discourse on the function of prayers focusing on the temple.[29]

4. Forming and Transforming the Image of the Temple

Solomon's prayer is also a discourse on the function of the temple. He picks up and discusses different ideas from tradition and on this basis redesigns the image of the temple and its function. When Solomon starts to redefine the expectations and hopes associated with the temple, he inevitably modifies the role of the king as well. It shifts from the image of the builder and guardian of the temple, the wealthy and glorious king, to a wise petitioner who is aware of human weaknesses and faults and, for this reason, is trying to provide support for the seemingly unavoidable disasters to come by reinterpreting the function of the temple.

4.1. The Temple: Between a Royal Building and a Place to Remember

The narrating voice offers the readers a detailed tour through the temple building in 1 Kgs 6–7. It presents the temple together with Solomon's palace and other buildings as part of the king's representation. Thus Solomon, the royal builder, re-creates space according to his visions. Furthermore, an adequate temple building is also part of a king's responsibility to care for the appropriate representation of the deity, and it thus expresses respect and fear of God. Vice versa, the divine order to build a temple shows divine benevolence for the king and his reign (1 Kgs 8:19). According to the will of the deity, the temple is the place where God can dwell in the midst of Israel and where a cultic encounter can take place. Hence, the temple becomes the central space, "constructed and enacted through both divine choice and human maintenance of sacred spaces."[30] This designation of the temple building, and thus the start of its function

---

29. See Hans-Peter Mathys, *Dichter und Beter: Theologen aus spätalttestamentlicher Zeit*, OBO 132 (Freiburg: Universitätsverlag; Göttingen: Vandenhoeck & Ruprecht, 1994), 51; Moshe Weinfeld, *Deuteronomy 1–11: A New Translation with Introduction and Commentary*, AB 5 (New York: Doubleday, 1991), 37; see also O'Kennedy, "Prayer of Solomon," 74.

30. Melody D. Knowles, *Centrality Practiced: Jerusalem in the Religious Practice of Yehud and the Diaspora in the Persian Period*, ABS 16 (Atlanta: Society of Biblical Literature, 2006), 6.

as a center, is emphasized in several ways. The previous symbols for God's representations (the ark of the covenant, the tent of meeting, and the holy vessels) are transferred to the temple, and the priests begin their service at the temple. This action is accompanied by the king's sacrifices. Parallel to the elaborate description of the temple building in all its glory, the narrative voice mentions the huge quantity of Solomon's sacrifices (1 Kgs 8:62–64). The king thus offers all he is able to give. This ceremony is further complemented by Solomon's prayer.[31] Corresponding to the visual inspection of the temple by the narrating voice, the prayer offers an insight into another function of the temple: as the place toward which prayers are directed and where God will listen to them. Only Solomon's prayer makes this explicit connection between the temple and the people's prayer, thus shifting the focus from the temple as a royal-divine project to its function for the people.[32] Although Solomon in his prayer emphasizes his initiative to build the temple and its significance, at the same time he sets aside the importance of the temple building for the royal demonstration of power and wealth. This aspect, which dominated the narrative account, fades into the background, and thereby the detailed description of the temple as a magnificent building is put into perspective. Solomon's prayer puts two concepts of the temple side by side: On the one hand, the temple is the visible expression of Solomon's legitimacy as king and David's successor and is a highlight of Israel's history with its deity. On the other hand, the temple is a place of remembrance. The prayer marks the temple as a reminder for Israel that God takes an interest in the events related to the temple, and also as a place God may remember and pay attention to. Thus the temple is a point of intersection between the divine and the human world, a place to remember God and a place God remembers.

Another reinterpretation strategy is connected to the aspect of time. While the narrative voice presents the dedication of the temple as a single event, Solomon's prayer focuses on the temple throughout different times: its building was commanded by Moses, promised to David, and executed

---

31. Newman pointed out that "prayers do not supersede sacrifices, they rather complement them" (*Praying by the Book*, 52). Furthermore, the combination of royal sacrifice and royal prayer is not unique but can also be found in several ancient Near Eastern narratives of the construction of a temple. See also Knoppers, "Prayer and Propaganda," 231.

32. Newman, *Praying by the Book*, 52; Michael Avioz, "The Characterization of Solomon in Solomon's Prayer (1 Kings 8)," *BN* 126 (2005): 20.

by Solomon, and it will function for generations to come. In this place, past, present, and future come together, and thus it is compatible for times to come.[33] There the hope passed on through time gains a spatial body.

4.2. The Temple: Between God's Dwelling Place and a Place of Divine Attention

While the narrating voice elaborates on the building of the temple, Solomon's prayer questions the whole project by his critical reflections. Once Solomon has finished building the temple, he emphasizes his legitimacy to do so, but he also problematizes the temple's function and its suitability. Continuing the narration, Solomon first picks up the aspect of darkness (1 Kgs 8:12) connected with God's appearance in the cloud (8:10–11). He points out that God wants to dwell in darkness and that he, Solomon, has built the desired temple as a divine dwelling forever (8:13). Thus God's presence does not reveal the deity, who remains concealed.[34] Further on, facing the assembly of Israel, Solomon repeats God's promise to David and thereby introduces another concept of God's presence; it is not God but his name (שם) that dwells in the temple (8:17–20, 29).[35] With this theological construction, the far-away deity can be imagined as present, and thus God's שם is the way God is present on earth, while God dwells in heaven. Subsequently, however, Solomon calls the temple's purpose into question (8:27): will it really offer an appropriate dwelling place for God? The point of comparison is the image of YHWH's dwelling in heaven, whereby, on second thought, even heaven does not offer sufficient space (cf. the polemic question in Isa 66:1–2).[36] Hence, already at the dedication of the

---

33. The temple does not become insignificant; on the contrary, its importance is continued beyond its destruction. See Haarmann, *JHWH-Verehrer der Völker*, 199.

34. See Jürgen van Oorschot, "Die Macht der Bilder und die Ohnmacht des Wortes? Bilder und Bilderverbot im alten Israel," *ZTK* 96 (1999): 317.

35. See Michael Rohde, "Wo wohnt Gott? Alttestamentliche Konzeptionen der Gegenwart Jahwes am Beispiel des Tempelweihgebets 1 Könige 8," *BTZ* 26 (2009): 176. For a discussion of the different images of God's dwelling, see also Brettler, "Interpretation and Prayer," 19–21.

36. Images of God's dwelling have always been connected to heaven, but the explicit localization in heaven follows the destruction of the temple in Jerusalem. In the exile, the image of God's throne in heaven unfolds. See Friedhelm Hartenstein, "Wolkendunkel und Himmelsfeste: Zur Genese und Kosmologie der Vorstellung des himmlischen Heiligtums JHWHs," in *Das biblische Weltbild und seine altorientali-*

newly built temple, Solomon challenges its function as an adequate divine dwelling place. This fundamental questioning marks the starting point for a new definition of the temple as a space of remembrance for God and people alike.

In the following petitions (8:28–30), Solomon asks God to pay attention to his prayer and to turn toward the place of the temple. What Solomon hopes for, and what he exemplifies in his pleas, is that God will concentrate his attention on the temple, especially on the prayers that are performed there or that are offered toward the temple. Solomon's petitions focus on the temple as the predominant place of prayers, and thereby the spatial concept of the temple is modified. The temple is not foremost the place where God takes up residence, but rather it is the place God gives his attention to. The temple remains the point of intersection between the divine and the human world, but it is no longer necessary to be at the temple, neither for God nor for the people.[37] In his prayer, Solomon thus modifies the image of the temple. At that point in time, when the glory of YHWH (כבוד־יהוה) was going to take permanent residence in the temple, the prayer emphasizes the people's and the deity's distance from it.[38] Thus the temple is not only a place to appear before God in person but also a place where God and people can meet without being actually present at the temple. In this way, a different concept of the temple is outlined. The focus is no longer on the temple as a place where an encounter between God and humans may take place through their mutual presence. Rather, the space of the temple as a meeting place is separated from a bodily presence, and hence the temple also becomes virtually accessible. Both concepts may coexist; the second concept, however, can also outlast the first. Even if the temple is destroyed and/or is no longer accessible, the place can still fulfill its function.

---

schen Kontexte, ed. Bernd Janowski and Beate Ego, FAT 32 (Tübingen: Mohr Siebeck, 2001), 127.

37. In the exemplary situations presented in the seven petitions, only the first, second, and fifth petitions are offered in/at the temple; all other prayers are offered only in the direction of the temple.

38. The temple marks the transition from the idea that God is only present at the tabernacle during the time of an encounter between God and humans to the idea that God takes permanent residence in the temple. See Rohde, "Wo wohnt Gott?," 179.

4.3. The Temple: Between the Center of the Land and Hope for the Land

In Solomon's prayer, the concept of the temple is closely linked to the idea of "the land." The temple is not only the place prayers are directed to, but also, as a hoped for consequence, the space where people's lives are transformed. The second, third, and fourth petitions ask for the possibility to dwell in the land; this includes not only God's care for it (1 Kgs 8:36) but also the opportunity for the people to return to the land God has given to their ancestors (8:34, 40).[39] The people's longing for the land is again picked up in the metaphor of the people as God's inheritance (נחלה) in the seventh petition, whereby the people's yearning for their land blends with God's relation to his people (8:53). Thus the strong and essential tie to one's inheritance puts the people on a level with the land.[40] The help these petitions ask for aims at a restoration of the experienced space as it is depicted in the well-known spatial concept of the "promised land." Solomon's petitions remind God of this spatial construction and ask him to restore this concept.[41] The space the petitions hope for thus takes its shape from a collective memory and transfers it to a yet-unknown but hoped-for future. Yet the hope of the seventh petition (8:46–53) exceeds the remembered space and extends the hopes to "Israel's surviving as a community in exile."[42]

The place where such memories and hopes may be expressed is the temple. Solomon's prayer presents the temple as a space in the middle of the land but on the margins of the experienced reality. The space of the temple is presented as a space of resistance able to redefine the reality of the actually experienced space.[43] To partake in this space, it is not

---

39. Boda points out that it is typical for later penitential prayers to emphasize the close connection between the people and the land, especially the hope to dwell in the land and to regain control of the land (Boda, "Confession," 44). 1 Kgs 8 already points in this direction.

40. The prayer uses the foundational narrative of the exodus to highlight the opportunity for divine rescue at any later time. See Boda, "Confession," 38.

41. Similar to Deut 30:1–10, Solomon's petitions express the hope for a divine intervention and a restoration of the expatriates to the land.

42. J. Gordon McConville, "1 Kings VIII 46–53 and the Deuteronomic Hope," *VT* 42 (1992): 76.

43. According to the critical spatial theory of Soja, such a space is a *Thirdspace*. For Soja, "Thirdspace is an act of resistance, a way of using space that points out its constructed nature.... Thirdspace always presents possibilities for resistance, for popular activity that redefines the realities of space" (Jon L. Berquist, "Introduction: Criti-

necessary to offer a prayer at the temple, but only to adjust the praying position (8:38; 42; 44; 48). The body or parts of the body should be turned toward the temple/Jerusalem when praying in a different place, thus referring to the temple. In this way, the geographic reach of the temple and its significance is expanded. "Like pilgrimage, the practice emphasizes the singularity of Jerusalem for worship and also explicitly includes the possibility of participation by foreigners."[44] Hence, Solomon's prayer does not focus only on Israel, but foreigners are also mentioned as beneficiaries of God's attention to the temple. Thus the divine focus on this place Solomon asks for will change social settings and redefine boundaries.

5. Solomon's Prayer:
A Crossroad between Monarchic and (Post)exilic Israel?

At the grand finale of the temple building, the royal prayer also looks into the future and anticipates further developments. The image of the king, the function of the temple, and the idea of prayer are therein modified. What Solomon prays for in 1 Kgs 8 remains relevant for times to come. After the exile, the community of Yehud draws its identity from the foundational past, and it looks to an ideal future.[45] In this way, Solomon's prayer initiates a discourse of different perspectives and thus opens the possibility for a relecture of preexilic and exilic discourses in postexilic times.

The most obvious changes introduced in Solomon's prayer affect the concept and the function of the temple. While classically the temple was "the locus of legitimate sacrifice and of divine revelation," 1 Kgs 8:23–53 presents the temple mainly as "a place of prayer and supplication."[46] This

---

cal Spatiality and the Uses of Theory," in *Constructions of Space I: Theory, Geography, and Narrative*, ed. Claudia V. Camp and Jon L. Berquist, LHBOTS 481 [London: T&T Clark, 2007], 5).

44. Knowles, *Centrality Practiced*, 92.

45. Ben Zvi points out that it is typical for postexilic discourses to marginalize the present and glorify the now-classical past and ideal future ("What Is New in Yehud?," 47).

46. Jon D. Levenson points out that such a reinterpretation of the temple as a place of prayer is well known from other sixth-century literature, especially Isa 56–66; see, e.g., Isa 56:6–8 (Levenson, "From Temple to Synagogue: 1 Kings 8," in *Traditions in Transformation: Turning Points in Biblical Faith; To Frank Moore Cross on the Occasion of his 60. Birthday, July 13, 1981*, ed. Baruch Halpern et al. [Winona Lake, IN: Eisenbrauns, 1981], 158–59).

different function is also reflected in the idea of the divine presence at the temple, which does not stress God's dwelling in the temple but rather emphasizes God's persistent attention that is focused on the temple. Within the logic of this concept, the temple can fulfill its function even if the petitioners are not at the temple or the temple is temporarily inaccessible. It is sufficient that they direct their prayers to the temple and that God pays attention to everything that is addressed toward the temple. Thus the idea of the centrality of the temple remains, while its function and also its accessibility are expanded and varied. This holds true not only regarding a spatial aspect but also concerning a social aspect as well, as Solomon's vision includes Israelites and foreigners. In this way, Solomon's prayer foresees the change of the temple's function for the times of exile and beyond and makes the new temple transparent to various situations to come. The literary presentation of the building of the temple as a narration and the reflection on its function in Solomon's speech make it possible to juxtapose different concepts of the temple as a discourse. In the course of this, none of the concepts are rejected; rather, they are interlocked and developed further.

Solomon's prayer is an elaborate reflection on the relationship of God and people, in the past but also in the future. It also thereby widens the concept of prayer by presenting it as a way of communication with God in various situations. Solomon drafts a theory of prayer and asks God to acknowledge it as a (new) standard. Describing such prayers, Solomon even anticipates penitential prayer as an important genre of prayer for the times to come. Solomon, the wise king, thus proclaims the theological message of exilic/postexilic times—namely, that in order to rebuild the temple and the community, Israel must confess their sins and pray for forgiveness.[47] In this way, Solomon's prayer presents a paradigm applicable to future periods.[48] Furthermore, it "may offer reassurance to many generations that their own prayers would be answered by God."[49] It thus emphasizes that prayer is nothing less than a way to initiate change and to (re)define the experienced world.[50]

---

47. O'Kennedy, "Prayer of Solomon," 77; see also Arnold Gamper, "Die heilsgeschichtliche Bedeutung des Salomonischen Tempelweihgebets," *ZKT* 85 (1963): 60.

48. See Newman, *Praying by the Book*, 54.

49. Newman, *Praying by the Book*, 52.

50. Rodney A. Werline points out that "biblical authors and editors demonstrate a special ability to use prayer to tie Israel's larger history to the peoples' lived experi-

Concerning the image of the king, 1 Kgs 8 emphasizes the image of a wise king. At the height of his power, Solomon is portrayed as a king who summarizes Israel's history and fulfils open promises but who also reinterprets traditional religious concepts so that they may be helpful for Israel's future. Complementing the image of the magnificent and wise king with the image of a prudent and foresightful praying man makes Solomon relevant for times to come. Solomon is presented as the one who makes such a transition possible, from Moses and David to his reign, but also to a time without a monarchy.[51] It thus becomes obvious that neither the monarchy nor the king is able to guarantee identity for the people. Rather, identity and belonging can be achieved through prayer toward the temple. The praying king may thus be seen as a role model. Solomon's words not only initiate a new understanding of prayers; he also demonstrates how such a prayer should be performed. If "the people stretch out their hands toward the temple, the prayer also establishes the power of the temple over their actions. In their petitions and in their posture, the people imitate Solomon.... In speech and in body the king and the people become united."[52]

To summarize, Solomon's prayer anticipates a far-reaching transition. It does not address the issue of how, when, or why a change will happen, but rather it focuses on how the people may still communicate with their God and in which way the temple will remain the center of their hopes. In this process, the figure of the king is also transformed. The monarch is presented as an intercessor for his people, who tries to secure their relationship with God and thus to protect their future. In this way, Solomon prepares the ground for intercessors and religious leaders to come. Solomon's prayer thus refers to a crossing point, where specific ideas and conceptions from different eras are juxtaposed and linked in order to emphasize the connecting aspects. The authority of King Solomon and the importance of the narrated context, the dedication of the temple, in turn highlight the significance of this transformation.[53] Hence, at the climax of the narration of the monarchy, it is to no less a king than Solomon, the exemplary wise sovereign, that the task of negotiating the border between

---

ences and the micropolitics of everyday life" (Werline, "Prayer, Politics, and Power in the Hebrew Bible," *Int* 68 [2014]: 16).

51. See McConville, "1 Kings VIII 46–43," 79.
52. Werline, "Prayer, Politics, and Power," 13.
53. See O'Kennedy, "Prayer of Solomon," 84.

the remembrance of a magnificent past, the experience of disaster, and an uncertain future is attributed—a task that, as 1 Kgs 8 makes clear, can (only) be mastered through prayer.

Bibliography

Avioz, Michael. "The Characterization of Solomon in Solomon's Prayer (1 Kings 8)." *BN* 126 (2005): 19–28.

Ben Zvi, Ehud. "What Is New in Yehud? Some Considerations." Pages 32–48 in *Yahwism after the Exile: Perspectives on Israelite Religion in the Persian Era*. Edited by Rainer Albertz and Bob Becking. STR 5. Assen: Van Gorcum, 2003.

Berquist, John L. "Introduction: Critical Spatiality and the Uses of Theory." Pages 1–12 in *Constructions of Space I: Theory, Geography, and Narrative*. Edited by Claudia V. Camp and Jon L. Berquist. LHBOTS 481. London: T&T Clark, 2007.

Boda, Mark J. "Confession as Theological Expression: Ideological Origins of Penitential Prayer." Pages 21–50 in *Seeking the favor of God*. Vol. 1 of *The Origins of Penitential Prayer in Second Temple Judaism*. Edited by Mark J. Boda, Daniel K. Falk, and Rodney A. Werline. EJL 21. Atlanta: Society of Biblical Literature, 2006.

Brettler, Marc Zvi. "Interpretation and Prayer: Notes on the Composition of 1 Kings 8.15–53." Pages 17–35 in *Minḥah le-Naḥum: Biblical and Other Studies Presented to Nahum M. Sarna in Honour of His 70th Birthday*. Edited by Marc Zvi Brettler and Michael Fishbane. JSOTSup 154. Sheffield: JSOT Press, 1993.

Falk, Daniel K. "Scriptural Inspiration for Penitential Prayer in the Dead Sea Scrolls." Pages 127–57 in *The Development of Penitential Prayer in Second Temple Judaism*. Vol. 2 of *Seeking the Favor of God*. Edited by Mark J. Boda, Daniel K. Falk, and Rodney A. Werline. EJL 22. Atlanta: Society of Biblical Literature, 2007.

Gamper, Arnold. "Die heilsgeschichtliche Bedeutung des Salomonischen Tempelweihgebets." *ZKT* 85 (1963): 55–61.

Groß, Walter. *Zukunft für Israel: Alttestamentliche Bundeskonzepte und die aktuelle Debatte um den Neuen Bund*. SBS 176. Stuttgart: Katholisches Bibelwerk, 1998.

Haarmann, Volker. *JHWH-Verehrer der Völker: Die Hinwendung von Nichtisraeliten zum Gott Israels in alttestamentlichen Überlieferungen*. ATANT 91. Zurich: TVZ, 2008.

Hartenstein, Friedhelm. "Wolkendunkel und Himmelsfeste: Zur Genese und Kosmologie der Vorstellung des himmlischen Heiligtums JHWHs." Pages 125–79 in *Das biblische Weltbild und seine altorientalischen Kontexte*. Edited by Bernd Janowski and Beate Ego. FAT 32. Tübingen: Mohr Siebeck, 2001.

Hoppe, Leslie J. "The Afterlife of a Text: The Case of Solomon's Prayer in 1 Kings 8." *LASBF* 51 (2001): 9–30.

Knoppers, Gary N. "Prayer and Propaganda: Solomon's Dedication of the Temple and the Deuteronomist's Program." *CBQ* 57 (1995): 229–54.

Knowles, Melody D. *Centrality Practiced: Jerusalem in the Religious Practice of Yehud and the Diaspora in the Persian Period*. ABS 16. Atlanta: Society of Biblical Literature, 2006.

Levenson, Jon D. "From Temple to Synagogue: 1 Kings 8." Pages 143–66 in *Traditions in Transformation: Turning Points in Biblical Faith; To Frank Moore Cross on the Occasion of His 60. Birthday, July 13, 1981*. Edited by Baruch Halpern et al. Winona Lake, IN: Eisenbrauns, 1981.

Linville, James R. *Israel in the Book of Kings: The Past as a Project of Social Identity*. JSOTSup 272. Sheffield: Sheffield Academic, 1998.

Mathys, Hans-Peter. *Dichter und Beter: Theologen aus spätalttestamentlicher Zeit*. OBO 132. Freiburg: Universitätsverlag; Göttingen: Vandenhoeck & Ruprecht, 1994.

Matlock, Michael D. *Discovering the Traditions of Prose Prayers in Early Jewish Literature*. LSTS 81. London: T&T Clark, 2012.

———. "Prayer Changes Things or Things Change Prayer: Innovations of Solomon's Temple Prayer in Early Jewish Literature." Pages 159–86 in *The Letters and Liturgical Traditions*. Vol. 2 of *"What Does the Scripture Say?" Studies in the Function of Scripture in Early Judaism and Christianity*. Edited by Craig A. Evans and H. Daniel Zacharias. LNTS 470. SSEJC 18. London: T&T Clark, 2012.

McConville, J. Gordon. "1 Kings VIII 46–53 and the Deuteronomic Hope." *VT* 42 (1992): 67–79.

Newman, Judith H. *Praying by the Book: The Scripturalization of Prayer in Second Temple Judaism*. EJL 14. Atlanta: Scholars Press, 1999.

Newsom, Carol A. *The Self as Symbolic Space: Constructing Identity and Community at Qumran*. STDJ 52. Leiden; Boston: Brill, 2004.

O'Kennedy, Daniel F. "The Prayer of Solomon (1 Ki 8:22–53): Paradigm for the Understanding of Forgiveness in the Old Testament." *OTE* 13 (2000): 72–88.

Oorschot, Jürgen van. "Die Macht der Bilder und die Ohnmacht des Wortes? Bilder und Bilderverbot im alten Israel." *ZTK* 96 (1999): 299–319.

Rohde, Michael. "Wo wohnt Gott? Alttestamentliche Konzeptionen der Gegenwart Jahwes am Beispiel des Tempelweihgebets 1 Könige 8." *BTZ* 26 (2009): 165–83.

Schniedewind, William M. *The Word of God in Transition: From Prophet to Exegete in the Second Temple Period*. JSOTSup 197. Sheffield: JSOT Press, 1995.

Stipp, Hermann-Josef. "Die sechste und siebte Fürbitte des Tempelweihegebets (1 Kön 8, 44–51) in der Diskussion um das Deuteronomistische Geschichtswerk." *JNSL* 24 (1998): 193–216.

Weinfeld, Moshe. *Deuteronomy 1–11: A New Translation with Introduction and Commentary*. AB 5. New York: Doubleday, 1991.

Werline, Rodney A. "Defining Penitential Prayer." Pages xiii–xvii in *The Origins of Penitential Prayer in Second Temple Judaism*. Vol. 1 of *Seeking the Favor of God*. Edited by Mark J. Boda, Daniel K. Falk, and Rodney A. Werline. EJL 21. Atlanta: Society of Biblical Literature, 2006.

———. *Penitential Prayer in Second Temple Judaism: The Development of a Religious Institution*. EJL 13. Atlanta: Scholars Press, 1998.

———. "Prayer, Politics, and Power in the Hebrew Bible." *Int* 68 (2014): 5–16.

Hannah's Prayer(s) in 1 Samuel 1–2 and in Pseudo-Philo's Liber antiquitatum biblicarum

Hannes Bezzel

1. Introduction

From a redaction-critical point of view, it can be stated that in what is commonly called late postexilic times, there was a tendency to insert prayers into important passages of the growing scrolls of what later would become biblical books. This holds true for the prophetic literature of the Latter Prophets, a topic that has been given its proper attention with the recent monograph by Alexa Wilke.[1] This likewise holds true for the narrative books, whether within the context of the later Former Prophets or the Writings: Dan 9; Ezra 9; Neh 1; 9–10; and 1 Chr 16, often called "psalms outside the psalter."[2] One of the best-known specimens of prayers within the corpus of the Former Prophets is, of course, Hannah's psalm in 1 Sam 2.

In the following, I will briefly consider the diachronic development of the prayer(s) in 1 Sam 1–2 before examining their reception in the pseudepigraphic document commonly referred to as Pseudo-Philo's Liber antiquitatum biblicarum.[3]

---

1. See Alexa Wilke, *Die Gebete der Propheten: Anrufungen Gottes im "Corpus Propheticum" der Hebräischen Bibel*, BZAW 451 (Berlin: de Gruyter, 2014).

2. See Kurt Galling, *Die Bücher der Chronik, Esra, Nehemia*, ATD 12 (Göttingen: Vandenhoeck & Ruprecht, 1954), 51–52; quote from Hans-Peter Mathys, *Dichter und Beter: Theologen aus spätalttestamentlicher Zeit*, OBO 132 (Göttingen: Vandenhoeck & Ruprecht, 1994), 125.

3. On the history of this title, see Howard Jacobson, *A Commentary on Pseudo-Philo's Liber Antiquitatum Biblicarum: With Latin Text and English Translation*, AGJU 31 (Leiden: Brill, 1996), 195–99.

2. Hannah's Prayers in 1 Samuel 1–2

Hannah's thanksgiving prayer, which she brings forth in reaction to the birth of her firstborn Samuel, is regarded as a typical example of shaping and interpreting a narrative context by secondarily inserting a psalm—and rightly so. Both the continuation of the narrative flow in 1 Sam 2:11 and the slightly differing position of the song in the LXX make it obvious that the piece should be seen as a rather late addition to what is generally called the birth narrative of Samuel, though in its final shape it is actually more interested in Hannah, the mother of the prophet to come, than in Samuel himself.[4]

Regardless of whether independent old traditions were worked into its creation or the poem should be seen as a literary unit, in its present position, it serves several purposes for the composition of its closer and wider contexts.[5] First, the numerous intratextual links with 2 Sam 22, David's psalm in the "appendix" to the books of Samuel, illustrate that both prayers intend to encircle the history of the early Israelite monarchy while focusing on its climax: the reign of David.[6] Even though the confident statement in 2:10 that the Lord will raise the horn of his anointed (וירם קרן משיחו) in the context of the following stories seemingly refers to Saul, David makes it clear in 2 Sam 22:51 that the word *anointed* refers to him alone: "He shows lovingkindness to his anointed, to David and to his seed forever" (ועשה־חסד למשיחו לדוד ולזרעו עד־עולם).[7] Put in other terms, 1 Sam 2 and

---

4. See A. Graeme Auld, *I and II Samuel: A Commentary*, OTL (Louisville: Westminster John Knox, 2011), 20.

5. Dietrich has developed the fascinating idea that two "Vor-Texte," once independent, had been worked together by a redactor: an ancient royal hymn on the one side and the prayer of a pious person in postexilic times on the other (Walter Dietrich, *1 Samuel 1-12*, BKAT 8.1 [Neukirchen-Vluyn: Neukirchener Verlag, 2010], 78–82). Anneli Aejmelaeus calls the poem a "Deuteronomistic composition" (Aejmelaeus, "Hannah's Psalm: Text, Composition, and Redaction," in *Houses Full of All Good Things: Essays in Memory of Timo Veijola*, ed. Juha Pakkala and Martti Nissinen, PFES 95 [Göttingen: Vandenhoeck & Ruprecht, 2008], 376). Mathys tends to a later dating and calls 1 Sam 2:1–10 "postdeuteronomistic" ("nachdeuteronomistisch") (Mathys, *Dichter und Beter*, 126).

6. On the intratextual links with 2 Sam 22, see, e.g., Erik Eynikel, "Das Lied der Hanna (1 Sam 2, 1–11) und das Lied Davids (2 Sam 22): Ein Vergleich," in *For and Against David: Story and History in the Books of Samuel*, ed. A. Graeme Auld and Erik Eynikel, BETL 232 (Leuven: Peeters, 2010), 57–72; Dietrich, *1 Sam 1-12*, 73–74.

7. Unless otherwise noted, all biblical translations are mine.

2 Sam 22 create what we know by the name of the books of Samuel or the Samuel scroll.

Second, with this outlook on an anointed king yet to come, Hannah reveals herself to be a prophetess or to be filled with a prophetic spirit in this special moment.[8]

Third, especially in the postbiblical Jewish reception history, Hannah serves as a role model of how to pray.[9] Commonly, this appraisal is not credited to her psalm but to her first, silent prayer in front of Eli. It may be a worthwhile endeavor, however, to take a look at the song of chapter 2 in its closer narrative context in chapter 1. From this point of view, both of her prayers, the silent one and the spoken one, appear to be closely connected.

Without a doubt, the literary history of 1 Sam 1–2 is complex and multilayered. To tell a long story short, I would suggest that its origins lie in a concise story of the miraculous birth of Samuel, with its core in something like 1 Sam 1:1–2, 5bβ, 7b, 8–9, (10a?), 10b, 13b, 14–15, 17a(b?), 18a(?), 18b–20; 3, 19aα.[10]

Hannah, a childless woman, prays to YHWH, and her prayer—which is not yet necessarily a silent one—is answered: she gives birth to a son. Several aspects of her prayer are explained and expanded in the course of the story's literary development: 1:12–13a, for example, deals with the question of why Eli reacted so harshly to her intense praying and crying. While this is not explicitly stated, it might be that he was offended because

---

8. See Dietrich, *1 Sam 1–12*, 97.

9. See Dietrich, *1 Sam 1–12*, 58; see also Leila L. Bronner, "Hannah's Prayer: Rabbinic Ambivalence," *Shofar* 17 (1999): 41–43, referring, inter alia, to y. Ber. 4:1; b. Ber. 31a; b. Yoma 73a–b.

10. I used to advocate a somewhat more extensive basic layer, such as 1:1–3a, 4, 5, 7aα.b, 8–10, 12–15, 17–20; 3, 19aα. See Hannes Bezzel, *Saul: Israels König in Tradition, Redaktion und früher Rezeption*, FAT 97 (Tübingen: Mohr Siebeck, 2015), 182–91. What made me change my mind was my reconsideration of the arguments put forth by Peter Porzig and Ernst Axel Knauf, especially regarding the tenses and some "suspicious" designations, such as אלהי ישראל in 1:17b, whose instances would not point "toward the oldest times" ("nicht unbedingt in früheste Zeit") (Porzig, *Die Lade im Alten Testament und in den Texten vom Toten Meer*, BZAW 397 [Berlin: de Gruyter, 2009], 114–15, quote at 115, n. 53; Knauf, "Samuel among the Prophets: 'Prophetical Redactions'" in *Is Samuel among the Deuteronomists? Current Views on the Place of Samuel in a Deuteronomistic History*, ed. Cynthia Edenburg and Juha Pakkala, SBLAIL 16 [Atlanta: Society of Biblical Literature, 2013], 149–69).

Hannah emphasized her prayer with some physical gesture. While our assumed basic layer in 1:10b, 13b, 14 suggests that it was some kind of loud disorderly conduct that gave the priest the impression of an uncontrolled and inebriated woman, 1:12–13a clearly state that Hannah behaved decently. She was muttering silently, and what gave rise to Eli's mistaken reproach was the mute moving of her lips. With this, Hannah is on her way to becoming the paradigm for an ideal supplicant. Verse 18a, as well as verse 16—a doublet to the preceding verse—emphasize her pious and humble character. Porzig speaks of "eine regelrechte Niedrigkeitsredaktion," and he does so with good reason.[11] In the end, Hannah represents "a curious combination of assertiveness and humility."[12]

The addition of 1:11 illustrates that once Hannahs's prayer was silent, later readers and editors were not satisfied but wanted to know more. Out of Hanna's own statement toward Eli that she was not drunk, they created a vow referring to the unborn child, making Samuel a Nazirite and establishing a link to the Samson story (see Judg 13:7).[13]

In another step, the character of the fertile Peninnah is developed not only as a counterpart to the seemingly barren Hannah but also as the latter's rival in 1:5–7, especially in 1:6. A new motif, Peninnah's mockery, is added to the story—at least in the masoretic version of the text. The LXX^B does not mention this mockery, neither in verses 6 and 7 nor in verse 16. In both 1:6 and 1:7, the LXX translates the root כעס in a reflexive way, with Hannah, not Peninnah, as its subject: "she was disheartened" (καὶ ἠθύμει; 1:7). Verse 16 has no equivalent in the Greek version at all for the Hebrew כעס.

Textual and literary criticism intermingle at this point.[14] Verse 6, a more or less obvious gloss, introduces Peninnah's rivalry—and clears the

---

11. Porzig, *Lade*, 114. He finds it in 1 Sam 1:7, 8, 16–18. His observations cannot be denied. They do not, however, affect the entire range of the verses mentioned. Furthermore, I would think that some pieces of these verses are indispensable to the basic layer of the story.

12. Bronner, "Hannah's Prayer," 37.

13. It can nicely be seen how Samuel's character as a Nazirite became more and more elaborated in the course of later reworking and rewriting: the LXX has an addition in 1 Sam 1:11 that is clearly inspired by Num 6:3, and 4Q51 (alias 4QSam^a) makes Samuel a Nazirite for life in 1:22. See also Sir 46:13 (in the Hebrew, not in the Greek version), according to which Samuel was a "Nazirite of YHWH in prophecy" (נזיר ייי בנבואה). See Bezzel, *Saul*, 184, n. 141.

14. For a detailed description of the problem, see Bezzel, *Saul*, 188–90.

way for a new understanding of Hannah's grief.[15] It is due not only to her seeming barrenness but also to the hostilities she has to endure at the hands of her enemy. This kind of mockery or trouble, כעס, in those instances in the Psalter where it does not describe in Deuteronomistic manner the anger of God (see Ps 78:58; 106:29), is the work of the wicked enemies of the supplicant or the result of their evildoing (see Pss 6:8; 10:14; 31:8).[16] With Peninnah constantly mocking Hannah, the latter's prayer appears not only to be a plea for a child but also a lament about unjust persecution by an enemy, a *Feindklage*.

The result of these and other *Fortschreibungen* of Samuel's birth narrative—or, that is to say, of the story of Hannah's answered prayer—is a multilayered and complex text. But however chaotic its history may be, evolving from several additions driven by various intentions at least partly unrelated to each other, there is something like a final form, and it appears to be well structured.[17] Taken together, 1 Sam 1–2 can be understood as a kind of individual lament in narrative guise.[18] The crucial elements of the genre, as identified classically by Hermann Gunkel and Joachim Begrich, are recognizable—albeit narratively transformed.[19]

Without an invocation of the deity (due to the narrative character of the passage), 1 Sam 1 starts with a depiction of Hannah's distress (1:1–8), namely, her infertility and her oppression by her rival, the latter expressed by means of the rather rare root כעס, as in Pss 6:8; 10:14; 31:10 for the supplicant's distress.

The next verses include Hannah's plea for salvation (1:10–13), followed by a declaration of her innocence (1:15–16)—taken with a grain of salt— which she is forced to produce by Eli, the priest: "I am not drunk." Verse 17 brings about the change typical for the genre, and Eli's blessing "go in peace" (לכי לשלום) appears to be the salvation oracle—and ironically, it is presented in precisely the context of an individual lament that Gunkel and

---

15. On 1 Sam 1:6 as a gloss, see, e.g., Hans Joachim Stoebe, *Das erste Buch Samuelis*, KAT 8.1 (Gütersloh: Gütersloher Verlagshaus, 1973), 91, 96.

16. See Bezzel, *Saul*, 181–82.

17. As the reference to the different versions of the MT and the LXX in 1:6, 7, 17 and 4Q51 exemplarily reveals, this so-called final form exists only in the plurality of several appearances.

18. For the following, see also Bezzel, *Saul*, 181–82.

19. See Hermann Gunkel and Joachim Begrich, *Einleitung in die Psalmen: Die Gattungen der religiösen Lyrik Israels*, 4th ed. (Göttingen: Vandenhoeck & Ruprecht, 1985), 212–51.

Begrich postulated for its *Sitz im Leben*.[20] Hannah's mood changes accordingly in 1:18: "Her features were no longer (like they were before)."[21]

One element of the individual lament is still missing: the vow of praise. But in the very position where one would expect such a vow, the text states that Hannah does exactly what the supplicant of the Psalter promises: she pays her vow and donates her boy to the sanctuary (1:21–28). From this perspective, chapter 2 is the natural continuation of chapter 1: Hannah's plea has been answered; now she reacts with a psalm of thanksgiving (which, as is well known, in 1 Sam 2 transcends the limitations of the genre by far).

To sum up: the development of Hannah's character as a praying woman begins with 1 Sam 1:10b, 13b. She prays and cries, presumably loudly, before YHWH, and Eli the priest regards her as drunk. Nevertheless, her prayer will be answered. As a result, Hannah, the literary character, was able to serve as an exemplar of successful praying. Step by step, certain features were added to her story with the purpose of demonstrating what would make up a successful prayer according to the views of the scribes who rewrote the chapters in postexilic times. These characteristics were a true vow, decent conduct, and, more and more, humbleness. From the perspective of some kind of *Armenfrömmigkeit*, this last aspect would implicate hostilities by the wicked, a part Peninnah was ready to play. In the masoretic version of 1 Samuel, her behavior is even more pronounced than in the LXX. This indicates that the "psalmification" of the narrative in 1 Sam 1 still continued after the separation of the two textual lines. Thus on the one hand, Hannah becomes something like another role model for the poor and humble pious. On the other hand, the great thanksgiving psalm in 1 Sam 2 is added to the story, depicting Hannah as a self-assured prophetess. These two images, however, are not contradictory but complementary: no one but the poor and the humble righteous see themselves as addressees of the prophetic revelation.

3. Hannah's Prayers in Pseudo-Philo

Let us now look at Hannah and her prayers in Pseudo-Philo's Liber antiquitatum biblicarum. Pseudo-Philo, whoever he (or she) was, must have

---

20. See Gunkel and Begrich, *Einleitung*, 243–47, esp. 246–47.
21. The translation of the singular and difficult phrase ופניה לא־היו־לה עוד follows Dietrich, *1 Sam 1–12*, 20.

regarded the first chapters of the books of Samuel as quite important. In his rewritten Bible, the Liber antiquitatum biblicarum, most probably to be dated to the end of the first century CE, he gave some attention to them.[22] While Josephus, his contemporary, mentions only Hannah's plea "to give her progeny and make her a mother" (δοῦναι γονὴν αὐτῇ καὶ ποιῆσαι μητέρα; A.J. 5.344[23]) and leaves the song of 1 Sam 2:1–10 totally aside, Liber antiquitatum biblicarum reports both her supplication in the presence of Eli and her thanksgiving song in an expanded form.

Her silent prayer, which in 1 Sam 1:11 is secondarily presented as a vow with the structure "if you give me, I will give you," is turned into a plea beginning with a statement of complete submission to the divine will: "Did you not, Lord, examine the heart of all generations before you formed the world? Now what womb is born opened or dies closed unless you wish it?"[24] This alteration may bear witness to a skeptical attitude toward vows

---

22. Liber antiquitatum biblicarum is dated between the first century BCE and the end of the first century CE, with early daters locating the document before the destruction of the Second Temple and late daters afterward. On the dating, see Jean Hadot, "Le milieu d'origine du 'Liber antiquitatum biblicarum,'" in *La littérature intertestamentaire: Colloque de Strasbourg (17–19 octobre 1983)*, ed. André Caquot, BCESS (Paris: Presses Universitaires de France, 1985), 163. For early daters, see, among others, Pierre-Maurice Bogaert, "Introduction Littéraire," in *Introduction Littéraire, Commentaire et Index*, vol. 2 of *Pseudo-Philon: Les Antiquités Bibliques*, ed. Charles Perrot and Pierre-Maurice Bogaert, SC 230 (Paris: Cerf, 1976), 74. For late daters, see, e.g., Louis Feldman, "Prolegomenon," in *The Biblical Antiquities of Philo: Now First Translated from the Old Latin Version*, ed. Montague R. James, 2nd ed., LBS (New York: Ktav, 1971), xxviii–xxxi; Christian Dietzfelbinger, *Pseudo-Philo: Antiquitates Biblicae (Liber Antiquitatum Biblicarum)*, 2nd ed., JSHRZ 2.2 (Gütersloh: Gütersloher Verlagshaus, 1979), 95–96. For a further overview of introductory matters, see Jacobson, *Commentary*, 195–280; Gerbern S. Oegema, "Pseudo-Philo: Antiquitates biblicae (Liber antiquitatum biblicarum)" in *Einführung zu den Jüdischen Schriften aus hellenistisch-römischer Zeit: Unterweisung in erzählender Form*, JSHRZ 6.1.2 (Gütersloh: Gütersloher Verlagshaus, 2005), 66–77.

23. English translation according to Christopher Begg, *Judean Antiquities Books 5-7: Translation and Commentary*, FJTC 4 (Leiden: Brill, 2005), 87. For an interpretation of the overall portrayal of Hannah by Josephus, see Cheryl A. Brown, *No Longer Be Silent: First Century Jewish Portraits of Biblical Women; Studies in Pseudo-Philo's Biblical Antiquities and Josephus's Jewish Antiquities*, GBT (Louisville: Westminster John Knox, 1992), 163–73.

24. LAB 50:4: "Nonne tu Domine inspeculatus es cor omnium generationum, antequam plasmares seculum? Que autem metra aperta nascitur, aut que clausa moritur, nisi tu volueris?" Latin quotations of Liber antiquitatum biblicarum are all

in general, but it demonstrates Pseudo-Philo's concept of predetermination, which in some cases (although not in this one) tends to be at strife with his idea of consequent divine retribution.[25] In any case, it can be seen how the tendency to stress Hannah's piety, understood as her humbleness, which we observed in the redaction history of 1 Sam 1, is picked up and continued by Pseudo-Philo. Hannah's loud weeping has been turned into a silent prayer, explained as a vow of a woman who designates herself as a humble handmaid. Now, although she is pleading, she is humbleness personified, stating that she totally resigns herself to the prescient will of God. The reason why she prays silently follows from her modesty and piety as well—she wants to prevent anyone hearing her from seeing her action as blasphemy in case her prayer might stay unanswered in the end, if she might be found unworthy by God: "Ne forte non sim digna exaudiri" (LAB 50:5). In this way, as Erich S. Gruen points out, stressing Hannah's piety dialectically comes dangerously close to doubting God's reliability: "Even the most faithful have reason to question the efficacy of reliance on the Lord."[26]

In a recent publication, Benjamin J. Lappenga wants to stress another aspect of Hannah's piety in the context of her silent prayer. In LAB 50:5, the first reason given is not her concern about potential blasphemy of other people but her apprehension of further mockery by Peninnah: "and it will be that Peninnah, even more railing against me, will taunt me."[27] Lappenga's theory is that Hannah with her silent prayer, as an antithesis to the "zelans" Peninnah, gives an example of better zealotry and challenges the idea of militant zealous action as pleasing to God.[28] For this, Lappenga

---

according to Daniel J. Harrington, *Introduction et Texte Critique*, vol. 1 of *Pseudo-Philon: Les Antiquités Bibliques*, SC 229 (Paris: Cerf, 1976). For textual problems of Liber antiquitatum biblicarum in general, especially the relation between the Δ and Π families of the manuscripts, see Jacobson, *Commentary*, 257–73. All translations of Liber antiquitatum biblicarum, unless otherwise specified, are according to Jacobson, *Commentary*.

25. See Jacobson, *Commentary*, 1089, with reference to LAB 18:4; 21:2, 7.

26. Erich S. Gruen, "Subversive Elements in Pseudo-Philo," in *Constructs of Identity in Hellenistic Judaism: Essays on Early Jewish Literature and History*, DCLS 29 (Berlin: de Gruyter, 2016), 478.

27. "Et erit ut plus me zelans improperet mihi Fenenna"; Jacobson understands *plus* as belonging to *improperet*: "will mock me more" (*Commentary*, 176).

28. See Benjamin J. Lappenga, "'Speak, Hannah, and Do Not Be Silent': Pseudo-

starts from a "monosemic bias,"[29] meaning that "we view all instances of *zelo/zelus* together, rather than treating them as distinct lexical inputs from separate domains."[30] It is not least this very method, as well as Lappenga's comprehensive survey of the usage of the words *zelare* and *zelus* in Liber antiquitatum biblicarum, that makes me question his result.

First, using Liber antiquitatum biblicarum, we are working with a translation—probably even the translation of a translation.[31] It is rather uncertain whether in an assumed Hebrew original we would have found the same root in every instance where we read *zelare* in Latin, such as קנא. In our case, Pseudo-Philo might as well have taken the root כעס over from his *Vorlage*. Even if it is plausible that *zelare* was translated from קנא, we just cannot know.

Second, and more importantly, Hannah's activities are in no instance labeled "zealous." Lappenga's chart of comparable instances of the connection "divine command—zealous action—intercessory prayer—divine acceptance"[32] illustrates perfectly that in LAB 50–51 the case is totally different from Moses or Phinehas. The pattern just does not fit.

Third, as obvious as Hannah and Peninnah are pictured as opposites with the pious woman here and the wicked woman there, I cannot see how *zelare* in 50:5 would serve to emphasize this contrast. Within the pragmatics of the respective sentence, Peninnah's zeal does not work as a background of or contrast to the "better zeal" of Hannah's silent prayer. It provides its motivation: Hannah fears Peninnah's zeal in case she is not answered by God.

As to Hannah's thanksgiving psalm itself, it differs strongly from the version given by 1 Sam 2. Marc Philonenko has regarded it as "une exégèse bien qoumrânienne du cantique d'Anne."[33] Nowadays, one would certainly be more careful with the use of the adjective "qumranic," but nevertheless the appellation "exegesis" certainly grasps the character of the piece cor-

---

Philo's Deconstruction of Violence in Liber antiquitatum biblicarum 50–51," *JSP* 25 (2015): 91–110.

29. Lappenga, "Speak, Hannah," 95.
30. Lappenga, "Speak, Hannah," 96 (emphasis original).
31. See Dietzfelbinger, *Pseudo-Philo*, 92.
32. Lappenga, "Speak, Hannah," 106.
33. Marc Philonenko, "Une paraphrase du cantique d'Anne," *RHPR* 42 (1962): 168.

rectly. It may be that LAB 51 "has little to do with 1 Sam 2"[34] at first glance. But it clearly is based on it, taking up keywords and key phrases from its *Vorlage*, quite similar in its way of reworking and rewriting to the way Targum Jonathan deals with the same text.[35]

What is stressed is first and foremost the prophetic character of the piece.[36] We have seen above that with the expectation of an anointed one yet to come and his reign in 1 Sam 2:10, which is mirrored in 2 Sam 22:51, the focus is set on David. Now, in Liber antiquitatum biblicarum, Hannah's sight reaches a great deal farther than just until David, who is by no means neglected: "until they will give the horn to his anointed one, and the power of the throne of his kin will be present."[37] Targum Jonathan is even more explicit in this context. Here the anointed one clearly means the messiah: וירבי מלכות משיחיה ("and he will magnify the kingdom of his anointed one") concludes here a passage describing the eventual destruction of Gog.[38]

Nevertheless, based on 1 Sam 2:6, "YHWH kills and brings to life, he brings down to sheol and raises up" (יהוה ממית ומחיה מוריד שאול ויעל), together with 2:10a, "YHWH will judge the ends of the earth" (יהוה ידין אפסי־ארץ), some eschatological clarifications can be found in Liber antiquitatum biblicarum, too:

> For the Lord kills with righteous judgement, and brings to life with mercy. For the unjust exist in this world, but he brings the just to life

---

34. "Der folgende Hymnus hat mit 1 Sam 2 nur wenig zu tun" (Dietzfelbinger, *Pseudo-Philo*, 237).

35. See Jacobson, *Commentary*, 1098–99.

36. See Targum Jonathan, where it is in 1 Sam 2:1 explicitly stated that Hannah sang her song "in a spirit of prophecy" (ברוח נבואה).

37. LAB 51:6: "quousque dent cornu christo suo, et aderit potentia thronis regis eius." As in 1 Sam 2:10, it is possible to understand this as a reference to Saul in LAB 51:6 (see Jacobson, *Commentary*, 1107), but the overall picture of Saul as drawn in Liber antiquitatum biblicarum makes me think otherwise. Frederick J. Murphy does not see here any reference to "any other than the earthly Israelite monarch" (Murphy, *Pseudo-Philo: Rewriting the Bible* [Oxford: Oxford University Press, 1993], 193, 260–61). Given the eschatological character of Hannah's psalm in Liber antiquitatum biblicarum, I would rather doubt that.

38. See Klaus Koch, "Das apokalyptische Lied der Profetin Hanna: 1 Sam 2, 1–10 im Targum," in *Die aramäische Rezeption der hebräischen Bibel: Studien zur Targumik und Apokalyptik*, vol. 4 of *Gesammelte Aufsätze* (Neukirchen-Vluyn: Neukirchener Verlag, 2003), 146–47.

when he wishes. The unjust he will shut up in darkness, but for the just he saves his light. When the unjust have died, then they will perish. After the just have slept, then they will be delivered. So will every judgement endure, until he who holds power be revealed.[39]

Key words such as *life*, *death*, and *judgment* are taken up and expanded into little treatises about a certain subject; this is a typical technique of biblical rewriting, innerbiblically as well as extrabiblically. In this way, Hannah appears to be not only a prophetess but also a bearer of apocalyptic knowledge concerning the end of days and the final fate of the just and the wicked.

Another method of reworking is subtler and harder to detect than the classical addition: the transformation of what was a poetical saying in the *Vorlage* into a little scene. This can be found when we take a closer look at Peninnah's mockery. In 1 Sam 1, it is only stated that Peninnah provoked Hannah, and this is mentioned twice, in 1:6 and in 1:7—in the Masoretic version of the story, as we have seen above, not in the LXX. Pseudo-Philo knows more. Not only does he report the fact of her "railing" (*improperare*; LAB 50:1, 2; see 50:5); he also knows how Peninnah did so. On the second occasion, she uses a kind of sapiential saying for her mean purpose, when she states, "A wife is not beloved even if her husband loves her or her beauty. Let Hannah not glory in her appearance; but she who glories, let her glory when she sees her offspring before her."[40] Following this, as an example to support her argumentation, she cites Rachel, whose being loved by Jacob would have been without any use. Obviously, the first part of Peninnah's defamatory speech refers to 1 Sam 1:5 (Elkanah loved Hannah, not Peninnah). Hannah's beauty is a piece of information that is special to Pseudo-Philo and associates her once more with her sister-in-fate, Rachel (see Gen 29:17).[41] The third part of the statement, however, sounds familiar—to everybody who knows Paul's First Letter to

---

39. LAB 51:5: Quia Dominus mortificat in iudicio, et vivificat in misericordia. Quoniam iniqui sunt in hoc seculo, et vivificat iustos cum vult. Iniquos autem concludet in tenebris, nam iustis conservat lumen suum. Et cum mortui fuerint iniqui tunc peribunt, et cum dormierint iusti tunc liberabuntur. Sic autem omne iudicium permanebit, quousque reveletur qui tenet.

40. "Non est dilectus mulieris, si diligat eam vir eius aut pulchritudinem illius. Ne glorietur in specie sua Anna, sed qui gloriatur glorietur cum videt semen suum ante conspectum suum"; LAB 50:2

41. See Jacobson, *Commentary*, 1086; see also Murphy, *Pseudo-Philo*, 189.

the Corinthians: ὁ καυχώμενος ἐν κυρίῳ καυχάσθω ("Let him who boasts boast in the Lord"; 1:31) The apostle refers to this as a quotation from, or rather an allusion to, Scripture, where, of course, the relevant passage can be found in Jer 9:22–23 (9:23–24 LXX). But as is well known, the LXX version of 1 Sam 2 has a similar though slightly different sapiential maxim in the mouth of Hannah, in 1 Sam 2:10 (LXX[B]), and with all necessary carefulness regarding the reconstruction by Frank Moore Cross and Eugene Ulrich, it can be said that a few consonants of it might have been preserved in 4Q51, too.[42] Considering the space in this scroll that must have been taken up by no longer existent text, "it would be a curious coincidence if the expansion in 4QSam[a] would not have contained the plus in the Septuagint."[43]

As Louis Feldman has already noted, Pseudo-Philo's Peninnah clearly refers to this dictum, and whatever the literary relationship between 1 Sam 2 LXX and Jer 9 may be, she most likely does so with Hannah's song in mind and not as an objection to Jeremiah, the prophet.[44]

Peninnah's allusion to Hannah's psalm according to its LXX version is interesting in several respects. From an analytical perspective, it demonstrates that Pseudo-Philo, who according to most scholars probably wrote his book in Hebrew or Aramaic, had in mind or in his hands a version of the Samuel scroll that, at least in this passage, was closer to the LXX than to the protomasoretic version of the book. On the other hand, he knew a tradition that included the aspect of Peninnah's mockery—a motif that is alien to the LXX. In this respect, he at least read כעס in his version of the Samuel scroll more in a protomasoretic way than did the LXX translators.[45]

---

42. See Frank Moore Cross et al., *Qumran Cave 4.XII: 1–2 Samuel*, DJD 17 (Oxford: Clarendon, 2002), 30–37 and pl. 2.

43. Anneli Aejmelaeus, "Hannah's Psalm in 4QSam[a]," in *Archaeology of the Books of Samuel: The Entangling of the Textual and Literary History*, ed. Philippe Hugo and Adrian Schenker, VTSup 132 (Leiden: Brill, 2010), 35.

44. See Feldman, "Prolegomenon," cxxx; Jacobson, *Commentary*, 1086–87. Dietrich argues that the aphorism would not have found its way into one of the first-century CE adaptations of Hannah's psalm: "In den um die Zeitenwende entstandenen Nachdichtungen des Hanna-Liedes … fehlt jegliche Erwähnung des *G*-Plus in 1 Sam 2, 10" (Dietrich, *1 Samuel 1–12*, 97). For a summary of the discussion on 1 Sam 2 LXX and Jer 9, see Dietrich, *1 Sam 1–12*, 96–97.

45. On the question of Pseudo-Philo's *Vorlage*, see Feldman, "Prolegomenon," xxx–xxxi; Jacobson, *Commentary*, 254–56.

But above that, his way of dealing with his *Vorlage* is worth an interpretation. He takes Hannah's saying on boasting and puts it—contradicted—into the mouth of her adversary. Everybody who knows the biblical, that is, in this case the LXX^B or 4Q51, version of Hannah's song will know immediately not only that what Peninnah states will be proven to be wrong, and very soon, but also that her words are foolish and presumptuous at best. But *only* the person who knows the biblical text will be able to grasp that hint. For a full understanding of Pseudo-Philo's rewritten Bible, one must know the *Vorlage* quite well. Or put in other terms: the biblical Samuel Scroll is always present even where it is not quoted literally, and even where Pseudo-Philo knows details of which his source is totally silent.

The phrase *qui gloriatur glorietur* appears in Liber antiquitatum biblicarum only in the context of Peninnah's mockery, but it nevertheless has its direct counterpart in Hannah's hymn. It can be found connected with the admonition of 1 Sam 2:3, "do not talk so very proudly, let no arrogance come forth from your mouth" (אל־תרבו תדברו גבהה גבהה יצא עתק מפיכם), "but," so Pseudo-Philo says, "delight in praise, for the light from which wisdom will be born will come forth, that not those who possess many things will be called rich, nor those who have borne in abundance will be called mothers,"[46] followed by 1 Sam 2:5.

Taken together, by the issue of "boasting," the contrast between Peninnah and Hannah is sharpened and put onto a different level. In 1 Sam 1–2, Peninnah is mean, while Hannah is unhappy but pious. According to Pseudo-Philo, Peninnah is also foolish, while Hannah is wise.[47] And even more: Hannah's wisdom includes the things to come, with the final judgment of the good and the bad, between the *iusti* and the *iniqui*, the צדקים and the רשעים.[48] With Peninnah's statement that appropriate boasting should be seen in the self-glorification of a fertile woman—and, as one

---

46. LAB 51:4: "sed delectamini in gloriationem. Dum enim exiet lumen ex quo nascetur sapientia, ut non qui possident plurima dicantur divites, sed que pepererunt in habundantia matres audient."

47. Accordingly, Hannah's song in LAB 51:3 opens up like a typical wisdom speech with a call to attention, *Aufmerksamkeitsruf*. On the wisdom motif in this context, see Brown, *No Longer Be Silent*, 158.

48. Brown also observes the development of the taunting motif by Pseudo-Philo as a means of depicting Hannah as righteous (see Brown, *No Longer Be Silent*, 145, 151).

must add with 1 Sam 2 LXX in mind, *not* in understanding and knowing the Lord—she reveals herself to be a representative of precisely these wicked people. As a further confirmation of her character, she explicitly associates herself with the enemies of the pious supplicant of the Psalter when she—as Hannah fears that she might do—joins in *their* mockery, saying, "Where is your god in whom you trust."[49] By putting the words of Ps 42:4, 11 into Peninnah's mouth, the psalmification of the narrative of 1 Sam 1–2 continues. While in 1 Sam 1:6 and 1:7 Peninnah was described in the style of a typical enemy of a psalm of lamentation, in Liber antiquitatum biblicarum she even makes these enemies' words their own.

This sheds further light on the contrast between life and death that is interwoven throughout the entire passage. At first glance, Peninnah, the fertile woman, seems to be on the life side, while Hannah, the barren one, is on the other. But Peninnah's wicked words, along with Samuel's birth interpreted as a symbol of divine truth, makes things turn. *Sub specie aeternitatis*, Peninnah represents the foolish and wicked people destined to eternal death, while Hannah stands for the wise and pious who in the end will be woken up to eternal living.

4. Conclusion

Taken together, it can be seen in Hannah's prayers in Liber antiquitatum biblicarum that Pseudo-Philo understood his biblical *Vorlage* with a sensitive intuition for its literary history. In his rewriting of the history of Israel, several aspects and tendencies that determined the diachronic development of 1 Sam 1–2 are taken up and continued. This can be summarized in four points.

First, there is what we called above psalmification. In 1 Sam 1, the story of Hannah's answered prayer is developed step by step along the lines of an individual lamentation psalm, with Peninnah increasingly assuming the role of a typical supplicant's enemy. In Liber antiquitatum biblicarum, she is ready to play this part even better by taking on a speaking role, quoting Ps 42:4, 11.

Second, the redaction history of 1 Sam 1–2 results in a twofold image of Hannah mirrored in both of her prayers. Again, both sides of her persona are expanded in Liber antiquitatum biblicarum. There is, for one,

---

49. LAB 50:5: "ubi Deus tuus in quo confidis"; see Ps 42:4, 11.

the humble and pious woman who utters her plea silently in 1 Sam 1:13. Pseudo-Philo exaggerates Hannah's piety so that it almost turns into its opposite: his Hannah prays silently in order to avoid a charge of blasphemy from anyone overhearing, in case she might not be answered by God (LAB 50:5). On the one hand, she is extremely pious, totally deferring to the will of God; on the other hand, this comes close to doubting God's willingness or power to intervene on her behalf.

Third, there is Hannah, the confident and self-assured singer of the hymn in 1 Sam 2. After the birth of her son Samuel, she reveals herself as a wise theologian and a true prophetess— Liber antiquitatum biblicarum makes her a bearer of apocalyptic wisdom. In Liber antiquitatum biblicarum, Hannah is not the only woman filled with a prophetic spirit: Melcha, the biblically unknown wife of Reu (see Gen 11:20) prophesies Abraham's birth in LAB 4:11, Miriam dreams about the future task of her yet unborn brother Moses in LAB 9:10, and Deborah is pictured as a veritable seer in LAB 31:1, when she calls Barak to battle; Hannah's sight, however, reaches farthest.

Fourth, together with its counterpart in 2 Sam 22, Hannah's song in 1 Sam 2 can be seen as part of the redactional tendency to structure the narrative books by means of inserting prayers at important moments, such as the dawn of kingship in Israel. In this series of inserted prayers, Hannah is the only female person praying. Pseudo-Philo takes over the biblical usage, but, again, he does not leave it at that. Aside from Hannah, there are additional women praying: In LAB 31:5, 7, Jael prays before killing Sisera—similar to Judith in Jdt 13:4.[50] Finally, Eluma, the wife of Manoah, who is biblically not known by name, finds herself in a similar situation to Hannah—and, in addition to what is known of her out of Judg 13, she behaves similarly. In LAB 42:2, she prays, demanding from God to know the reason for her or her husband's infertility. She is, as one might say, in Liber antiquitatum biblicarum modeled on Hannah, her narrative successor.

It was said above that in parts of the rabbinic literature, the story of Hannah in 1 Sam 1–2 served as a paradigm for how to pray. Her female fellow supplicants, like Jael and especially Eluma, elucidate that already in Liber antiquitatum biblicarum—as well as in the masoretic version of the biblical text, Hannah has come very close to becoming a role model—for female and male supplicants alike.

---

50. See Dietzfelbinger, *Pseudo-Philo*, 192.

Bibliography

Aejmelaeus, Anneli. "Hannah's Psalm in 4QSam^a." Pages 23–37 in *Archaeology of the Books of Samuel: The Entangling of the Textual and Literary History*. Edited by Philippe Hugo and Adrian Schenker. VTSup 132. Leiden: Brill, 2010.

———. "Hannah's Psalm: Text, Composition, and Redaction." Pages 354–76 in *Houses Full of All Good Things: Essays in Memory of Timo Veijola*. Edited by Juha Pakkala and Martti Nissinen. PFES 95. Göttingen: Vandenhoeck & Ruprecht, 2008.

Auld, A. Graeme. *I and II Samuel: A Commentary*. OTL. Louisville: Westminster John Knox, 2011.

Begg, Christopher. *Judean Antiquities Books 5–7: Translation and Commentary*. FJTC 4. Leiden: Brill, 2005.

Bezzel, Hannes. *Saul: Israels König in Tradition, Redaktion und früher Rezeption*. FAT 97. Tübingen: Mohr Siebeck, 2015.

Bogaert, Pierre-Maurice. "Introduction Littéraire." Pages 9–78 in *Introduciton Littéraire, Commentaire et Index*. Vol. 2 of *Pseudo-Philon: Les Antiquités Bibliques*. Edited by Charles Perrot and Pierre-Maurice Bogaert. SC 230. Paris: CERF, 1976.

Bronner, Leila L. "Hannah's Prayer: Rabbinic Ambivalence." *Shofar* 17 (1999): 36–48.

Brown, Cheryl A. *No Longer Be Silent: First Century Jewish Portraits of Biblical Women; Studies in Pseudo-Philo's Biblical Antiquities and Josephus's Jewish Antiquities*. GBT. Louisville: Westminster John Knox, 1992.

Cross, Frank Moore, Donald W. Parry, Richard J. Saley, and Eugene Ulrich, *Qumran Cave 4.XII: 1–2 Samuel*. DJD 17. Oxford: Clarendon, 2002.

Dietrich, Walter. *1 Samuel 1–12*. BKAT 8.1. Neukirchen-Vluyn: Neukirchener Verlag, 2010.

Dietzfelbinger, Christian. *Pseudo-Philo: Antiquitates Biblicae (Liber Antiquitatum Biblicarum)*. 2nd ed. JSHRZ 2.2. Gütersloh: Gütersloher Verlagshaus, 1979.

Eynikel, Erik. "Das Lied der Hanna (1 Sam 2, 1–11) und das Lied Davids (2 Sam 22): Ein Vergleich," Pages 57–72 in *For and Against David: Story and History in the Books of Samuel*. Edited by A. Graeme Auld and Erik Eynikel. BETL 232. Leuven: Peeters, 2010.

Feldman, Louis. "Prolegomenon." Pages xxviii–xxxi in *The Biblical Antiquities of Philo: Now First Translated from the Old Latin Version*. Edited by Montague R. James. 2nd ed. LBS. New York: Ktav, 1971.

Galling, Kurt. *Die Bücher der Chronik, Esra, Nehemia*. ATD 12. Göttingen: Vandenhoeck & Ruprecht, 1954.

Gruen, Erich S. "Subversive Elements in Pseudo-Philo." Pages 473–85 in *Constructs of Identity in Hellenistic Judaism: Essays on Early Jewish Literature and History*. DCLS 29. Berlin: de Gruyter, 2016.

Gunkel, Hermann, and Joachim Begrich. *Einleitung in die Psalmen: Die Gattungen der religiösen Lyrik Israels*. 4th ed. Göttingen: Vandenhoeck & Ruprecht, 1985.

Hadot, Jean. "Le milieu d'origine du 'liber antiquitatum biblicarum.'" Pages 153–71 in *La littérature intertestamentaire: Colloque de Strasbourg (17–19 octobre 1983)*. Edited by André Caquot. BCESS. Paris: Presses Universitaires de France, 1985.

Harrington, Daniel J. *Introduction et Texte Critique*. Vol. 1 of *Pseudo-Philon: Les Antiquités Bibliques*. SC 229. Paris: Les éditions du CERF, 1976.

Jacobson, Howard. *A Commentary on Pseudo-Philo's Liber Antiquitatum Biblicarum: With Latin Text and English Translation*. AGJU 31. Leiden: Brill, 1996.

Knauf, Ernst Axel. "Samuel among the Prophets: 'Prophetical Redactions.'" Pages 149–69 in *Is Samuel among the Deuteronomists? Current Views on the Place of Samuel in a Deuteronomistic History*. Edited by Cynthia Edenburg and Juha Pakkala. AIL 16. Atlanta: Society of Biblical Literature, 2013.

Koch, Klaus. "Das apokalyptische Lied der Profetin Hanna: 1 Sam 2, 1–10 im Targum." Pages 132–57 in *Die aramäische Rezeption der hebräischen Bibel: Studien zur Targumik und Apokalyptik*. Vol. 4 of *Gesammelte Aufsätze*. Neukirchen-Vluyn: Neukirchener Verlag, 2003.

Lappenga, Benjamin J. "'Speak, Hannah, and Do Not Be Silent': Pseudo-Philo's Deconstruction of Violence in Liber antiquitatum biblicarum 50–51." in *JSP* 25 (2015): 91–110.

Mathys, Hans-Peter. *Dichter und Beter: Theologen aus spätalttestamentlicher Zeit*. OBO 132. Göttingen: Vandenhoeck & Ruprecht, 1994.

Murphy, Frederick J. *Pseudo-Philo: Rewriting the Bible*. Oxford: Oxford University Press, 1993.

Oegema, Gerbern S. "Pseudo-Philo: Antiquitates Biblicae (JSHRZ II/2)." Pages 66–77 in *Einführung zu den Jüdischen Schriften aus hellenistisch-römischer Zeit: Unterweisung in erzählender Form*. Edited by Gerbern S. Oegema. JSHRZ 6.1. Gütersloh: Gütersloher Verlagshaus, 2005.

Philonenko, Marc. "Une paraphrase du cantique d'Anne." *RHPR* 42 (1962): 157–68.

Porzig, Peter. *Die Lade im Alten Testament und in den Texten vom Toten Meer*. BZAW 397. Berlin: de Gruyter, 2009.

Stoebe, Hans Joachim. *Das erste Buch Samuelis*. KAT 8.1. Gütersloh: Gütersloher Verlagshaus, 1973.

Wilke, Alexa. *Die Gebete der Propheten: Anrufungen Gottes im "Corpus Propheticum" der Hebräischen Bibel*. BZAW 451. Berlin: de Gruyter, 2014.

(Re-)constructing Identity in the Prayers of the Psalter

Psalm 37 and the Devotionalization of Instruction in the Postexilic Period

Scott C. Jones

1. Introduction

By the Hellenistic period, wisdom instruction and prayer had become so intertwined that entire compositions grew out of their confluence. One thinks especially of the book of Ben Sira in this regard. Though the grandfather's instruction is styled after the book of Proverbs at every turn, he is also a tradent of the Psalter. His work is filled with hymns and prayers, and he portrays the ideal sage as a praying sage (39:5–8).[1] Moreover, the book closes with a thanksgiving psalm in Sir 51:1–12, followed in manuscript B by a litany of thanksgivings modeled on Ps 118:1–4 and Ps 136.[2] The very last portion of the book is an acrostic in which the sage declares his love for wisdom (51:13–30). The fact that this closing poem is attested in a psalms manuscript from Qumran (11QPs^a) shows that the text history

---

Much of the research for this essay was undertaken with the funding and support of the Alexander von Humboldt foundation during a research stay at the University of Göttingen in 2014. An earlier version of this essay was presented at the European Association for Biblical Studies Annual Meeting in Córdoba, Spain, July 13, 2015, and yet another version was offered in honor of Prof. Dr. Hermann Spieckermann at the University of Hamburg, November 7, 2015. I thank each of those audiences and the editors of this volume, whose questions, comments, and corrections greatly improved it.

1. See recently Hermann Spieckermann, "Der betende Weise: Jesus Sirach," in *Lebenskunst und Gotteslob in Israel: Anregungen aus Psalter und Weisheit für die Theologie*, FAT 91(Tübingen: Mohr Siebeck, 2014), 117–19.

2. On this later insertion between Sir 51:1–12 and 51:13–30, see Patrick W. Skehan and Alexander A. Di Lella, *The Wisdom of Ben Sira: A New Translation with Notes*, AB 39 (New York: Doubleday, 1987), 568–73.

of Ben Sira is inextricably linked to the text history of the Psalter.[3] This combination of instruction and prayer is continued in the Thanksgiving Hymns from Qumran, many of which are stamped by sapiential language and themes.[4]

Such a confluence of instruction and prayer, however, was already well attested in Persian-period compositions in the Psalter, especially in Ps 37. But to what end? This essay argues that Ps 37 devotionalizes instruction in order to foster a way of life that can sustain one in times of trial. With respect to postexilic communities in particular, Ps 37 can be read as an exercise in identity construction that encourages a way of being in the world that is at odds with the regnant way of seeing reality. It is an identity formed not only by reflection upon sociological status or intellectual theory but also through pious praxis. Contrary to those who argue that Ps 37 "reflects unqualified trust in the system" or that it "denies the reality of life," Ps 37 exhorts trust, patience, and integrity, with full recognition that such ways of being often offer no advantage in reality as it is currently perceived.[5] Moreover, these very themes—trust and patience during times of affliction—are the contribution of the psalm to the theology of the first Davidic Psalter (Pss 3–41) and, more particularly, to the theology of the subcollection in Pss 35–41.

The thesis of this essay, therefore, is that Ps 37 devotionalizes instruction as an exercise in identity formation through pious practice. Through trust and patience during times of trial, the poor can maintain their

---

3. Sir 51:13–30 is attested in 11QPs^a (11Q5 XXI, 11–17; XXII, 1) and also in MS B. On the text of Ben Sira, see Pancratius C. Beentjes, *The Book of Ben Sira in Hebrew: A Text Edition of All Extant Hebrew Manuscripts and a Synopsis of All Parallel Hebrew Ben Sira Texts*, VTSup 68 (Atlanta: SBL Press, 2006); www.bensira.org.

4. An authoritative edition of the Thanksgiving Hymns from Qumran is now available: Hartmut Stegemann and Eileen Schuller, *Qumran Cave 1.3: 1QHodayot^a: With Incorporation of 1QHodayot^b and 4QHodayot^{a-f}*, trans. Carol Newsom, DJD 40 (Oxford: Clarendon, 2009). A manual edition is also available: Eileen M. Schuller and Carol A. Newsom, *The Hodayot (Thanksgiving Psalms): A Study Edition of 1QH^a*, EJL 36 (Atlanta: SBL Press, 2012). For the sake of convenience, all citations of 1QHodayot^a in this essay will be from the manual edition. On sapiential influence in the Hodayot, see especially Sara J. Tanzer, "The Sages at Qumran: Wisdom in the Hodayot" (PhD diss., Harvard University, 1987); Matthew J. Goff, "Reading Wisdom at Qumran: 4QInstruction and the Hodayot," *DSD* 11 (2004): 263–88.

5. Quotes from Leonard P. Maré, "The Ethics of Retribution in Psalm 37," *EP* 92 (2010): 273.

integrity despite the fact that such righteous behavior seems to offer little advantage in the present. In order to establish this thesis, this essay will focus on four points: (1) the identity of the poor, (2) the hope of the poor in the areas of justice and land, (3) the contribution of Ps 37 to the final subcollection of the first Davidic Psalter (Pss 35–41), and (4) the contribution of Ps 37 to postexilic prayer in general.

2. Two Ways of Reading Psalm 37: Sectarian and Pious

Before turning to the psalm itself, it is instructive to focus on two different streams of interpretation that have shown up in one form or another throughout the centuries. While the key to the theology of Ps 37 lies in its presentation of the poor, the meaning of the vocabulary of poverty is flexible. This flexibility has prompted both ancient and modern interpreters to construe "the poor" of Ps 37 in different ways.

The first known exegesis of Ps 37 is found at Qumran in 4QpPs^a (4Q171).[6] This interpretation equates the poor with the community of the elect, who will soon inherit "the high mountain of Israel": "The interpretation of it concerns the congregation of the poor ones [האביונים]; [their]s is the inheritance of all the great [ones;] they will take possession of the high mountain of Isra[el, and on] his holy [moun]tain they will delight" (4QpPs^a 1–10 III, 10–11).[7] This interpretation encourages the Qumranites to identify with the poor in the psalm who will soon inherit the land, and it accents their election and group identity. This and other readings that treat "the poor" as a sociological marker serve as examples of what one might call a *sectarian reading* of Ps 37.

Other interpreters, however, have emphasized the psalm's exhortation to righteous acts. Like the Qumran pesher, Martin Luther encourages his audience to identify with the poor of Ps 37. But rather than focusing on their election and future inheritance, as in 4Q171, he exhorts them to action in the present. In a comment on Ps 37:3, Luther states,

---

6. The literature on this pesher is extensive. The *editio princeps* is John M. Allegro and A. A. Anderson, *Qumrân Cave 4.I (4Q158–4Q186)*, DJD 5 (Oxford: Clarendon, 1968), 42–49.

7. Transcription and translation here follow Maurya P. Horgan, *Pesharim: Qumran Interpretations of Biblical Books*, CBQMS 8 (Washington, DC: Catholic Biblical Association, 1979), 197.

You might get the idea that you want to run away and move to some other place, in order to be rid of them and get away from them. Not so! Remain in the land; go on dwelling where you are. Do not on their account transfer your home or change your country. Rather you should make your living in faith and go on doing your job as you did before. If they frustrate or harm you and provoke you to run away, never mind. Keep your faith, and do not doubt. God will not forsake you. Just do your part, go on working and making a living, and let him prevail.[8]

Here Luther focuses on the torments that the righteous undergo at the hands of the wicked, which may tempt them to abandon all hope and leave their rightful home. Keying in on the phrase "make your living in faith" in 37:3, Luther exhorts the righteous not to give in to frustration but to "go on working and making a living," placing all trust in God.[9] This interpretation no doubt assumes a group identity for the poor, but it emphasizes ethics and action in a way that the sectarian reading does not. I call this second interpretation a *pious reading* of Ps 37.

It is important to underscore that these readings are not really separate from one another and that any interpretation of Ps 37 will contain both sectarian and pious elements. In truth, these are not discreet, and it is important to hold on to both. Of these two ways of reading, however, the sectarian reading has received the greatest assent among recent interpret-

---

8. Martin Luther, *Selected Psalms III*, ed. Jaroslav Pelikan, vol. 14 of *Luther's Works*, ed. Jaroslav Pelikan and Helmut T. Lehmann (St. Louis: Concordia, 1958), 212. In this volume, Ps 37 is grouped among the "four psalms of comfort" (Pss 37, 62, 94, 109).

9. The reading that evoked Luther's comment ("make your living in faith") itself has an interesting history. In his *First Lectures on Psalms (Dictata super Psalterium, 1513/1514)*, Luther had suggested that this phrase denoted that the righteous would be "fed by the riches of the land." This seems to be related to the LXX's rendering (καὶ ποιμανθήσῃ ἐπὶ τῷ πλούτῳ αὐτῆς; Ps 36:3 LXX), where πλούτῳ translates המון ("riches"; see Vulgate's *divitiis*) where the MT attests אמונה ("faithfulness"). See Martin Luther, *First Lectures on the Psalms I (Psalms 1–75)*, ed. Hilton C. Oswald, vol. 10 of *Luther's Works*, ed. Jaroslav Pelikan and Helmut T. Lehmann (St. Louis: Concordia, 1958), 174. In Luther's *Selected Psalms III*, his translation is closer to the Hebrew with "make your living in faith" (212), though by the time of his final revisions of the Psalms translation for the *Lutherbibel* in 1545, he translates, "make your living uprightly." On these readings, see Erwin Mülhaupt, "Luthers Übersetzung und Auslegung des 37. Psalms: Ein Beispiel zunehmender Verchristlichung, aber nicht Christologisierung," *ZLG* 34 (1963): 49–60.

ers. The work of the late Frank-Lothar Hossfeld and Erich Zenger is a case in point.

According to Hossfeld and Zenger, Ps 37 is a sapiential instruction to the poor that reflects the concrete social realities of the postexilic period (fifth to fourth century BCE).[10] Within the subcollection of Pss 35–41, Ps 37 offers a comprehensive explanation of the meaning of poverty, an *Armenfrömmigkeit*. The postexilic redaction of which Ps 37 is a part is a response to the collapse of religious, political, and social institutions during the exile. As a comfort to God's people, this redaction offers them a new group consciousness as the "true Israel." Psalm 37 in particular focuses on the possession of land as a central component of this *Armenfrömmigkeit*, and it reinvests the existence of the poor with meaning by focusing on their future land inheritance and the eventual establishment of YHWH's world order. In sum, according to Hossfeld and Zenger, persecution and cultural collapse led to problems of self-understanding and loss of meaning. Psalm 37 addresses these problems by offering a new group identity and instruction about cosmic order.[11]

While Ps 37 undoubtedly bears on the self-understanding and intellectual worldview of its audience, Hossfeld and Zenger's interpretation overshadows or even intentionally excludes the psalm's exhortations to piety, especially those that resonate with the worldview of the book of Proverbs. Perhaps this reflects a modern preference for theory over praxis, or even a suspicion of piety, such as that which informed Albrecht Ritschl's influential *Geschichte des Pietismus*.[12] Whatever the case may be, I contend that the sapiential theology of Ps 37 is at least as practical as it is intellec-

---

10. The summary of Frank-Lothar Hossfeld and Erich Zenger's position in the following paragraph is from their *Die Psalmen: Psalm 1–50*, NEchtB 29 (Würzburg: Echter, 1993), 14–15, 229–39; and Hossfeld and Zenger, "'Selig, wer auf die Armen achtet' (Ps 41,2): Beobachtungen zur Gottesvolk-Theologie des ersten Davidpsalters," in *Volk Gottes, Gemeinde und Gesellschaft*, ed. I. Balderman et al., JBTh 7 (Neukirchen Vluyn: Neukirchener Verlag, 1992), 21–50.

11. It is worth noting that one key difference between the sectarian reading at Qumran and the sectarian reading of Hossfeld and Zenger is that Hossfeld and Zenger do not encourage their contemporary audience to identify with the poor. Rather, the poor are simply a historical and sociological reconstruction. As far as I can tell, every interpretation up to the modern period always assumed that the audience was to identify with the poor in the psalm.

12. See Albrecht Ritschl, *Geschichte des Pietismus*, 3 vols. (Bonn: Adolph Marcus, 1880–1886).

tual. Indeed, these two are inseparable. Even while Ps 37 attempts to shape the audience's self-understanding in light of future realities, it also aims to form their identity through action and ethics. It is the righteous acts of the poor—and not only their reflections on world order and sociology—that set them apart as an identifiable group. In what follows, I aim to rehabilitate a pious reading of Ps 37.

3. Who Are the Poor in Psalm 37?

The question of the identity of the poor in the Psalms revolves around the relationship between "poor" as a description of a concrete social reality and as a term for a religious attitude. Furthermore, there is the question of whether "the poor" is primarily intended as a sociological marker, denoting membership in a particular group. The issue vis-à-vis Ps 37 is how to render ענוים in 37:11 and the phrase עני ואביון in 37:14, and how these terms describe the plight of those whom the psalm addresses.

Since the nineteenth century, biblical scholars have associated the term ענו with a particular sociological party or movement. Particularly influential was Alfred Rahlfs's Göttingen dissertation in 1892. While Heinrich Graetz had identified the ענוים with the Levites, Rahlfs argued instead that ענוים should be identified with the suffering servant of Deutero-Isaiah.[13] The exile, Rahlfs said, was the period in which Israel as a people became a group identified as ענו. This was the moment when their outward humiliation was transformed into inward humility. Thus the ענוים were a distinct party of the Jewish people, and the Psalms was their prayer book. More recently, Christoph Levin has expressed a view similar to Rahlfs's group identification theory, though it goes even further in de-emphasizing any connotation of humility or trust in the term "poor." Levin says that when the psalmist identifies himself as poor in the individual laments, he is "not so much describing his individual need as acknowledging his membership of a particular group. It is as if he were presenting YHWH with his membership card."[14]

---

13. See Heinrich Graetz, *Kritischer Commentar zu den Psalmen: Nebst Text und Uebersetzung*, 2 vols. (Breslau: Schottlaender, 1882–1883), 2:16–37; Alfred Rahlfs, עָנִי und עָנָו *in den Psalmen* (Göttingen: Dieterich, 1892), 80–90.

14. Christoph Levin, "The Poor in the Old Testament: Some Observations," in *Fortschreibungen: Gesammelte Studien zum Alten Testament*, trans. M. Kohl, BZAW 316 (Berlin: de Gruyter, 2003), 333. See also Levin, "Das Gebetbuch der Gerechten:

I wonder, however, how confidently one can draw such conclusions from these terms in the psalms, where the language is so often traditional. As Levin himself notes, the self-description "poor" in the Psalter is a "stereotype in the language of prayer" that is used to "win [the deity's] attention and commitment."[15] Given both the stereotypical and traditional nature of designations such as "the poor," as well as the great diversity of settings in which such language is found, it is the literary and rhetorical context of each psalm, rather than a reconstructed social theory, that should be decisive in determining the sense.[16]

Psalm 37:11 states, "And ענוים will inherit the land, and they will delight in an abundance of well-being."[17] The psalm, however, uses several other designations for those who will receive the same inheritance:

37:9 For evildoers will be cut off,
      but as for *those who wait on YHWH* [וקוי יהוה], they will inherit the land. (cf. 37:34)

37:22 For *those who are blessed by him* [מברכיו] will inherit the earth, but those who are cursed by him will be cut off.

37:29 *Righteous ones* [צדיקים] will inherit the land,
      and they will dwell upon it forever. (cf. 37:16–17)

Beyond the issue of land inheritance, Ps 37 refers to its addressees as "the blameless" (תמימם; v. 18), "the devout" (חסיד; v. 28), and "one who has integrity" (איש שלום; v. 37). The expression עני ואביון in 37:14 has a similar sense, though it is noteworthy that in every occurrence in the Psalter, the

---

Literargeschichtliche Beobachtungen am Psalter," *ZTK* 90 (1993): 355–81; Levin, "Das Amosbuch der Anawim," *ZTK* 94 (1997): 407–36.

15. Levin, "Poor in the Old Testament," 324. The presentation of oneself as humble in order to win the commitment of the deity seems to apply especially well to the use of ענה ('*nh*) in the Zakkur inscription (*KAI* 202), where Zakkur claims in lines 2–3, "I am a humble man (*'š 'nh 'nh*), but Baalshamayn [gave] me [victory] and stood with me." Translation from Choon Leong Seow, "West Semitic Sources," in *Prophets and Prophecy in the Ancient Near East*, by Martti Nissinen, with contributions by C. L. Seow and Robert K. Ritner, WAW 12 (Atlanta: Society of Biblical Literature, 2003), 205. My thanks to Prof. Seow for pointing this out to me.

16. Compare the comments of Sue Gillingham, "The Poor in the Psalms," *ExpTim* 100 (1988): 15–19, 16.

17. All translations in this essay are mine, unless otherwise noted.

phrase is found in the context of a request for deliverance from oppression (Ps 35:10; 37:14; 40:18; 70:6; 86:1; 109:16, 22). As Sue Gillingham notes, the expression עני ואביון is a stereotyped phrase for a pious sufferer who seeks vindication from God.[18]

Each of these expressions is essentially synonymous with ענוים in Ps 37, suggesting that ענו is a religious honorific for the righteous.[19] The antonyms of ענו in Ps 37 underscore this interpretation. Those who oppose the ענוים are called "evildoers" (מרעים; e.g., vv. 1, 9), "those who practice injustice" (עשה עולה; v. 1), "those who carry out schemes" (איש עשה מזמות; v. 7), "the wicked" (רשע; e.g., vv. 12, 14, 17), "enemies of YHWH" (איבי יהוה; v. 20), "transgressors" (פשעים; v. 38), and possibly also "unjust ones" (עול; v. 28 [reconstructed]).[20] These data suggest that the language of poverty in Ps 37 is at least as much a description of pious actions as it is a group designation. It is, in fact, the piety or impiety that they practice that forms the basis for their being identified as a particular group.

The reception of Ps 37 and its echoes in the Qumran literature offer helpful comparisons and contrasts to the viewpoint of the biblical psalm. While the Qumran Hodayot use terms for poverty to accent the sage's theology of humility and dependence upon God, the pesher on Ps 37 in 4Q171 uses such terminology to accent group identity and election. Thus the two streams of interpretation of the poor in Ps 37, the sectarian and the pious, are already represented at Qumran.

In the Qumran Hodayot, ענו and its cognates are religious terms that describe a person who is oppressed by enemies and who cries out to God for salvation (see especially 1QH^a IX, 38; X, 36; XIII, 15–16, 23). Especially interesting is the conclusion of the creation hymn in column IX. There the sage, having cast off self-reliance and reaffirmed his utter dependence on God, turns with new power and purpose to address others in the wisdom

---

18. See Gillingham, "Poor in the Psalms," 17.

19. Ps 25:12 calls whose who are to inherit the land "Godfearers" (ירא יהוה).

20. The ע strophe in Ps 37:28–29 MT lacks an ע in the first line, reading only לעולם נשמרו. I read עולם לעולם נצמתו ("the unjust are destroyed forever"), assuming that the initial עולם fell out of the text by haplography, based on its similarity to the following phrase, לעולם. The reconstruction of עולים was already suggested by Wilhelm M. L. de Wette in *Die Psalmen*, 3rd ed. (Heidelberg: J. C. B. Mohr, 1829), 297, n. 28. I reconstruct נצמתו based on LXX^A (ἐκδιωχθήσονται). The root ἐκδιώκω elsewhere renders Hebrew צמת (Ps 69:5 [68:4 LXX], Ps 101:5 [100:5 LXX]), and a niphal suffix conjugation, נצמתו, is close enough graphically to explain the MT's נשמרו as an inner-Hebrew error.

mode.²¹ In lines 37–38, he calls his audience "sages" (חכמים), "those who ponder knowledge" (שחי דעת), "those who are straight of way" (ישרי ד[רך]), "righteous ones" (צדיקים), and "those crushed by poverty" (נד[כא עני]).²²

> O sages, and those who ponder knowledge. May those who are eager become firm in purpose. [All who are straight of wa]y become more discerning. O righteous ones, put an end to injustice. And all you whose way is perfect, hold fast [...O you who are cru]shed by poverty, be patient.

The lexical similarities to Ps 37 are remarkable and, like Ps 37, 1QHodayot^a teaches patience, steadfastness, and discernment in the face of oppressors. In contrast to this view, 4Q171 identifies the עדת האביונים (e.g., 1–10 II, 10) with the "congregation of [God's] chosen ones" (עם בחירו; 1–10 IV, 11–12), who are led by the Righteous Teacher and opposed by the "Man of the Lie" (איש הכזב; 1–10 IV, 14).²³ Here the notions of election and group identity are given a stronger accent than in 1QHodayot^a or in Ps 37.

The theology of this passage in 1QHodayot^a is instructive for the interpretation of Ps 37. Like the creation hymn in 1QHodayot^a, Ps 37 uses terms for the poor to describe those who are oppressed by evildoers and who rely on God for deliverance. In the face of unjust oppression, theirs is a total religious commitment. As Emanuel Podechard states, in Ps 37, "Les humbles sont … ceux qui sont soumis à Iahvé et lui obéissent."²⁴ It is no doubt true that they are a group of righteous ones who are oppressed by another group whom both Ps 37 and 1QHodayot^a call the "ruthless" (עריץ, Ps 37:35; ער[יצים], 1QH^a IX, 41). Yet an exclusively sociological explanation for the use of terms denoting the poor in the psalm do not do justice to its emphasis on ethics. In much the same way as in the creation hymn

---

21. See Carol A. Newsom, "What Do Hodayot Do? Language and the Construction of the Self in Sectarian Prayer," in *The Self as Symbolic Space: Constructing Identity and Community at Qumran*, STDJ 52 (Leiden: Brill, 2004), 191–286, here paraphrasing her analysis of several passages on 226–29.

22. Transcription and translation of 1QHodayot^a follow Schuller and Newsom, *Hodayot*.

23. For translation and notes, see Horgan, *Pesharim*, 194–226.

24. Emmanuel Podechard, *Le Psautier: Traduction littérale et explication historique*, 2 vols. (Lyon: Facultés Catholiques, 1949), 1:170. See Albert Gélin, *The Poor of Yahweh*, trans. Kathryn Sullivan (Collegeville, MN: Liturgical Press, 1964), 36–37 (translation of Gélin, *Les pauvres de Yahvé* [Paris: Cerf, 1953]).

in 1QHodayot[a], the power of "the poor" in Ps 37 comes from a rejection of autonomy and utter reliance upon God, from whom wise speech comes.[25]

4. What Is the Hope of the Poor in Psalm 37?

The second issue of interpretation concerns the hope of the poor. Their hope is twofold: hope for justice and hope for land.

4.1. Justice

The problem of injustice is the occasion for Hossfeld and Zenger's theory that Ps 37 was written, in part, as a reflection on *Weltordnung*. There is a long history in the scholarship on Israel's wisdom literature of treating this order as an abstract, universal principle to which reality must conform in order to produce justice. This notion led to comparison with *Maat*, which was thought by some to be the Egyptian equivalent to Israel's world order.[26] But as Jan Assmann and others have shown, *Maat* is social and ethical in its core meaning; it is not so much the order itself as it is the expressions of social justice that maintained that order.[27] In my opinion, the same can be said for Israel's notion of justice, especially in Ps 37. This is not world order in the abstract but justice that is socially embedded. As Walter Brueggemann and W. H. Bellinger have recently noted, "This psalm is not a piece of theory that articulates a universal structure of reality."[28] Finally, at least since the early nineteenth century, scholars have often claimed that Ps 37 is a theodicy. In his Psalms commentary, Wilhelm M. L. de Wette stated, "Dieser Psalm ist gleichsam eine Theodicee, eine Lösung der Zweifel, die

---

25. Here again I paraphrase Newsom's remarkable characterization of several passages in 1QHodayot[a] and apply those comments by analogy to Ps 37. See Newsom, "What Do Hodayot Do," 226–29, especially 229.

26. One thinks especially of the monograph of Hans Heinrich Schmid, *Gerechtigkeit als Weltordnung: Hintergrund und Geschichte des alttestamentlichen Gerechtigkeitsbegriffes*, BHT 40 (Tübingen: Mohr Siebeck, 1968).

27. See especially Jan Assmann, *Ma'at: Gerechtigkeit und Unsterblichkeit im Alten Ägypten* (Munich: Beck, 1990); Michael V. Fox, "World Order and Ma'at: A Crooked Parallel," *JANESCU* 23 (1995): 37–58; James P. Allen, *Middle Egyptian: An Introduction to the Language and Culture of the Hieroglyphs* (Cambridge: Cambridge University Press, 2000), 115–17.

28. Walter Brueggemann and W. H. Bellinger Jr., *Psalms*, NCBC (New York: Cambridge University Press, 2014), 183.

man gegen die Gerechtigkeit Gottes in Rücksicht des Schicksals der Frommen erheben könnte."²⁹ This sentiment is restated in the work of Hermann Gunkel and others.³⁰

The psalm undoubtedly offers its audiences scenarios and metaphors for reflection. But the heart of the argument in this essay is that its vision of justice is not meant simply for the construction of a philosophical argument. Rather, it is meant to spur the poor to action. Psalm 37 speaks of those who "*do* injustice" (עשה עולה; v. 1) and of those who "*speak* justice" (תדבר משפט; v. 30), not just the notions of justice or injustice in the abstract. Furthermore, Ps 37 frequently expresses its exhortation to action in imperatives. In the face of the apparently enviable position of the wicked, God's people are to "trust in YHWH and do good" and "strive for faithfulness,"³¹ as verse 3 says. Finally, the psalm is characterized by practical themes typical of wisdom literature: moneylending (vv. 22, 26) and speech (v. 30). In addition, God's people recite the law of God (v. 31), practice integrity (v. 37), and strive for uprightness (v. 37).³² By doing these things, they prove that they are YHWH's חסדים (v. 28), and on this basis they have a future (v. 37). As Amos Ḥakham says, "The righteous man is involved at all times in acts of lovingkindness."³³

4.2. Land

The second aspect of the hope of the poor is land. Their hope has both a present and a future orientation. As Ps 37:27 says, "Turn from evil and do

---

29. De Wette, *Psalmen*, 293.

30. See Hermann Gunkel and Joachim Begrich, *Einleitung in die Psalmen: Die Gattungen der religiösen Lyrik Israels*, 3rd ed. (Göttingen: Vandenhoeck & Ruprecht, 1975), 386.

31. Many interpret the MT's רעה אמונה as meaning "shepherd faithfulness" or the like, deriving רעה from רעה I ("to tend, shepherd"). The Peshitta, however, reads "seek faithfulness" (*bʿy hymnwtʾ*), correctly deriving the sense from רעה III ("to strive after"). The root רעה III occurs regularly in the book of Ecclesiastes, where it refers to the "strivings" or "longings" of the wind (Eccl 1:14; 2:11, 17, 26; 4:4, 6; 6:9). The point in Ps 37:3 is striving to do good and to be faithful in the face of the prosperity of the wicked. On אמונה, see n. 9 above.

32. This recitation of the law is, of course, a form of meditation, but it is not disconnected from the *practice* of the law.

33. Amos Ḥakham, *Psalms 1–57*, vol. 1 of *The Bible: Psalms with Jerusalem Commentary* (Jerusalem: Mossad Harav Kook, 2003), 290 (commenting on Ps 37:26).

good; dwell forever." Remarkably, both commands here are present tense imperatives. Just as God's people are to "turn from evil and do good," so also they are to "dwell in the land" even in the present (cf. v. 3: "dwell in the land" // "Trust in YHWH and do good").[34] Such commands suggest that, under the present circumstances, the poor might be tempted to leave the land and to abandon their righteousness. And yet the psalm commands them to remain in the land and continue to strive for faithfulness.

The psalm also has a future orientation with respect to the land. It states that when evildoers are cut off, the righteous will receive their inheritance (vv. 9, 11, 29, 34). On the basis of this future orientation, some have argued that Ps 37 is eschatological in focus. Markus Witte, for example, reads the psalm as a wisdom poem that combines elements of apocalyptic with Deuteronomic and Deuteronomistic torah theology.[35] For Witte, the psalm's view of land inheritance is cosmic; it envisions the inheritance of the whole world.

Witte's view is quite similar to the viewpoint of the Qumran pesher in 4Q171, which speaks of the congregation of the poor "taking possession of the high mountain of Israel" ([אל]ירשו את הר מרום ישר; 1–10 III, 11) and, according to Stegemann's reconstruction, even inheriting the "whole world" (כול ת[ב]ל; 1–10 III, 10).[36] This cosmic, eschatological interpretation is also evident in the citation of the LXX version of Ps 37:11a [Ps 36:11a LXX] in Matt 5:5: μακάριοι οἱ πραεῖς, ὅτι αὐτοὶ κληρονομήσουσιν τὴν γῆν.[37]

As Ulrich Luz notes, this text transposes the traditional promise of land into the cosmic realm.[38] But the phrase κληρονομήσουσιν γῆν in the

---

34. See especially the discussion in Ḥakham, *Psalms 1–57*, 282.
35. See Markus Witte, "Psalm 37 im Spannungsfeld von Weisheit und Eschatologie," in *Weisheit als Lebensgrundlage: Festschrift für Friedrich V. Reiterer zum 65. Geburtstag*, ed. Renate Egger-Wenzel, Karin Schöpflin, and Johannes Diehl, DCLS 15 (Berlin: de Gruyter, 2013), 411–36.
36. See the various readings offered and discussion in Horgan, *Pesharim*, 217.
37. Matthew's gospel adds the definite article to the object, and by translating ענוים in 37:11 [36:11 LXX] with πραΰς, the Septuagint paves the way for the gospel's emphasis on the active, ethical connotations of "the poor" over the material ones. See Ulrich Luz, *Matthew 1–7: A Commentary*, trans. J. E. Crouch, Hermeneia (Minneapolis: Augsburg Fortress, 2007), 194–95. Takamitsu Muraoka glosses πραΰς in the Septuagint as "modest, unassuming" (Takamitsu Muraoka, *A Greek-English Lexicon of the Septuagint* [Leuven: Peeters, 2009], 581–82, s.v.).
38. Luz, *Matthew 1–7*, 194–95.

LXX version of Ps 37, Ps 36 LXX, is equally at home in the Greek text of the pentateuchal narratives concerning land inheritance, as Michaela Bauks has shown.[39] This suggests that both the Greek and Hebrew texts of Ps 37 may be read in light of the more mundane expectations of land, such as those in the patriarchal narratives, in addition to the cosmic perspective more common in later Jewish traditions, such as 4Q171 and the Gospel of Matthew.

In my estimation, the closest point of contact with Ps 37 is not apocalyptic eschatology but the worldview of Prov 1–9. Especially comparable to Ps 37 is Prov 2:21–22: "For the upright will dwell in the land, and people of integrity will remain in it; but the wicked will be cut off from the land, and the treacherous will be torn out of it." In the context of Prov 2, "dwelling in the land" refers to long life in the land, both for oneself and one's descendants, while "being torn out of the land" refers to dying early and being dislocated from the land.[40]

Psalm 37 is intensely focused on inheritance. As is common in the ancient Near East, the psalm expresses this concept in agricultural metaphors. The central claim of the elderly teaching voice in verse 25 is that the sage has not seen the "seed" (זרע) of the righteous ever reduced to a state of beggary. He goes on to say in verse 26 that the "seed" of the righteous is a gracious moneylender and is therefore a blessing. These verses suggest that the righteous should practice generosity even when they may lack basic needs, for they can be assured that this will not always be so. The wicked, on the other hand, are compared throughout the poem to green grass (v. 2), beautiful meadows (v. 20), and luxuriant trees (v. 25).[41]

---

39. See Michaela Bauks, "'Das Land erben' oder 'die Erde in Besitz nehmen' in Ps 36 (37 MT): Ein Übersetzungsvergleich," in *Die Septuaginta—Texte, Kontexte, Lebenswelten: Internationale Fachtagung veranstaltet von Septuaginta Deutsch (LXX.D), Wuppertal 20.–23. Juli 2006*, ed. Martin Karrer and Wolfgang Kraus, WUNT 219 (Tübingen: Mohr Siebeck, 2008), 518–20.

40. This description paraphrases the analysis of James Alfred Loader, *Proverbs 1–9*, HCOT (Leuven: Peeters, 2014), 134–35. See also Michael V. Fox, *Proverbs 1–9*, AB 18A (New York: Doubleday, 2000), 124; Ḥakham, *Psalms 1–57*, 284.

41. The MT's ביקר כרים (37:20) is the first major exegetical and textual difficulty in the poem, and space does not permit a full survey of the readings in the texts and versions or all proposed emendations. Julius Wellhausen's emendation to כרים בקיד ("like a fire in the stove") has been the most influential among modern interpreters. One might call on 4Q171 for support of this reading, as it attests בורים, which looks like the plural of בור ("furnace"). In 1954, however, John Allegro argued that the Qumran

Despite the fact that they seem to be verdant, they will wilt and vanish in an instant. The green growth in Ps 37 is not an indication of long-term flourishing, as it is in Ps 1; rather, it is a temporary state that will not last (cf. Wis 4:3–5).

Fittingly, the end of the poem begins to focus more acutely on the "future" (אחרית) of both the "person of integrity" (v. 37) and the "transgressors" (v. 38). The term אחרית may be understood both in a temporal sense and with reference to one's descendants.[42] In Ps 37, these meanings should not be separated too sharply, for the future is tied directly to one's progeny. While the present may seem intolerable, it is those who continue to strive for uprightness who will be blessed with the "seed" whose inheritance will be eternal. As Rashi commented, "Though [the איש שלום] may not have a past, he will have a future."[43]

5. The Contribution of Psalm 37 to the Final Subcollection of the First Davidic Psalter

According to Hossfeld and Zenger, Ps 37 was added to the subcollection in Pss 35–41 during the postexilic period. While the addition of Pss 35,

---

commentator likely understood the form as a variant of the MT's כרים, rendering a pronunciation of a short *o* with a ו (Allegro, "A Newly Discovered Fragment of a Commentary on Psalm XXXVII from Qumrân," *PEQ* 86 [1954]: 74, n. 4a). The primary question that faces the interpreter, then, is whether to read the MT's כיקר כרים as "like the wealth of meadows" or "like the valuable (portion) of rams" (see Aquila, Peshitta, and Targum). The first interpretation understands the MT's יקר as signifying wealth and honor (see especially Esth 1:4) and reads כרים as deriving from כר II ("meadow, pasture"). The second interpretation reads כרים as deriving from כר I ("young ram") and must extend the sense of יקר by taking it to mean the most valuable portion of the animal, i.e., the fat. The first interpretation best fits the agricultural metaphors in the near context (Ps 37:19) and in other portions of the psalm (37:2).

42. The word אחרית most commonly carries a temporal sense of "future," especially in phrases such as באחרית הימים, "in the latter days" (see Aramaic באחרית יומיא in Dan 2:28; Akkadian *ina aḫrât ūmē* [*CAD*, A/1, 194, s.v. *aḫrâtu*]). Yet אחרית may also be used with the meaning "posterity" or "descendants," as in Jer 31:17; Ps 109:13; Sir 16:4 MS B. Thus the LXX renders with "descendants" (ἐγκατάλειμμα), while Aquila (ἔσχατον) and Symmachus (μέλλοντα; then with ἔσχατον in 37:38) translate with a focus on the temporal sense. Cognates in Akkadian (*aḫrâtu*), Ugaritic (*uḫry*), and inscriptional Aramaic (*'ḥrh*) may all be used in either sense.

43. Mayer I. Gruber, *Rashi's Commentary on Psalms*, BRLJ 18 (Philadelphia: Jewish Publication Society of America, 2007), 315.

38, and 41 made the first Davidic Psalter into a compositional unit, the postexilic redaction of the four smaller collections from the late exilic period (Pss 3–14 [not 9–10]; 15–24 [not 16, 19, or 23]; 26–32; and 35–41 [not 37, 39, or 40]) reworked these earlier psalms and added several that focused on a deep divine mysticism (e.g., Pss 16, 23, 40) and on "true Israel" and their knowledge of divine world order (e.g., Pss 19; 25; 33; 34; 37; 39).[44] They state,

> Ihr Anliegen ist es, in den Psalmenbetern die typischen Armen als Vertreter des angefeindeten und angefochtenen "wahren Israel" zu sehen, die aufgrund der beiderseitigen engen Beziehung zwischen JHWH und "den gerechten Knechten JHWHs" den Feinden im Gottesvolk Widerstand leisten können, weil sie wissen, daß JHWH und seine Weltordnung (vgl. besonders den "reflektierten" JHWH-Psalm 19, die Erweiterung Ps 18$^{26-32}$ sowie die Weisheitspsalmen 25 34 37 39) sich durchsetzen werden.[45]

It is, of course, true that Ps 37 represents a kind of system of cosmic order and retribution.

One of the main points of this essay, however, is that the theology of Ps 37 should not be reduced to instruction about a system *as such*. The psalm is not merely an abstract intellectual or sociological exercise, something that Hossfeld and Zenger's characterization of Ps 37 comes very close to suggesting. Reflections on the way YHWH has ordered the world leads the poor to trust in YHWH in the face of present affliction and to continue to do justice and righteousness even though it seems to afford little advantage.

In addition to Hossfeld and Zenger's suggestion that Ps 37 contributes to Pss 35–41 by focusing on world order, Ps 37 also brings to light the themes of trust and waiting during times of affliction, rather than turning aside to join in the (presently) successful schemes of evildoers. The affliction of the poor and the upright by transgressors is a common theme in Pss 35; 36; 37; 39; and 41. Several excerpts will suffice to illustrate the point:

35:1 Contend, YHWH, with the one who contends with me!
Fight the one who fights me!

35:10b One who rescues the עָנִי from one who is stronger than he,
the עָנִי וְאֶבְיוֹן from one who robs him.

---

44. See Hossfeld and Zenger, *Psalm 1–50*, 14–15.
45. Hossfeld and Zenger, *Psalm 1–50*, 14–15.

36:12   Do not let the foot of the proud travel over me,
        and do not let the hand of the wicked make me wander away.

37:12   The wicked schemes against the righteous
        and gnashes his teeth at him.

39:9   Rescue me from all my offenses,
        do not make me the object of a fool's scorn.

41:6–8 My enemies speak evil of me:
        "When will he die, and his name perish?"
        And if one comes to see (me), his heart speaks emptiness.
        He gathers wickedness for himself (and) he goes outside speaking (it).
        Together all those who hate me whisper against me,
        against me they devise my ruin.

In the face of this oppression, the righteous are to trust in YHWH, who will support the poor in their integrity and reward them with their inheritance, while dispensing with their oppressors. A few excerpts from Pss 36; 38; 40; and 41 will serve illustrate these themes:

36:13   There are evildoers, fallen.
        They are thrust down, and they are not able to get up.

37:5   Entrust your path to YHWH,
        Trust in him, and he will make (it).

37:17   For the arms of the wicked will be broken,
        but YHWH upholds the righteous.

38:16   For I wait for you, YHWH.
        You will answer, O lord, my God.

40:5   How fortunate is the man who places his trust in YHWH,
        who does not turn toward the arrogant or to those who follow lies.

40:14–18   Show me favor, YHWH, by saving me,
        YHWH, rush to my aid.
        May they be shamed and disgraced together—

>   those who seek to snatch away my life.
>   May they be turned back and put to shame—
>   those who delight in my harm.
>   …
>
>   As for me, I am עָנִי וְאֶבְיוֹן,
>   may the lord devise for me—
>   you are my help and my deliverer.
>   My God, do not delay!

41:13   As for me, you will support me on account of my integrity,
and you will station me before you forever.

6. The Contribution of Psalm 37 to Postexilic Prayer

Many have been quick to point out that Ps 37 is not a prayer. As Norbert Lohfink says bluntly, "Psalm 37 ist kein Gebet."[46] Indeed, from the very first line, the poem is shot through with allusions to the book of Proverbs, and it exudes an air of instruction, both in tone and in its acrostic form.[47] Most scholars think that Ps 37 would have fit better in the book of Proverbs than in the Psalter, and on this basis, Ludin Janzen raised the possibility that the psalm had its *Sitz im Leben* in the school rather than in the worship service.[48]

Such conclusions, however, privilege the hypothetical original setting of the text over its use and its current place in a collection. In the case of Ps 37, one may say that whatever Ps 37 once was, by the time of the postexilic period, it was assembled among prayers and praises, and it could be

---

46. Norbert Lohfink, "Die Besänftigung des Messias: Gedanken zu Psalm 37," in *"Den Armen eine frohe Botschaft": Festschrift für Bischof Franz Kamphaus zum 65. Geburtstag*, ed. Josef Hainz, Hans-Winfried Jüngling, Reinhold Sebott (Frankfurt am Main: Knecht, 1997), 79.

47. The acrostic form, however, is not necessarily associated with instruction or with wisdom literature. On the acrostic form in the Bible and ancient Near Eastern literature, see William M. Soll, "Babylonian and Biblical Acrostics," *Bib* 69 (1988): 305–23.

48. On its fit with Proverbs, note especially the comments of Bernhard Duhm: "Das Gedicht hätte eigentlich besser in die Sprüche Salomos als in den Davidpsalter hineingepasst" (Duhm, *Die Psalmen*, KHC 14 [Freiburg im Breisgau et al.: Mohr Siebeck, 1899], 110). See Herman L. Jansen, *Die spätjüdische Psalmendichtung, ihr Entstehungskreis und ihr "Sitz im Leben": Eine literaturgeschichtlich-soziologische Untersuchung*, SNVAO 2.3 (Oslo: Dybwad, 1937), 139.

used as such. The combination of wisdom, the acrostic form, and prayer is hardly unusual in ancient Near Eastern literature. It is on full display in the Mesopotamian masterpiece we call the Babylonian Theodicy. William M. Soll states, "While the *Theodicy* as a whole is undeniably wisdom literature, the text of its poetic acrostic seems to borrow something from the realm of prayer, in order to anchor the poem in a sense of the author's fundamental religious and social loyalty."[49] This combination of wisdom instruction and prayer is precisely that which becomes pronounced in biblical and parabiblical literature of the Hellenistic and Roman periods—in the Hellenistic period in the book of Ben Sira, in the Roman period in 11QPs[a] and 1QHodayot[a]. But even before these great Jewish works, the postexilic substratum of the first Davidic Psalter drew together wisdom and prayer in such a way that one is justified of speaking not only of the sapientializing of the Psalter, but also of the devotionalizing of instruction.[50] This was not an invention of the tradent who set Ps 1 as the prologue to the Psalter; rather, it reflects the fact that the editor recognized a union of wisdom and prayer that was already before him. The postexilic community could look to the psalms—and to Ps 37 in particular—for instruction for everyday life during their moments of most pressing need. Those who devoted themselves to the worldview of Ps 37 did so not only by intellectual reflection or sociological identification but also by prayerful trust in a God who rescues the needy and who would reward them for their integrity in times of trial.

Bibliography

Allegro, John M. "A Newly Discovered Fragment of a Commentary on Psalm XXXVII from Qumrân." *PEQ* 86 (1954): 69–75.
Allegro, John M., and A. A. Anderson. *Qumrân Cave 4.I (4Q158–4Q186)*. DJD 5. Oxford: Clarendon, 1968.
Allen, James P. *Middle Egyptian: An Introduction to the Language and Culture of the Hieroglyphs*. Cambridge: Cambridge University Press, 2000.
Assmann, Jan. *Maʿat: Gerechtigkeit und Unsterblichkeit im Alten Ägypten*. Munich: Beck, 1990.

---

49. Soll, "Babylonian and Biblical Acrostics," 312.
50. For sapientalizating, see Joseph Reindl, "Weisheitliche Bearbeitung von Psalmen: Ein Beitrag zum Verständnis der Sammlung des Psalters," in *Congress Volume: The Tenth Congress of the International Organization for the Study of the Old Testament, Vienna 1980*, ed. J. A. Emerton, VTSup 32 (Leiden: Brill, 1981), 333–56.

Bauks, Michaela. "'Das Land erben' oder 'die Erde in Besitz nehmen' in Ps 36 (37 MT): Ein Übersetzungsvergleich." Pages 502–22 in *Die Septuaginta—Texte, Kontexte, Lebenswelten: Internationale Fachtagung veranstaltet von Septuaginta Deutsch (LXX.D), Wuppertal 20.–23. Juli 2006.* Edited by Martin Karrer and Wolfgang Kraus. WUNT 219. Tübingen: Mohr Siebeck, 2008.

Beentjes, Pancratius C. *The Book of Ben Sira in Hebrew: A Text Edition of All Extant Hebrew Manuscripts and a Synopsis of All Parallel Hebrew Ben Sira Texts.* VTSup 68. Atlanta: SBL Press, 2006.

Brueggemann, Walter, and William H. Bellinger Jr. *Psalms.* NCBC. New York: Cambridge University Press, 2014.

Duhm, Bernhard. *Die Psalmen.* KHC 14. Freiburg im Breisgau: Mohr Siebeck. 1899.

Fox, Michael V. *Proverbs 1–9.* AB 18A. New York: Doubleday, 2000.

———. "World Order and Ma'at: A Crooked Parallel." *JANESCU* 23 (1995): 37–58.

Gélin, Albert. *Les pauvres de Yahvé.* Paris: Cerf, 1953.

———. *The Poor of Yahweh.* Translated by Kathryn Sullivan. Collegeville, MN: Liturgical Press, 1964.

Gillingham, Sue. "The Poor in the Psalms." *ExpTim* 100 (1988): 15–19.

Goff, Matthew J. "Reading Wisdom at Qumran: 4QInstruction and the Hodayot." *DSD* 11 (2004): 263–88.

Graetz, Heinrich. *Kritischer Commentar zu den Psalmen: Nebst Text und Uebersetzung.* 2 vols. Breslau: Schottlaender, 1882–1883.

Gruber, Mayer I. *Rashi's Commentary on Psalms.* BRLJ 18. Philadelphia: Jewish Publication Society of America, 2007.

Gunkel, Hermann, and Joachim Begrich. *Einleitung in die Psalmen: Die Gattungen der religiösen Lyrik Israels.* 3rd ed. Göttingen: Vandenhoeck & Ruprecht, 1975.

Ḥakham, Amos. *Psalms 1–57.* Vol. 1 of *The Bible: Psalms with Jerusalem Commentary.* Jerusalem: Mossad Harav Kook, 2003.

Horgan, Maurya P. *Pesharim: Qumran Interpretations of Biblical Books.* CBQMS 8. Washington, DC: Catholic Biblical Association, 1979.

Hossfeld, Frank-Lothar, and Erich Zenger. *Die Psalmen: Psalm 1–50.* NEchtB 29. Würzburg: Echter, 1993.

———. "'Selig, wer auf die Armen achtet' (Ps 41,2): Beobachtungen zur Gottesvolk-Theologie des ersten Davidpsalters." Pages 21–50 in *Volk Gottes, Gemeinde und Gesellschaft.* Edited by I. Balderman et al. JBTh 7. Neukirchen Vluyn: Neukirchener Verlag, 1992.

Jansen, Herman L. *Die spätjüdische Psalmendichtung, ihr Entstehungskreis und ihr "Sitz im Leben": Eine literaturgeschichtlich-soziologische Untersuchung.* SNVAO 2.3. Oslo: Dybwad, 1937.

Levin, Christoph. "Das Amosbuch der Anawim." *ZTK* 94 (1997): 407–36.

———. "Das Gebetbuch der Gerechten: Literargeschichtliche Beobachtungen am Psalter." *ZTK* 90 (1993): 355–81.

———. "The Poor in the Old Testament: Some Observations." Pages 322–38 in *Fortschreibungen: Gesammelte Studien zum Alten Testament.* Translated by M. Kohl. BZAW 316. Berlin: de Gruyter, 2003.

Loader, James A. *Proverbs 1–9.* HCOT. Leuven: Peeters, 2014.

Lohfink, Norbert. "Die Besänftigung des Messias: Gedanken zu Psalm 37." Pages 75–87 in *"Den Armen eine frohe Botschaft": Festschrift für Bischof Franz Kamphaus zum 65. Geburtstag.* Edited by Josef Hainz, Hans-Winfried Jüngling, Reinhold Sebott. Frankfurt am Main: Knecht, 1997.

Luz, Ulrich. *Matthew 1–7: A Commentary.* Translated by J. E. Crouch. Minneapolis: Augsburg Fortress, 2007.

Muraoka, Takamitsu. *A Greek-English Lexicon of the Septuagint.* Leuven: Peeters, 2009.

Newsom, Carol A. "What Do Hodayot Do? Language and the Construction of the Self in Sectarian Prayer." Pages 191–286 in *The Self as Symbolic Space: Constructing Identity and Community at Qumran.* STDJ 52. Leiden, Boston: Brill, 2004.

Maré, Leonard P. "The Ethics of Retribution in Psalm 37." *EP* 92 (2010): 264–74.

Mülhaupt, Erwin. "Luthers Übersetzung und Auslegung des 37. Psalms: Ein Beispiel zunehmender Verchristlichung, aber nicht Christologisierung." *ZLG* 34 (1963): 49–60.

Luther, Martin. *First Lectures on the Psalms I (Psalms 1–75).* Edited by Hilton C. Oswald. Vol. 10 of *Luther's Works.* Edited by Jaroslav Pelikan and Helmut T. Lehmann. St. Louis: Concordia, 1958.

———. *Selected Psalms III.* Edited by Jaroslav Pelikan. Vol. 14 of *Luther's Works.* Edited by Jaroslav Pelikan and Helmut T. Lehmann. St. Louis: Concordia, 1958.

Podechard, Emmanuel. *Le Psautier: Traduction littérale et explication historique.* 2 vols. Lyon: Facultés Catholiques, 1949–1954.

Rahlfs, Alfred. עָנִי *und* עָנָו *in den Psalmen.* Göttingen: Dieterich, 1892.

Reindl, Joseph. "Weisheitliche Bearbeitung von Psalmen: Ein Beitrag zum Verständnis der Sammlung des Psalters." Pages 333–56 in *Congress*

Volume: The Tenth Congress of the International Organization for the Study of the Old Testament, Vienna 1980. Edited by J. A. Emerton. VTSup 32. Leiden: Brill, 1981.

Ritschl, Albrecht. *Geschichte des Pietismus*. 3 vols. Bonn: Adolph Marcus, 1880–1886.

Schmid, Hans Heinrich. *Gerechtigkeit als Weltordnung: Hintergrund und Geschichte des alttestamentlichen Gerechtigkeitsbegriffes*. BHT 40. Tübingen: Mohr Siebeck, 1968.

Soll, William M. "Babylonian and Biblical Acrostics." *Bib* 69 (1988): 305–23.

Schuller, Eileen M., and Carol A. Newsom. *The Hodayot (Thanksgiving Psalms): A Study Edition of 1QH^a*. EJL 36. Atlanta: SBL Press, 2012.

Seow, Choon Leong. "West Semitic Sources." Pages 201–18 in *Prophets and Prophecy in the Ancient Near East*. By Martti Nissinen, with contributions by Choon L. Seow and Robert K. Ritner. WAW 12. Atlanta: Society of Biblical Literature, 2003.

Skehan, Patrick W., and Alexander A. Di Lella. *The Wisdom of Ben Sira: A New Translation with Notes*. AB 39. New York: Doubleday, 1987.

Spieckermann, Hermann. "Der betende Weise: Jesus Sirach." Pages 116–40 in *Lebenskunst und Gotteslob in Israel: Anregungen aus Psalter und Weisheit für die Theologie*. By Hermann Spieckermann. FAT 91. Tübingen: Mohr Siebeck, 2014.

Stegemann, Hartmut, with Eileen Schuller. *Qumran Cave 1.3: 1QHodayot^a with Incorporation of 1QHodayot^b and 4QHodayot^{a-f}*. Translated by Carol Newsom. DJD 40. Oxford: Clarendon, 2009.

Tanzer, Sara J. "The Sages at Qumran: Wisdom in the Hodayot." PhD diss., Harvard University, 1987.

Wette, Wilhelm M. L. de. *Die Psalmen*. 3rd ed. Heidelberg: Mohr, 1829.

Witte, Markus. "Psalm 37 im Spannungsfeld von Weisheit und Eschatologie." Pages 411–36 in *Weisheit als Lebensgrundlage: Festschrift für Friedrich V. Reiterer zum 65. Geburtstag*. Edited by Renate Egger-Wenzel, Karin Schöpflin, and Johannes Diehl. DCLS 15. Berlin: de Gruyter, 2013.

To Sanction and to Subvert:
The Reuses of Psalm 132 in the Hebrew Bible

Melody D. Knowles

In the examination of the production and reception of texts and prayers in the Persian and Hellenistic periods, Ps 132 plays a signal role. This text is unique in that it underwent two distinct receptions into the biblical canon during this time—both into the collection of Songs of Ascents (שיר המעלות; Pss 120–134) and into the Chronicler's presentation of Solomon's prayer to dedicate the temple (2 Chr 6:41–42). It also represents key concepts of Israelite identity, namely, the role of David and Jerusalem and the temple. Yet even as the editors of Pss 120–134 and the Chronicler repeat the same text, they nevertheless authorize and subvert very different understandings of identity and religious practice. By examining the presentations in turn, what emerges are two distinct visions of identity conveyed in the same words of prayer.

1. Psalm 132

Ps 132 begins with David's oath to establish a place for the deity, with the king's oath quoted directly (vv. 1–5). Then, after an account of what seems to be a liturgical procession (with the ark? vv. 6–7), the people utter a three-part prayer to God (vv. 8–10). The second half of the psalm begins in verse 11 with God's response to David's oath and the people's prayer. First, God promises to set and support obedient Davidic heirs on the throne in verses 11b–12, then God claims Zion as a place to dwell, makes provisions for Zion's priests and inhabitants, and promises security to the "anointed one" and shame to the enemies (vv. 13–18). As such, the psalm is finely balanced between two sections of ten lines each (vv. 1b–10 and 11–18), with the two sets of direct quotes from the human community (David's vow in vv. 3–5; the worshipers' entreaty in vv. 8–10) mirrored by two divine addresses (vv. 11b–12; 14–18).[1]

The poetic balance of the text that satisfies on the literary level also has implications for identity construction. That is, the literary artistry sustains claims for the authority of particular religious practices, sacred geography, and the capacity of the human community to influence the divine world.

1.1. Sanctioning God's Choice of David and Jerusalem

On the most obvious level, the text champions the divine chosenness of David and Jerusalem. Although the central place of David and Jerusalem in the divine economy is assumed throughout the Psalter, outside of Ps 132 very few other psalms explicitly mention a covenant between them and God or name either as "chosen" (בחר)—only two for David (Pss 78:70; 89) and one for Jerusalem (Pss 78:68; and cf. 87:2). Thus Ps 132 contains one of the few explicit assertions of chosenness, presented alongside a "backstory" that describes the way this came to be.

This assertion is especially significant given the text's placement within the "Songs of Ascents" in Pss 120–134.[2] In many ways, Ps 132 is distinctive within this collection in that the other fourteen psalms are much shorter, make frequent use of anadiplosis as a literary feature, contain formulas repeated throughout the collection but absent in Ps 132, and focus more on individuals and families rather than national leaders.[3] Yet Ps 132's origin

---

1. In contrast, Terence E. Fretheim and Frank-Lothar Hossfeld argue that the text of Ps 132 divides at vv. 1–9 and 10–18, with v. 10 "introductory to vv. 11–12, just as vs. 1 is to vss. 2–4" (Fretheim, "Ps 132: A Form-Critical Study," *JBL* 86 [1967]: 289–300, quote at 292; Hossfeld, "König David im Wallfahrtspsalter," in *Ein Herz so weit wie der Sand am Ufer des Meeres: Festschrift für Georg Hentschel*, ed. Susanne Gillmayr-Bucher, Anette Giercke, and Christina Nießen, ETS 90 [Würzburg: Echter, 2006], 219–33, esp. 220–21).

2. For more on the collection and the place of Ps 132 within it, see Klaus Seybold, *Die Wallfahrtspsalmen: Studien zur Entstehungsgeschichte von Psalm 120–34*, BThSt 3 (Neukirchen-Vluyn: Neukirchener Verlag, 1978); Loren D. Crow, *The Songs of Ascents (Psalms 120–34): Their Place in the Israelite History and Religion*, SBLDS 148 (Atlanta: Scholars Press, 1996); Erich Zenger, "Der Zion als Ort der Gottesnähe: Beobachtungen zum Weltbild des Wallfahrtspsalters Ps 120–134," in *Gottes Nähe im Alten Testament*, ed. Gönke Eberhardt and Kathrin Liess, SBS 202 (Stuttgart: Katholisches Bibelwerk, 2004), 84–114.

3. Examples of repeated formulas absent from Ps 132 include "maker of heaven

story for Jerusalem and David explains and promotes the practice of pilgrimage to the holy city (perhaps even the rebuilding campaign itself) and thus fits within the larger themes and purposes of the collection.[4] It may be that the presentation of this story in Ps 132 explains the distinctive archaistic and/or archaizing elements that appear in the text alongside later forms—in the Persian period, Ps 132 is deliberately signaling that pilgrimage to Jerusalem is based on an ancient tradition.[5] When shaping the

---

and earth" (Pss 121:2; 124:8; 134:3) and "from this time forth and for evermore" (Pss 121:8; 125:2; 131:3).

4. As Erich Zenger puts it, "Psalm 132 … offers a theological etiology of Zion as the place of YHWH's presence and the liturgy celebrated there" (Zenger, "Psalm 132," in *Psalms 3: A Commentary on Psalms 101–150*, ed. Klaus Baltzer, trans. Linda M. Maloney, Hermeneia [Minneapolis: Fortress, 2011], 454–68, esp. 468).

5. It has been suggested that the older elements in Ps 132 include terminology such as ישבו ל (v. 12) and מושב (v. 13), as well as grammatical forms such as the long imperfect (used twice in v. 7) and the emphatic use of the infinitive absolute in vv. 15 and 16. Probable postexilic grammatical elements include four instances of a verb with a direct object suffix (vv. 6 [2x], 12, 14), four instances of possession indicated by use of the preposition ל (vv. 11, 12, 13, 17), long imperative in v. 8, and plene spelling in v. 1, as well as late vocabulary such as אוה (v. 13) and פה (v. 14). See Avi Hurvitz, *The Transition Period in Biblical Hebrew: A Study in Post-exilic Hebrew and Its Implications for the Dating of Psalms* (Jerusalem: Bialik Institute, 1972), 152–63; Avi Hurvitz, "The Chronological Significance of 'Aramaisms' in Biblical Hebrew," *IEJ* 18 (1968): 234–40; Gary A. Rendsburg, *Linguistic Evidence for the Northern Origin of Selected Psalms*, SBLMS 43 (Atlanta: Scholars Press, 1990), 87–90. The text's date is also argued via reconstructions of its non/dependence on Deuteronomistic theology and Canaanite influence. For arguments about the text's antiquity, see Matitiahu Tsevat, "Studies in the Book of Samuel III: The Steadfast House; What Was David Promised in II Sam. 7:11b–16?," *HUCA* 34 (1963): 71–82; Frank Moore Cross, *Canaanite Myth and Hebrew Epic: Essays in the History of the Religion of Israel* (Cambridge: Harvard University Press, 1973), 232–38, 97 n. 24; Hartmut Gese, "Der Davidsbund und die Zionserwählung," in *Vom Sinai zum Zion: Alttestamentliche Beiträge zur biblischen Theologie*, BEvT 64 (Munich: Kaiser, 1974), 113–29; C. L. Seow, *Myth, Drama, and the Politics of David's Dance*, HSM 44 (Atlanta: Scholars Press, 1989), 145–203; Antti Laato, "Psalm 132 and the Development of the Jerusalemite/Israelite Royal Ideology," *CBQ* 54 (1992): 49–66; Laato, "Psalm 132: A Case Study in Methodology," *CBQ* 61 (1999): 24–33. For arguments for a postexilic (or later) date, see Lothar Perlitt, *Bundestheologie im Alten Testament*, WMANT 36 (Neukirchen-Vluyn: Neukirchener Verlag, 1969), 51–52; Tryggve N. D. Mettinger, *King and Messiah: The Civil and Sacral Legitimation of the Israelite Kings*, ConBOT 8 (Lund: Gleerup, 1976), 256–57, 277–78; Timo Veijola, *Verheißung in der Krise: Studien zur Literatur und Theologie des Exilszeit anhand des 89. Psalms*, AASF 220 (Helsinki: Suomalainen Tiedeakatemia, 1982),

collection, it may be that the editors retained (or created?) the distinctive voice of Ps 132 to register the text as a secondary incorporation of an older text in order to bolster its authority.

1.2. Sanctioning God's Choices as Responses to Prayer

The authorization of ancient religious practice and geography combines in Ps 132 with an emphasis on the role of the human community to shape the divine will. This is seen especially in the way that God's oaths in the second half of the text mirror the words of David and the human community in the first half.

Initially, this is marked by the linguistic mirroring of David and God. David's vow is immediately preceded by the introductory phrase: "which/how he swore to YHWH" (אשר נשבע ליהוה; v. 2). In parallel, YHWH's vow is introduced in a very similar way: "YHWH swore to David" (נשבע־יהוה לדוד; v. 11). Significantly, both parties enact the same action, using the same verb (שבע niphal). Thus in the world of the text, David mirrors something for God, acting in a way that God subsequently imitates. God's vow is portrayed as a sympathetic response to David's preceding act.

This dynamic of divine responsiveness continues with God's answer to the people's prayer (vv. 8–10). Given the several problems in interpreting verse 8, I will begin with the more straightforward section in verses 9–10. Here are two petitions, one for the priesthood/godly ones and one for David/[God's] anointed one. A direct comparison with God's later speech is illuminating:

132:9   Let your priests be clothed with righteousness, and let your godly ones sing for joy.[6]

132:15   "I will abundantly bless [Zion's] provision; I will satisfy its needy with bread.

132:16   "[Zion's] priests will I clothe with salvation; its godly ones will sing aloud for joy."

161–62; Heinz Kruse, "Psalm CXXXII and the Royal Zion Festival," *VT* 33 (1983): 279–97; Karel A. Deurloo, "Gedächtnis des Exils: Psalmen 120–34," *T&K* 55 (1992): 28–34; Corrine L. Patton, "Psalm 132: A Methodological Inquiry," *CBQ* 57 (1995): 643–54; Zenger, "Psalm 132," 454–68.

6. Unless otherwise noted, all biblical translations are mine.

132:10 For the sake of *David* your servant, do not reject *your anointed one*.

132:17 "There I will cause the horn of *David* to spring forth, I have prepared a lamp for *my anointed*.

132:18 His enemies I will clothe with shame, but upon him his crown will shine."

In both cases, God repeats key vocabulary from the initial prayer but also includes additional elements. Physically, there is an obvious enlargement in size: each one-line petition is answered with a two-line response. But there is also an expansion in degree or scope. That is, even while God *repeats* key aspects of the original requests, God also *magnifies* the proffer. Zion's priests do not simply appear in garments of righteousness, they are clothed by God with salvation. At the same time, God promises to "abundantly bless" the city's provisions (v. 15). The holy ones will not simply sing, they will "sing aloud with joy" (v. 16). And it is not just the priests and the holy ones in view in verses 15–16 but the needy as well. Finally, to the request that David not be refused, God responds with a promise to have the king's horn spring forth, a shining crown upon his head, and his enemies put to shame (v. 17).

This pattern of prayer in verses 9–10 and response in verses 15–18 sets up the emerging consensus that verse 8, in parallel with 13–14, should be read together with verses 9–10.[7]

132:8 Come, O Lord, to/on behalf of *your resting place*, you and the ark of your strength.

132:13 For the Lord has chosen Zion; he has desired it for his habitation.

132:14 "This is *my resting place* forever; Here I will dwell for I have desired it."

---

7. This grouping works even if one reads the ל with Elizabeth F. Huwiler as "for the sake of," or, with most others, as "to" (see Huwiler, "Patterns and Problems in Psalm 132," in *The Listening Heart: Essays in Wisdom and the Psalms in Honor of Roland E. Murphy*, ed. Kenneth G. Hoglund and Elizabeth F. Huwiler, JSOTSup 58 [Sheffield: JSOT Press, 1987], 199–215). For the argument that the ל should be read as "from," see Delbert R. Hillers, "Ritual Procession of the Ark and Ps 132," *CBQ* 30 (1968): 48–55.

As with the other two petitions in verses 9 and 10, there is both a repetition of key vocabulary as well as a lavish response from God. The request that YHWH "arise" and protect his "resting place" is answered with a report that God has "chosen" Zion and "desired" it as a place to dwell. This report is affirmed and amplified by God in the following verse, confirming this choice with a strategic and new possessive suffix, and adding a new horizon of permanence: "your resting place" (v. 8) becomes "my resting place forever" (v. 14).

Thus the three imperatives prayed for in the "we" section (vv. 8–10) and answered by God in the second half (vv. 13–18), nicely extend David's own earlier vow (vv. 3–5), which also initiates a divine response (vv. 11–12). Just as God responds to David's vow with a divine oath, so, too, does God respond to the several requests of the larger group with emphatic and expansive pronouncements. In Ps 132, human prayer is answered by a sympathetic and empathic deity.

David's vow to find a place for God and God's subsequent vow that he will set Davidides on the throne in Ps 132 inevitably brings to mind 2 Sam 7, where David notices that he is dwelling in a house of cedar and God promises him a dynasty. The play on "house" is not present in Ps 132, but there is a similar interchange between concern for divine space and promises of dynasty.[8]

Where the two accounts differ is in the portrayal of God's responsiveness. In 2 Sam 7, David places the ark in the city, then briefly notes the architectural discrepancy: "I am dwelling in a house of cedar, while the ark of YHWH abides in a tent." In response, God utters an eleven-verse-long objection: "You are not the one to build the house for me to live in. Indeed, I have not lived in a temple from the day I brought Israel out of Egypt until now.... I will raise up your descendent.... He will build a temple for my name, and I will establish his royal throne forever" (2 Sam 7:5–16). One might summarize this exchange as an extended "Okay, but..." interchange. In Ps 132, by contrast, there is more of a "Yes, and even more!" dynamic at play. David swears to God with a three-lined oath, and then God swears to David with a three-lined oath. In addition, God also responds to the

---

8. Possible linguistic plays at work in Ps 132 include the fact that David's vow (נדר; v. 2) results in the promise of a crown (נזרו; v. 18), as well as the interaction between the verbs ישב and שוב: "do not turn away..." (v. 10), "he will not turn back" (v. 11), "their sons shall sit enthroned" (v. 12), "for his seat" (v. 13), and "I will sit enthroned" (v. 14).

prayers of the people with a lavish extension of their request. The human community models and initiates, and God responds in kind.

Thus the signal features of identity that Ps 132 builds are the pilgrimage to Jerusalem and the Davidic dynasty as the result of the agency of human prayer. In the world of Ps 132, many of the traditional aspects of the Zion tradition are claimed, such as YHWH's choice of David and of Jerusalem as a dwelling place and the prosperity that ensues. Uniquely, however, these features emerge not as a result of a cosmic battle, or as a prior idea in the mind of God, but in direct response to the prayers of the community. This is regardless of whether or not earlier portions of liturgies or oracles were reused or even whether or not the divine speeches are simply somehow modeling something to God; as the text stands now, in its own internal timeline, the requests motivate the response, and the response is more than simply a divine *reaction* to the prayer, as scholars like Erich Zenger claim.[9] By repeating key features of the requests, God's promises appear closely *shaped* by the prayers. In Ps 132, the acts and prayers of the human community are valorized as influential on the divine world.

2. 2 Chronicles 6:41–42

In the second reception of Ps 132 into the biblical corpus during the Persian-Hellenistic period, the Chronicler also reuses verses 8–10 to promote a distinctive vision of religious geography and practice as well as communal identity. Even as the reused text remains substantively the same, however, the new literary context, small strategic changes, and omission of the entirety of the psalm enable the author to construct a very different program of identity.

2.1. Sanctioning the Account's Authority, Jerusalem's Priority, and David's Cultic Initiatives

The Chronicler includes a close paraphrase[10] of Ps 132:8–10 to conclude Solomon's prayer dedicating the newly built temple (2 Chr 6:41–42):

---

9. Zenger, "Psalms 132," 458. See also J. Clinton McCann Jr.'s assertion that Ps 132:11–18 maintains a "clear emphasis on God's initiative" in *The Book of Psalms*, NIB 4 (Nashville: Abingdon, 1996), 1212.

10. The changes are fairly minimal and include the addition of ועתה to introduce the quote, the expansion of the divine name יהוה to יהוה אלהים (and used two additional

> 6:41   Now come, YHWH God, to/for the sake of your resting place,
>   You and the ark of your might.
>   Let your priests, YHWH God, be clothed with salvation;
>   And your faithful ones rejoice in prosperity.
>
> 6:42   YHWH God, do not reject your anointed ones,
>   Remember for the sake of (your) faithfulness to (לחסדי)[11] David
>   your servant.

This conclusion is absent in the parallel account in 1 Kgs 8:22–53, as is the following display of fire descending from heaven to consume the sacrifices and offerings and YHWH's glory filling the temple (2 Chr 7:1).

This is the second of two major quotations from the Psalms in Chronicles, and it lines up with the author's thematic emphases and literary style.[12] Earlier in the book, 1 Chr 16 included a blend of Pss 105:1–15; 96:1–13; and 106:1, 47–48, likewise in a cultic context with a connection to the ark.[13] And, like the Chronicler's adoption of the text of Samuel-Kings, these quotes from the Psalms are unattributed within the work.[14] Importing source texts (especially when absent in the parallel account

---

times); "resting place" in 132:8 (מנוחתך) replaced with "rest" in 6:41 (נוחך); "righteousness" in 132:9 replaced with "victory" in 6:41 (תשועה; but see ישע in 132:16); "let shout for joy" in 132:9 replaced with "rejoice in prosperity" in 6:41. According to Klein, the emphasis moves from the people's cultic actions to "a concern for their overall welfare" (Ralph W. Klein, *2 Chronicles: A Commentary*, Hermeneia [Minneapolis: Fortress, 2012], 99). I discuss the specific changes in the treatment of 132:10 later in this essay.

11. Read as a subjective genitive, with H. G. M. Williamson, "The Sure Mercies of David: Subjective or Objective Genitive?," *JSS* 23 (1978): 31–49. For an argument that it should be read as an objective genitive, in parallel with the use of חסדי in connection with other notable kings in Chronicles such as Hezekiah and Josiah (2 Chr 32:32; 35:26), see Pancratius C. Beentjes, *Tradition and Transformation in the Book of Chronicles*, SSN 52 (Leiden: Brill, 2008), 173–74.

12. See Howard N. Wallace, "What Chronicles Has to Say About Psalms," in *The Chronicler as Author: Studies in Text and Texture*, ed. M. Patrick Graham and Steven L. McKenzie, JSOTSup 263 (Sheffield: Sheffield Academic, 1999), 267–91; Pancratius C. Beentjes, *Tradition and Transformation in the Book of Chronicles*, SSN 52 (Leiden: Brill, 2008), esp. 169–75.

13. For more, see Ralph W. Klein, "Psalms in Chronicles," *CurTM* 32 (2005): 264–75.

14. For a discussion of the places where the author does cite or allude to sources, see Ralph W. Klein, *1 Chronicles: A Commentary*, Hermeneia (Minneapolis: Fortress, 2006), 39–44.

in 1 Kgs 8:22–54) ascribes authority to the account. With the use of Ps 132, the Chronicler signals that his version of the temple's dedication is ancient and reliable.

The use of Ps 132:8–10 relates well to the larger emphases of the book of Chronicles, especially the focus on Jerusalem and the significance of temple worship for national identity, as well as Davidic authority for the cult. Throughout the book of Chronicles, Jerusalem is mentioned repeatedly, much more frequently than the source text of Samuel-Kings and ten times before David even attempts to capture the city (1 Chr 11:4).[15] In addition to its ubiquity within the book, the city and its worship play a distinctive role in the identity construction of the people of God. With key ritual practices such as sacrifice disallowed outside of Jerusalem, the faithful are thus obliged to make regular pilgrimages to the central cult site.[16] And, although the author is clear that the northern kingdom (with its alternative worship sites and non-Davidic king) is illegitimate, he emphasizes the participation of "all Israel" in key moments of the Jerusalem cult. For instance, only David and his army capture Jerusalem and transfer the ark in the account in Samuel (2 Sam 5:6; 6:1), but in the Chronicler's account, the participants include "all Israel" (1 Chr 11:4–5; 13:2, 5, 6; 15:3, 28). In addition, the temple is the key vehicle for the north to obtain divine forgiveness and reunification with the south—as Hezekiah beseeches the apostate Israel: "yield yourselves to YHWH and come to his sanctuary" (2 Chr 30:8). Finally, the book concludes with the assertion that the return from exile has the single purpose of rebuilding the temple in Jerusalem (2 Chr 36:23).[17]

---

15. As Isaac Kalimi notes, "in Chronicles little happens without some connection to Jerusalem"; for more on this point, see his "Jerusalem—The Divine City: The Representation of Jerusalem in Chronicles Compared with Earlier and Later Jewish Compositions," in *The Chronicler as Theologian: Essays in Honor of Ralph W. Klein*, ed. M. Patrick Graham, Steven L. McKenzie, and Gary N. Knoppers, JSOTSup 371 (London: T&T Clark, 2003), 189–205, here 205; see also Hugh G. M. Williamson, *Studies in Persian Period History and Historiography*, FAT 38 (Tübingen: Mohr Siebeck, 2004), 150–61.

16. See Melody D. Knowles, "1 and 2 Chronicles," in *Theological Bible Commentary*, Gail R. O'Day and David L. Petersen (Louisville: Westminster John Knox, 2009), 145–54, esp. 151–54.

17. For more on exclusive ritual geography, sacrifice, and pilgrimage in Chronicles, see Melody D. Knowles, *Centrality Practiced: Jerusalem in the Religious Practice of Yehud and the Diaspora in the Persian Period*, ABS 16 (Atlanta: SBL Press, 2006), 32–38, 91–92.

Alongside the centrality of Jerusalem within the book of Chronicles is the emphasis on the role of David as the one who established its cult. Although it is Solomon who builds the temple, the Chronicler inserts many additional chapters into the Samuel-Kings source to detail David's procurement of the building materials, his setup of the priestly orders and singers, and more (see especially 1 Chr 22–26).

Given these emphases in the whole book of Chronicles, the insertion of a section of Ps 132 (a text that promotes both David as well as the temple) makes sense. The psalm also links up with immediate context of Solomon's prayer with its assertion of God's choice of Jerusalem and David (6:6), David's desire to build the house of God and Solomon's completion of the project (6:7–10), the placement of the ark in the temple (6:11), and the conditional dynastic promise (6:16).

2.2. Subverting David's Kingship and God's Responsiveness

In the quotation, the Chronicler changes some aspects of Ps 132, both explicitly via the textual alteration of verses 8–10 and implicitly via the omission of the rest of the verses. The verse that is the most altered is verse 42 (the Chronicler's version of Ps 132:10), as a direct comparison shows:

> Ps 132:10: For the sake of David your servant, do not reject your anointed one
> 2 Chr 6:42: YHWH God, do not reject your anointed ones, Remember for the sake of (your) faithfulness to (לחסדי) David your servant.

In addition to the typical insertion of "YHWH God" (used twice before in 6:41), the author also reverses the order of the two verses, changes "anointed one" into a plural, and expands the second half to include additional elements ("Remember for the sake of [your] faithfulness…").[18] These changes work to move the prayer away from God's ongoing protection of the king and dynasty, as well as downplaying David's distinctive role in the generation of the divine promises. In verse 42, God is less the responsive partner who supports the Davidic line and the Jerusalem cult and more the exalted deity whose past acts of faithfulness are the model for the future blessing of the temple cult.

---

18. The LXX changes "anointed one" to the singular in its version of 2 Chr 6:42, but, as the *lectio difficilior*, the MT is preferred.

Significantly, what the Chronicler changes and leaves out of Ps 132 also links up with central themes both in the immediate context of Solomon's prayer as well as throughout the larger work. Most clear is the lack of focus on the promise to David. By leaving out David's vow and God's response (Ps 132:3–5; 11–12) the king loses his primary place in the text, supplanted by the temple and the people.[19] This treatment of David is consonant with the rest of the book of Chronicles, where the emphasis is less on the king as founder of a dynasty and more on his role as cultic organizer and paragon of piety.[20] Any hope for the return of the Davidic monarchy or new messiah that Ps 132 may keep alive in the Persian Period is subverted by the Chronicler's treatment of the text.

The changes and omissions also highlight the overwhelming power of God that is singularly distinct from the human community. The king's dedicatory prayer in 2 Chr 6 emphasizes the signal role of God in the building of the temple: "Bless YHWH, the God of Israel, who spoke directly to my father David and now has kept his promise" (2 Chr 6:4). This stress on God's primary role is also seen in the earlier account of God's promise to David in 1 Chr 17:1–15, an account largely carried over from the source of 2 Sam 7:1–16. By leaving out David's vow (Ps 132:3–5) and God's response that repeats and expands the requests of the human community (Ps 132:11–18), the Chronicler avoids the implication that God is influenced by anything other than the divine world. Similar to the author of 2 Sam 7, the Chronicler champions a program for communal identity that downplays human agency as a precipitating cause of divine action. It is telling that, given the Chronicler's avoidance of any sense of divine reciprocity via repetition, God's response to Solomon's prayer is nonverbal. Instead of repeating (and expanding) the requests from the human community, God indicates approval by a bolt from the sky.

---

19. As Klein puts it, the Chronicler "inverts" the priorities of Ps 132 (Klein, "Psalms in Chronicles," 270–72).

20. For more on the treatment of David in the biblical text, see John Van Seters, *The Biblical Saga of King David* (Winona Lake, IN: Eisenbrauns, 2009); Jacob L. Wright, *David, King of Israel, and Caleb in Biblical Memory* (New York: Cambridge University Press, 2014). For more detailed studies of the treatment of David in Chronicles, see Gary N. Knoppers, "Images of David in Early Judaism: David as Repentant Sinner in Chronicles," *Bib* 76 (1995): 449–70; William M. Schniedewind, *Society and the Promise to David: The Reception History of 2 Samuel 7:1–17* (Oxford: Oxford University Press, 1999), 128–34.

Thus by inclusion, adaptation, and omission of parts of Ps 132, the Chronicler recasts the borrowed text to promote a program in harmony with the rest of the book but in many ways distinct from the entirety of the complete psalm. Using the same words of the same prayer, 2 Chr 6:41–42 constructs a very different vision of religious identity and practice. In the Chronicler's hands, the text retains the emphasis on the role of Jerusalem (and, by extension, pilgrimage to it) as the center of God's presence on earth. In the context of diaspora, the temple is a key site of identity for the entire nation. Yet the Chronicler's version also downplays the role of David and the human community to influence the divine choice of the dynasty and city. Instead it emphasizes God's power to promise and to fulfill promises to be present in the temple. In many ways, the Chronicler reflects the theological impulses of the author of 2 Sam 7, a text that retained a place for the agency of David even as the purposes of God marched on with an almost overwhelming power. As the larger picture of the production and reception of texts in this period emerges, the reuse of Ps 132 is a salutary notice that authors are able to construct very different views of communal identity even as they reuse the same words of prayer.

Bibliography

Beentjes, Pancratius C. *Tradition and Transformation in the Book of Chronicles*. SSN 52. Leiden: Brill, 2008.

Cross, Frank Moore. *Canaanite Myth and Hebrew Epic: Essays in the History of the Religion of Israel*. Cambridge: Harvard University Press, 1973.

Crow, Loren D. *The Songs of Ascents (Psalms 120–134): Their Place in the Israelite History and Religion*. SBLDS 148. Atlanta: Scholars Press, 1996.

Deurloo, Karel A. "Gedächtnis des Exils: Psalmen 120–34." *T&K* 55 (1992): 28–34.

Fretheim, Terence E. "Ps 132: A Form-Critical Study." *JBL* 86 (1967): 289–300.

Gese, Hartmut. "Der Davidsbund und die Zionserwählung." Pages 113–29 in *Vom Sinai zum Zion: Alttestamentliche Beiträge zur biblischen Theologie*. BEvT 64. Munich: Kaiser, 1974.

Hillers, Delbert R. "Ritual Procession of the Ark and Ps 132." *CBQ* 30 (1968): 48–55.

Hossfeld, Frank-Lothar. "König David im Wallfahrtspsalter." Pages 219–33 in *Ein Herz so weit wie der Sand am Ufer des Meeres: Festschrift für*

Georg Hentschel. Edited by Susanne Gillmayr-Bucher, Anette Giercke, and Christina Nießen. ETS 90. Würzburg: Echter, 2006.

Hurvitz, Avi. "The Chronological Significance of 'Aramaisms' in Biblical Hebrew." *IEJ* 18 (1968): 234–40.

———. *The Transition Period in Biblical Hebrew: A Study in Post-exilic Hebrew and Its Implications for the Dating of Psalms*. Jerusalem: Bialik Institute, 1972.

Huwiler, Elizabeth F. "Patterns and Problems in Psalm 132." Pages 199–215 in *The Listening Heart: Essays in Wisdom and the Psalms in Honor of Roland E. Murphy*. Edited by Kenneth G. Hoglund and Elizabeth F. Huwiler. JSOTSup 58. Sheffield: JSOT Press, 1987.

Kalimi, Isaac. "Jerusalem—The Divine City: The Representation of Jerusalem in Chronicles Compared with Earlier and Later Jewish Compositions." Pages 189–205 in *The Chronicler as Theologian: Essays in Honor of Ralph W. Klein*. Edited by M. Patrick Graham, Steven L. McKenzie, and Gary N. Knoppers. JSOTSup 371. London: T&T Clark, 2003.

Klein, Ralph W. *1 Chronicles: A Commentary*. Hermeneia. Minneapolis: Fortress, 2006.

———. *2 Chronicles: A Commentary*. Hermeneia. Minneapolis: Fortress, 2012.

———. "Psalms in Chronicles." *CurTM* 32 (2005): 264–75.

Knoppers, Gary N. "Images of David in Early Judaism: David as Repentant Sinner in Chronicles." *Bib* 76 (1995): 449–70.

Knowles, Melody D. "1 and 2 Chronicles." Pages 145–54 in *Theological Bible Commentary*. Edited by Gail R. O'Day and David L. Petersen. Louisville: Westminster John Knox, 2009.

———. *Centrality Practiced: Jerusalem in the Religious Practice of Yehud and the Diaspora in the Persian Period*. ABS 16. Atlanta: SBL Press, 2006.

Kruse, Heinz. "Psalm CXXXII and the Royal Zion Festival." *VT* 33 (1983): 279–97.

Laato, Antti. "Psalm 132: A Case Study in Methodology." *CBQ* 61 (1999): 24–33.

———. "Psalm 132 and the Development of the Jerusalemite/Israelite Royal Ideology." *CBQ* 54 (1992): 49–66.

McCann, J. Clinton, Jr. *The Book of Psalms*. NIB 4. Nashville: Abingdon, 1996.

Mettinger, Tryggve N. D. *King and Messiah: The Civil and Sacral Legitimation of the Israelite Kings*. ConBOT 8. Lund: Gleerup, 1976.

Patton, Corrine L. "Psalm 132: A Methodological Inquiry." *CBQ* 57 (1995): 643–54.

Perlitt, Lothar. *Bundestheologie im Alten Testament*. WMANT 36. Neukirchen-Vluyn: Neukirchener Verlag, 1969.

Rendsburg, Gary A. *Linguistic Evidence for the Northern Origin of Selected Psalms*. SBLMS 43. Atlanta: Scholars Press, 1990.

Schniedewind, William M. *Society and the Promise to David: The Reception History of 2 Samuel 7:1–17*. Oxford: Oxford University Press, 1999.

Seow, C. L. *Myth, Drama, and the Politics of David's Dance*. HSM 44. Atlanta: Scholars Press, 1989.

Seybold, Klaus. *Die Wallfahrtspsalmen: Studien zur Entstehungsgeschichte von Psalm 120–34*. BThSt 3. Neukirchen-Vluyn: Neukirchener Verlag, 1978.

Tsevat, Matitiahu. "Studies in the Book of Samuel III: The Steadfast House; What Was David Promised in II Sam. 7:11b–16?" *HUCA* 34 (1963): 71–82.

Van Seters, John. *The Biblical Saga of King David*. Winona Lake, IN: Eisenbrauns, 2009.

Veijola, Timo. *Verheißung in der Krise: Studien zur Literatur und Theologie des Exilszeit anhand des 89. Psalms*. AASF 220. Helsinki: Suomalainen Tiedeakatemia, 1982.

Wallace, Howard N. "What Chronicles Has to Say about Psalms." Pages 267–91 in *The Chronicler as Author: Studies in Text and Texture*. Edited by M. Patrick Graham and Steven L. McKenzie. JSOTSup 263. Sheffield: Sheffield Academic, 1999.

Williamson, H. G. M. *Studies in Persian Period History and Historiography*. FAT 38. Tübingen: Mohr Siebeck, 2004.

———. "The Sure Mercies of David: Subjective or Objective Genitive?" *JSS* 23 (1978): 31–49.

Wright, Jacob L. *David, King of Israel, and Caleb in Biblical Memory*. New York: Cambridge University Press, 2014.

Zenger, Erich. "Der Zion als Ort der Gottesnähe: Beobachtungen zum Weltbild des Wallfahrtspsalters Ps 120–134." Pages 84–114 in *Gottes Nähe im Alten Testament*. Edited by Gönke Eberhardt and Kathrin Liess. SBS 202. Stuttgart: Katholisches Bibelwerk, 2004.

———. "Psalm 132." Pages 454–68 in *Psalms 3: A Commentary on Psalms 101–50*. Edited by Klaus Baltzer. Translated by Linda M. Maloney. Hermeneia. Minneapolis: Fortress, 2011.

Aspects of Dynamic Remembering and Constructing in Psalm 145: A Contribution to the Study of Prayer in Persian and Hellenistic Times

Nancy Rahn

There is no sense to any political speech, theological innovation and scientific discovery; nor to any part of human dialogue in this world, if it is not understood as a variation of something. A variation of something that is shared by the speaker and his audience, something they have in common and want to preserve and perpetuate, but as a variation that leads into a new future.[1]

1. Introduction

"Talk to God as if humans would listen" is a well-known maxim ascribed to Seneca, one of the locals of Cordoba. His remark contains an apparently obvious insight: prayer talks not only to and about God but also to and about humans. This may be the reason why the topic of prayer is experiencing an upswing in all theological subject areas. Discussion of prayer has the potential to bring together people with different perspectives on theology, gather them around a table, and generate new questions together Many publications in the field of biblical studies and related sciences dem-

---

1. Eugen Rosenstock-Huessy, *Die Sprache des Menschengeschlechts: Eine leibhaftige Grammatik in vier Teilen; Erster und zweiter Teil*, vol. 1 of *Die Sprache des Menschengeschlechts: Eine leibhaftige Grammatik in vier Teilen* (Heidelberg: Schneider, 1963), 318, my translation (original: "Keine Parteirede, keine theologische Neuerung, keine wissenschaftliche Entdeckung, kein Teil eines Zwiegesprächs in dieser Welt ist sinnvoll, wenn es nicht verstanden wird als eine Variation von etwas, das der Sprecher und seine Zuhörerschaft gemeinsam haben und bewahren, aber als eine Variation, durch die der Sprecher in eine neue Zukunft führt.").

onstrate the potential of prayer texts to illuminate ancient theologies and anthropologies anew. These poetic and hymnal texts may be understood as testimonies that aim to create a relationship between God and humans, to paint a picture of reality—or even desired reality—and in that way shape the cultural memory of a certain community.[2] For a large number of these texts, the categories of *remembering* and *constructing* may be characterized as their own specific method: they remember traditional materials by gathering, reviving, and sharpening them, and they construct new entities, especially through new contextualization, as they speak into consistently changing realities. Thus texts of this kind involve their recipients in theological reasoning and its identity-shaping effects.

But what difference does it make if theological and anthropological insights are offered in the form of prayers? And what role do the Persian and Hellenistic periods as a time of remembering and constructing in literary production play in this? By examining a late text of the Hebrew Psalter, Ps 145, we will arrive at possible answers to these questions.

After giving a translation and an overview of the psalm's structure as well as examining hints to its possible origin in (late) Persian / (early) Hellenistic times, this essay aims to shed light on the question of which specific features characterize Ps 145 as a text of prayer. Special attention is given to its superscription, which is unique in the Psalter but has not received the scholarly consideration it deserves. Does it mark the text as a special type of prayer and what implications does it have for the understanding of the psalm as a whole within its context? Furthermore, we will trace aspects of dynamic remembering and constructing in Ps 145 by examining its images of God and humans, which are put into relationship throughout the entire text. Afterward, we will also analyze the text with respect to Israelite identity. Because of the text's universal character, two questions arise: To what extent does Ps 145 construct *Israelite* identity? What roles do different types of contextualization play in the history of the text. A short conclusion completes this study by positioning it within the wider context of this volume.

---

2. As an example, for the examination of prayer texts referring to a (relatively) distinct group, see Qumran studies such as Carol Ann Newsom, *The Self as Symbolic Space: Constructing Identity and Community at Qumran*, STDJ 52 (Leiden: Brill, 2004); Bilhah Nitzan, *Qumran Prayer and Religious Poetry*, trans. Jonathan Chipman, STDJ 12 (Leiden: Brill, 1994).

1.1. Text and Structure of Psalm 145[3]

(1) A Davidic praise	תהלה לדוד
I will exalt you, my God the king / O king! and I will bless your name for all times and further.	ארוממך אלוהי המלך ואברכה שמך לעולם ועד:
(2) Every day I will bless you, and I will praise your name for all times and further.	בכל־יום אברכך ואהללה שמך לעולם ועד:
(3) Great is YHWH and very praiseworthy, and to his greatness there is no limit ("in research").	גדול יהוה ומהלל מאד ולגדלתו אין חקר:
(4) One generation to the other will glorify your works, and your mighty deeds they will make known.	דור לדור ישבח מעשיך וגבורתיך יגידו:
(5) On the splendor of the glory of your majesty, and on the words / events of your wonders I will meditate.	הדר כבוד הודך ודברי נפלאותיך אשיחה:
(6) And the power of your awesome deeds they will tell, and your greatness I will recount.	ועזוז נוראתיך יאמרו וגדולתיך [ו][גדולתך] אספרנה:
(7) The memory of your abundant goodness they will pass on, and of your righteousness they will sing.	זכר רב־טובך יביעו וצדקתך ירננו:
(8) Gracious and compassionate is YHWH, slow to anger and great of faithfulness.	חנון ורחום יהוה ארך אפים וגדל־חסד:
(9) Good is YHWH to all, and his compassions are over all his works.	טוב־יהוה לכל ורחמיו על־כל־מעשיו:
(10) They will give thanks to you, YHWH, all your works, and your faithful ones will bless you.	יודוך יהוה כל־מעשיך וחסידיך יברכוכה:
(11) The glory of your kingdom they will tell, and of your mighty deeds they will speak,	כבוד מלכותך יאמרו וגבורתך ידברו:
(12) to make known to the children of humanity his mighty deeds, and the glory of the splendor of his kingdom.	להודיע לבני האדם גבורתיו וכבוד הדר מלכותו:

---

3. Unless otherwise noted, all biblical translations are mine.

(13) Your kingdom is a kingdom for all times, and your dominion from one generation to the other. מלכותך מלכות כל־עלמים
וממשלתך בכל־דור ודור:

(14) A supporter is YHWH to all who are falling, and one who lifts up all who are bent down. סומך יהוה לכל־הנפלים
וזוקף לכל־הכפופים:

(15) The eyes of all, to you they look, and you are the one who gives them their food in its time, עיני־כל אליך ישברו
ואתה נותן־להם את־אכלם
בעתו:

(16) opening your hand and satisfying every living being with desire. פותח את־ידך
ומשביע לכל־חי רצון:

(17) Righteous is YHWH in all his ways, and faithful in all his works. צדיק יהוה בכל־דרכיו
וחסיד בכל־מעשיו:

(18) Near is YHWH to all who cry out to him, to all who cry out to him in truth. קרוב יהוה לכל־קראיו
לכל אשר יקראהו באמת:

(19) The desire of the ones who fear him he fulfills, and their cry for help he hears and saves them. רצון־יראיו יעשה
ואת־שועתם ישמע ויושיעם:

(20) A guardian is YHWH over all who love him, but all the evildoers he will destroy. שומר יהוה את־כל־אהביו
ואת כל־הרשעים ישמיד:

(21) The praise of YHWH my mouth will speak, and all flesh will bless the name of his holiness for all times and further. תהלת יהוה ידבר־פי
ויברך כל־בשר שם קדשו
לעולם ועד:

Considering the structure of Ps 145, different solutions are arguably plausible, depending on the criteria being used to identify different sections of the text.[4] For the purpose of this study, a concentric structure proves helpful to enhance the understanding of the text's different dynamics.[5]

---

4. For an overview of different suggestions considering the structures of Ps 145 and the difficulty of deciding on the one with the most promising heuristic potential, see Friederike Neumann, *Schriftgelehrte Hymnen: Gestalt, Theologie und Intention der Psalmen 145 und 146–150*, BZAW 491 (Berlin: de Gruyter, 2016), 43.

5. Concentric structures for Ps 145 may also be found in the work of Weber, *Die Psalmen 73–150*, vol. 2 of *Werkbuch Psalmen* (Stuttgart: Kohlhammer, 2003), 367–68; Bernd Janowski, *Konfliktgespräche mit Gott: Eine Anthropologie der Psalmen*, 4th ed. (Neukirchen-Vluyn: Neukirchener Verlag, 2013), 370–72.

Superscription

Framework with characterizations: the praying subject (I) as always praising, the king (God) as the one who is always praised (vv. 1–2)
>   Part 1: YHWH's greatness as the content of the orator's praise / YHWH's deeds as theme of the proclamation of all generations (vv. 3–7)
>   Part 2: YHWH's goodness as the content of the praise of all his works (vv. 8–9)
>   Center: the universality of YHWH's kingdom (vv. 10–13)
>   Part 3: YHWH's care brought into focus—support and supply for all the living (vv. 14–17)
>   Part 4: YHWH's care brought into focus—his addressability and comprehensive action for mankind (vv. 18–20)

Framework: The praising subject (I) / the universality of praise (v. 21)

Other principles of construction, however, should be kept in mind, such as the alphabetical acrostic, with its rhetorical function and reader-leading indications. This most distinctive surface structure, which creates the basic frame for the message of the text, has often been neglected or was at least not evaluated as an important part of the psalm. Psalm 145 is one in a long history of acrostics—and, more specifically, abecedary compositions—that in a strikingly large number of cases appear with prayers, in both hymns of praise and laments.[6] This form has inspired a variety of different interpretations. One very important aspect for Ps 145 may be summarized with a quote by Adele Berlin: "The entire alphabet, the source of all words, is marshalled in praise of God. One cannot actually use all of the words in a language, but by using the alphabet, one uses all potential words. So, the form is made to serve the message."[7] Furthermore, the linear structure from א to ת underlines the notional path of prayer on which the praying subject may be shadowed by the reader through the text. Thus it adds a perspective that may supplement the concentric reading.

---

6. Besides other psalms of the Hebrew Bible, examples are the Apostrophe to Zion from Qumran, the long history of piyyutim in rabbinic literature, early Christian hymns, hymns from the Middle Ages, and many more.

7. Adele Berlin, "The Rhetoric of Psalm 145," in *Biblical and Related Studies Presented to Samuel Iwry*, ed. Ann Kort and Scott Morschauser (Winona Lake, IN: Eisenbrauns, 1985), 17–22, quote at 18.

Researchers of Ps 145 have made various attempts to date the text, ranging from the time of the Davidic kingdom well into Hellenistic times. Nonetheless, since the nineteenth century, a broad consensus has formed among biblical scholars that the text has a postexilic origin, probably in late Persian / early Hellenistic times. Frank-Lothar Hossfeld writes in his commentary on Ps 145:

> The final psalm of the last Davidic Psalter is, with a broad consensus in exegetical scholarship, a late postexilic psalm. Aspects in favor of this dating are the Aramaizing language (see, e.g., שבח, "to praise," and מלכות, "kingdom"), the anthological style, the acrostic that points to wisdom literature, the concentration on God's kingdom and the distinctive universalism. As a possible temporal classification, the fourth century BCE may be considered, rather toward the end of the Persian era.[8]

In terms of composition/redaction history, Ps 145 is most likely part of the final redaction of the book of Psalms in its manifestation as the Hebrew Psalter. Its role as a hinge between the last Davidic Psalter and the final *hallel* may even point to the conclusion that the text was originally designed for this position as the finale of the Psalter.[9] The Persian and Hellenistic eras, which were the context for the collection and formative redaction of the Psalter, can be considered as times with a special need for remembering and constructing, as may be seen in texts like Ps 145. Religious wisdom is gathered, sorted, recorded, and transformed; theological geography has to be reexamined; and political as well as religious concepts, such as questions of empire and power, have to be discussed against the background of changing realities. In all that, new concepts, such as the notion of God's kingdom,

---

8. Frank-Lothar Hossfeld and Erich Zenger, *Psalmen 101–50*, HThKAT (Freiburg im Breisgau: Herder, 2008), 789–807, here 796: "Der Schlusspsalm des fünften Davidspsalters ist mit breitem Konsens unter den Exegeten ein später nachexilischer Psalm. Dafür sprechen seine aramaisierende Sprache (vgl. שבח 'rühmen' und מלכות 'Königtum'), der anthologische Stil, die weisheitliche Form des Akrostichons, die Konzentration auf das Königtums JHWHs und der spezifische Universalismus. Möglich für eine zeitliche Einordnung erscheint das 4. Jh. v. Chr., eher gegen Ende der persischen Epoche."

9. I am not able to elaborate here on the exact relationship between the final groups of the Psalter, their internal coherence and possible development, and the place of Ps 145 in this composition. On the ongoing discussion, see, e.g., Neumann, *Schriftgelehrte Hymnen*, 429–49.

emerged.[10] This, however, is only one of several homes for Ps 145.[11] Its history encompasses a number of contexts, in antiquity and later on, that are equally interesting for generating different possibilities for understanding the psalm itself. The following aspects that illustrate the psalm's method of remembering and constructing may also prove helpful for analyzing the long history of Ps 145 and its central motif, God's kingdom.

2. Psalm 145: Prayer

Interestingly, the prayer aspects of Ps 145 are commonly underestimated in commentaries and studies on the text. This is a fate it shares with other hymnal texts of the Second Temple period that, at first sight, present theological reflection rather than communication between God and humans. A main point of the attraction of this literature, however, may precisely have been the combination of both aspects: theological reasoning and existential communication. In analyzing these texts, we should stay attentive to the questions we normally address to prayer texts, such as: Who is praying? Who is addressed? How may the relation between "I" and the community be characterized? Is there a possible liturgical setting? Texts like Ps 145 do reflect, in their particular ways, the situation of mankind *coram Deo*.[12] The dialogic structure of such texts refer to the relationship not only between God and humankind but also between the different members of creation. This feature of prayer texts points to the special role they play in the history of theological and anthropological insights.

2.1. Individual Prayer and Community

Already in verse 1 we encounter the two protagonists of prayer: the praising subject, as praying man or woman, and the praised, blessed God,

---

10. "New," of course, has a problematic notion here. As we will see later on, it is all about remembering "old(er)" traditions, gathering them in new forms of compilations, transforming them, and bringing them to a point in terms like מלכות יהוה.

11. For the idea of biblical texts as "nomadic" texts that, "wherever we encounter them, ... are not quite at home," see Brennan W. Breed, *Nomadic Text: A Theory of Biblical Reception History* (Bloomington: Indiana University Press, 2014), here 202.

12. See Janowski, "Konfliktgespräche," 11: "In der Situation 'vor Gott' (*coram Deo*) ereignet sich also nach alttestamentlichem Zeugnis die Menschwerdung des Menschen."

imagined as king and represented by his name in the second part of the verse. Subsequently, the prayer, the song of praise, is not restricted to the action of reciting a certain text, an action taking place between the individual and his or her God at a certain time and place. It is rather claimed as a way of life (see חי, v. 21) for all humankind, corresponding to the kingdom of God by its ability to encompass both time and space. In a more narrow sense, Ps 145 is a prayer of praise, which, like many others, weighs fundamental questions about God, man and the world. As such, it is not unanimous but polyphonic in itself, pervaded by changes in the direction of speech, confessional insertions, and/or meditations.[13]

By examining the different perspectives on God and the world in Ps 145, we encounter important dynamics that also have led to simplifying divisions of the psalm into two parts: the first one focusing on the praying individual(s) and the second one pointing to God in action.[14] In addition to the fact that the subject of the psalm does not change, the manifold perspectives and the plurivalent motifs preclude such a strict distinction. The perception of Ps 145 as a prayer leads to the recognition of a more complex, purposeful composition of the text. The development from the praying subject ("I") to the praying/praising collective of "all flesh" does not eliminate the individual but keeps it until the end as "my mouth." The prayer is directed to God but spoken by humanity on earth, and in time it appears as an explicitly social phenomenon. As such, it affects the individuals in their community, but it also transcends the group of actually present living beings, as it points both back into the past and also to the future of humanity. By paying attention to these social dimensions of the text, the prayer more comprehensively shows its theological potential. It raises hope and commitment for God's kingdom, but it also raises awareness of realities that fundamentally contradict the psalm's notion of God's kingdom.[15] Both may lead not only to a change in

---

13. A short definition of prayer that especially points to the diversity of voices can be found in Thomas Staubli and Silvia Schroer, *Menschenbilder der Bibel* (Ostfildern: Patmos, 2014), 541–51.

14. See, e.g., David Blumenthal, "Psalm 145: A Liturgical Reading," in *Hesed ve-emet: Studies in Honor of of Ernest S. Frerichs*, ed. Jodi Magness and Seymour Gitin, BJS 320 (Atlanta: Scholars Press, 1998), 17–18, 21. This view is rightly challenged also by Neumann, *Schriftgelehrte Hymnen*, 44.

15. On that, see Walter Brueggemann, *Israel's Praise: Doxology against Idolatry and Ideology*, 2nd ed. (Philadelphia: Fortress, 1988), 3.

the dynamics of identity shaping within a certain community but also to action, as the psalm itself illustrates.

2.2. Praise and Lament

Another dynamic tied to the prayer form of Ps 145 is the Psalter-enveloping dynamic of human action in praise and lament. In Ps 145, the prayer emanates from praise but does not exclude lament, which surfaces primarily in the second half of the text with the roots קרא and שוע. The experience of need and deprivation lingers under the immediate surface of the text and materializes in the various textual and historical contexts that the text may point to. Rather than focusing on the dangers of reality and strategies for coping with them, a prayer like Ps 145 may serve as a means to temporarily step into a world not yet in existence but reasonably hoped for. Steps of this kind may even reestablish a sense of life and inspire praise when the reader or subject experiences turmoil. This proleptic character links different (hymnal) prayers throughout the centuries of dialogue between God and humans, and it is an important point of comparison between Ps 145 and other (antique) Jewish and Christian attempts to describe God in the image of kingship. Moreover, it also shares a critical potential: the world is not (yet) as it should be. Prayer, including one that excessively and joyously praises God, may at the same time admonish him to show up as the God he is already praised as: the righteous and compassionate king.

In prayer, reasoning—or to use the text's Hebrew term, "research" (v. 3: חקר)—on God may be reflected in hymnal form. This mode of hymnal theology is decisive for the time- and culture-comprising history of prayer to the point of modern reasoning on the function of prayer texts in liturgical contexts and interreligious dialogue. In the way that Ps 145 is poetically designed as a text of theological meditation, it especially points to the later history of Jewish praying that in many cases put together new prayers from scribal tradition.[16] Thus it contributes not only to the audio-visual character of liturgy but also to liturgy as an intellectual experience. This art of constructing prayer texts through remembering—that is, through recomposition—by no means represents a reduction of artistry but rather raises a claim of its own.

---

16. For Ps 145 and the final *hallel* as "scribal hymns," see Neumann, *Schriftgelehrte Hymnen*, 481–83.

2.3. The Superscription

Psalm 145 may be seen as a piece of art, a description of God's action that is seemingly totally self-contained, starting with א ending with ת. The designation of the psalm, which was given to it during the history of its composition and integration into the known corpus of Psalms, is easily overlooked, even though it marks the text as a special type of prayer. A short look at the *Forschungsgeschichte* emphasizes this fact. In some commentaries, the superscription is not even displayed as part of the text, and only a few attend to its content and meaning for the psalm and the special position it has in the Psalter.[17] The annotators looking for an explanation widely agree that the superscription was inspired by the use of תהלה in verse 21, the ת-verse, and attributed to the text secondarily. The effect, achieved by this connection of keywords, would be the enhancement of the *inclusio* framing the psalm.[18] Even though this observation is undoubtedly persuasive, the designation of Ps 145 as תהלה may be further deciphered and clarified.[19] The designation תהלה occurs only once in the superscriptions of the (biblical) psalms, which raises the questions of why exactly this otherwise commonly used term is employed here, together with לדוד, and whether that might tell us something about the pragmatics and the understanding of the text as a whole.[20]

---

17. In more recent commentaries, one can often find short remarks considering the superscription; for example, Hossfeld and Zengeralso offer a short analysis of the vocabulary of praise within the psalm in *Psalmen 101–50*, 789–807. The latest study that includes an analysis of Ps 145 draws attention to the superscription and emphasizes the change in the picture of David that may be deduced from 145:1–21; see Neumann, *Schriftgelehrte Hymnen*, 54–55.

18. See Hossfeld and Zenger, *Psalmen 101–50*, 797.

19. A first step in this direction is made by Thijs Booij in "Psalm CXLV: David's Song of Praise," *VT* 58 (2008): 633–37. In a short note on Ps 145, he especially points to the connection between the Chronicles and Ps 145 and comes to the conclusion that the superscription of Ps 145 was not ascribed to the text by the hand of a redactor but rather can be traced back to the hand of the author. Nonetheless, it is important to point out that the superscription, whether original or already a piece of reception, is tightly connected to the text. This may be further illustrated by a careful examination of the term תהלה.

20. On the importance of the superscriptions of the biblical psalms, see now Bernd Janowski, "'Die Hindin der Morgenröte' (Ps 22,1): Ein Beitrag zum Verständnis der Psalmenüberschriften," in *Psalmen und Chronik: Aspekte ihres Verhältnisses*, ed. Friedhelm Hartenstein and Thomas Willi, FAT (Tübingen: Mohr Siebeck, forthcoming).

The term תהלה is part of a rich vocabulary of praise in the Hebrew Bible. Occurrences of the verbal root הלל, typically with reference to God, and the noun form תהלה are concentrated in the Psalter.[21] The evidence is spread throughout the whole book of תהלים, whereupon the group of psalms Pss 146–150, the final *hallel*, holds a special position. The verb הלל is here, as is well known, *the* leading verb, and the noun תהלה also appears repeatedly. Thus the actual superscription tightly connects Ps 145 with the following group of psalms that conclude the Hebrew Psalter in its present form.

In order to understand the special character of the superscription, we should take a closer look at the range of meanings of תהלה as it is used in Ps 145 and elsewhere. The verbal form of הלל, together with the derived noun, is one of the most common terms of praise, even outside the Psalter. Unsurprisingly, תהלה often appears in parallel to other words expressing the praise of God—for example, in Ps 100:4 (תודה // תהלה) or in Neh 9:5 (תהלה // ברכה), but see also Neh 12:46 and 2 Chr 20:22. In Ps 145, similarly, הלל and its parallels ידה and ברך are the leading verbs of praise. Furthermore, they play an important role for the last third of the Psalter as a whole.[22]

The noun תהלה, however, not only marks a mode of speaking but also has a very significant meaning. God and his engagement with man and the world are, with a few exceptions, the content of תהלה. The תהלת יהוה is expressed in the Psalms; it is narrated, declared, acclaimed, and remembered.[23] The practical embodiment, the praise one can hear, and its foundation and content are closely connected, so that God may be called "God of my תהלה" (Ps 109:1) or even "my תהלה" (Deut 10:21). In Exod 15:11, the תהלות are directly referring to the deeds of the "wonderworker" (עשה פלא) YHWH. This is similar to Isa 63:7, where the deeds of God's חסד are the content of remembrance and praise.

To further characterize the תהלה, spatial and temporal descriptions are used, ascribing a special realm of action to it. It is supposed to be heard from "the ends of the earth" (Isa 42:10; compare also Ps 48:11) and be declared "on the islands" (Isa 42:12). It "fills the earth" (Hab 3:3), but it also directly refers to Zion and Jerusalem in some places (Ps 65:2; Isa 62:7) and serves as a description for the people of Israel in others (Deut 26:19; Jer 13:11;

---

21. For more details on the different occurrences, see Helmer Ringgren, "הלל I and II," *ThWAT* 2:434–41.

22. See Hossfeld and Zenger, *Psalmen 101–50*, 794–95.

23. Ringgren, "הלל I and II," 2:433–41.

33:9; Zeph 3:19). Here it is often used as a counterpart to facing destruction, expulsion, and suppression and thus contains a hint of promise and expectation. Even the widely traveled camels from Saba are carrying not only gold and silver but also the account of the תהלת יהוה (Isa 60:6). Alongside the promising aspect, which points to the expected implementation of the תהלה in the future, we have a number of descriptions characterizing its temporal dimension as "everlasting, perpetual." So, for example, in Pss 34:2; 35:28; 71:8, 14; 79:13, it is often combined with an aspect that is important as well for Ps 145: the praise, תהלה, is passed on from one generation to another. In addition, and more subtle, there are connections of תהלה with the steadfast character of God in his actions, expressed through the parallelization or the close linking of תהלה with God's name (Exod 15:11; Isa 42:8; 63:7; and, of course, Ps 145). Together, the passages mentioned form the background for the use of תהלה as a superscription in Ps 145. They show that תהלה inseparably connects a hymnal form and its content. Furthermore, there are often universal descriptions referring to space and time directly linked to it. Thus the superscription of Ps 145, a text aiming to sing the praise of YHWH "from א to ת," already strikes a thematic note. The noun תהלה is, overall, a term that comprises temporal aspects and thus connects generations and establishes identity. Communicated by proclaimed audible—as well as legible—praise, it guarantees that the content of praise stays alive. Ben Sira 44:1, 11b–15 points that out by referring to special role models in the history of faith: "Let us praise [הלל] the famous man and our fathers, one by one ... their generation stays/endures forever and their praise [תהלה] will not fade. They are buried in peace, but their name is forever. Humanity speaks of their wisdom and the congregation narrates/chronicles/records [ספר] their praise [תהלה]."

Obviously striking, in connection with the superscription of Ps 145, is the pslam's version at Qumran, which uses תפלה instead of the word we have discussed thus far: תהלה.[24] Ulrich Dahmen noticed that this completely runs against a tendency—described, for example, by Karl-Heinrich Ostmeyer—of avoiding cultic terminology in Qumranic/Essenic texts

---

24. For a discussion of the version of Psalm 145 in 11Q5, see Reinhard Kratz, "'Blessed Be the Lord and Blessed Be His Name Forever': Psalm 145 in the Hebrew Bible and in the Psalms Scroll 11Q5," in *Prayer and Poetry in the Dead Sea Scrolls and Related Literature: Essays in Honor of Eileen Schuller on the Occasion of Her 65th Birthday*, ed. Jeremy Penner, Ken M. Penner, and Cecilia Wassen, STDJ 98 (Leiden: Brill, 2012), 229–43. Kratz does not, however, respond to the changed superscription.

and thus using תהלה for תפלה.²⁵ The reason for a deliberate change in the Qumran version is a matter for discussion elsewhere. Nonetheless, Dahmen interprets the change as a liturgization of the text, which changes the "merely profane תהלה" to תפלה, a term with the character of "liturgical prayer."²⁶ While the description of תהלה as profane is disputable, especially in the light of the foregoing analysis of this term in the Hebrew Bible, it may well be imaginable that the terms תהלה and תפלה became increasingly exchangeable and that תפלה was used more frequently than תהלה for liturgical prayers.²⁷ It should be mentioned, however, that the contextualization of the psalm at Qumran not only creates a new superscription and thus destroys the inclusion of the text, but it also establishes a completely new frame of the text by adding a *subscriptio* and framing the psalm with other texts than the ones in the MT.

To these, quite speculative, remarks one could add an observation on possible dynamics between תהלה and תפלה in the Psalter and beyond. These dynamics, which also crystallize in the character of David, are reflected by the second part of the superscription. David is both the one who is moaning, thronged, and in need of rescue and also the servant of YHWH and the paradigmatic singer of praise (see Neh 12:46). Focusing on Ps 145 in its context, Ps 144:9 praises YHWH, who "rescued David, his servant," while Ps 145:1 lets this very David utter the overall תהלה of the God and king YHWH. This connection is supported by the parallel drawn between being rescued by God and uttering his praise in other texts (Isa 60:18; Jer 17:14; Ps 9:5; Ps 106:47 // 1 Chr 16:35). Situations concerning life and thus prayer from א to ת are connected to David and held up for identification in all generations to come (see Ps 145). Susanne Gillmayr-Bucher writes, "The reading of the Psalms in light of generally acknowledged texts and the recollection of David and his life assures the readers of their own way and raises their hopes."²⁸

---

25. See Ulrich Dahmen, *Psalmen- und Psalter-Rezeption im Frühjudentum: Rekonstruktion, Textbestand, Struktur und Pragmatik der Psalmenrolle 11QPsa aus Qumran*, STDJ 49 (Leiden: Brill, 2003), 197.

26. Kratz, "Blessed Be the Lord," 197.

27. See Eileen Schuller, *Non-canonical Psalms from Qumran: A Pseudepigraphic Collection*, HSS 28 (Atlanta: Scholars Press, 1986), 27.

28. Susanne Gillmayr-Bucher, "The Psalm Headings. A Canonical Relecture of the Psalms," in *The Biblical Canons*, ed. J.-M. Auwers and H. J. de Jonge, BETL 163 (Leuven: Peeters, 2003), 253–54.

The superscription תהלה, similar to the superscription ספר תהלים for the whole Psalter, reveals a perspective focused on praise, but at the same time lament is not suppressed, as is shown by Ps 145 and its location in the Psalter. The ups and downs of Israel's history, David's biography, and the struggle of every single praying man and woman between lament and praise determine the dynamics of the Psalter (and its ability to connect with people to this very day), dynamics that reach a climax in the תהלה לדוד.[29]

3. Remembering and Constructing God and Humans in Psalm 145

The investigation of the psalm's superscription leads us to consider dynamic aspects of the description of God and humans in Ps 145 in light of God's מלכות.

The formation of the Hebrew Psalter as we understand it today is characterized by several acts of remembering and constructing, the superscriptions of the psalms being only one element worthy of note. Likewise, in the analysis of individual psalms, the aforementioned categories can be helpful tools for understanding what is actually going on *in* these texts and in elaborating Old Testament theology/anthropology *with* these texts. That Ps 145 remembers—for example, in its use of quotations from other biblical books—and constructs—for example, in its use of an acrostic structure—has been noted in different ways by various commentators. Yet, this has rarely lead to appreciative evaluations of the text as a piece of art.[30] In the following, I assume instead that Ps 145 purposefully applies resumptions from other texts as well as new semantic and poetic constructions to make fundamental statements about God and humans and their relationship, assembled under the letters of the Hebrew alphabet within a manageable text.[31] The categories of remembering and constructing thus appear as methods used, respectively, by the authors of the text and by its recipients to, for example, recontextualize the psalm. Filled with all

---

29. See Bernd Janowski, "Ein Tempel aus Worten: Zur theologischen Architektur des Psalters," in *Der nahe und der ferne Gott*, BThAT 5 (Neukirchen-Vluyn: Neukirchener Verlag, 2014), 287–314, esp. 298–99.

30. See, e.g., Bernhard Duhm's assessment of Ps 145 in his commentary on Psalms (Duhm, *Die Psalmen*, 2nd ed., KHC 14 [Tübingen: Mohr Siebeck, 1922]).

31. Neumann, *Schriftgelehrte Hymnen*, is the newest example of a lucid, comprehensive analysis of Ps 145 and its intertexts that enhances its understanding as a theologically dense text.

its theological and anthropological compactness, Ps 145 resembles an essence, a poetic digest.³² Its originality lies above all in the arrangement of its contents, in the way different motifs and traditions are assembled to illustrate the center of the text, God's kingdom and its effect on human action. Some selected examples may illustrate my point.

The path of prayer Ps 145 describes is shaded by striking constructions of time.³³ The temporal terms are eye-catching: they characterize the praise of humanity as perennial and everlasting, and they draw attention to the center of the psalm and its depiction of the everlasting kingdom of YHWH. The close contact between בכל יום and לעולם ועד within a single verse (v. 2) is unique in the Hebrew Bible, as singular as the enhancement of perpetuity in verse 13 with כל עולמים. The activities of God and human are thus already connected to one another on a temporal level. Psalm 145 unfurls along the lines established by עולם ועד, comprising the daily prayer of man as well as the everlasting kingdom of God. In the framework of עולם ועד (vv. 1–2 and v. 21) we find the chain of generations passing on the knowledge of God and his deeds (v. 4) and at the same time appearing as the sphere of action in which God's kingdom is manifested (v. 13). The same holds true for God's works as subjects of praise (v. 10) and as beneficiaries of God's mercy (v. 9). Together with the overall quantifier כל, used seventeen times in twenty-one verses, the temporal aspects of Ps 145 construct universality, global importance, and stability. These are topics that appear in many more texts within the tradition of prayer, connecting different times and religions.³⁴ This recurrent theme of tradition itself may be interpreted as a response to the experience of permanent threats to human life through integrative, universal figuration of perpetual stability. The threat, however, is not suppressed but is constantly resonating—as in the case of Ps 145, where it broaches the issue of the elimination of enemies.³⁵ In addition, Ps 144:3 asks (as the last ques-

---

32. This is enhanced by constructing it as an acrostic, as pointed out earlier.

33. These temporal aspects often led interpreters to construct a connection to the theological topos of eschatology. See, e.g., the commentary on Ps 145 from Peter Schegg, *Achtundsechzigster bis hundertundfünfzigster Psalm*, vol. 2 of *Die Psalmen: Übersetzt und erklärt für Verständnis und Betrachtung* (München: Lentner, 1847), 704–13.

34. On the visual and audible manifestations of the notion of universality in Ps 145, see Reuven Kimelman, "Psalm 145: Theme, Structure, and Impact," in *JBL* 113 (1994): 37–58, esp. 47 and 51.

35. Strikingly, this is in the mode of *yiqtol*, whereas God's action is otherwise continually described with participle constructions.

tion of the Psalter!) the fundamental question of anthropology: what is man? (see Ps 8:5).

With its overall construction, Ps 145 advises us to reflect on this very question and on what could be described as a fundamental anthropological question question: Who is God? The questions are entwined, or at least closely tied together.[36]

The human being is, according to Ps 145, first of all characterized by the ability to communicate on several levels. First, as a praising individual, it stands at the beginning of the psalm, it appears as part of humanity, as part of the whole of God's creation; the human being speaks about God and the world to others and to God as a personal God, imagined as king. Second, the human being is constituted by his or her neediness, expressed vividly in the second half of the psalm. Psalm 145 therefore features resonant fundamental insights into the essence of humanity, found throughout the Psalter, and closely ties these instances together with its notion of God. Aside from the framework of the psalm, which describes God as king, accessible through his name, every verse of the text contains numerous characterizations of God.[37] I will concentrate on some selected aspects. Among the epithets that Ps 145 attributes to God, his kingdom/kingship, מלכות, undoubtedly holds the central position. Exactly where the missing נ-line catches the eye, the initials of each verse form the root מלך, read from the bottom up, which was already introduced in verse 1. Some commentaries praise this stylistic element as a skillful poetic device; others modify its importance as an inevitable result of the Hebrew alphabet.[38] Without appealing to any argument regarding the true intention of the author(s) of Ps 145, one may assume that the close connection between form and content of these verses would have

---

36. Interestingly, questions of anthropology are often underrepresented in the discussion of Ps 145. For the understanding of the text, its concept of God's kingdom, and its relevance for the history of the picture of God as king, this human side of the coin is, however, very important.

37. For an overview with a strong theological accent, see Neumann, *Schriftgelehrte Hymnen*, 49–94. Hossfeld and Zenger also point to important aspects of the text and its semantic and poetic specialties, as well as to further reading (*Psalmen 101–50*, 789–807).

38. For example, Kimelman carves out the reverse acrostic and points to the strategy of addressing poems by means of such a play with letters in Babylonian acrostics (*Psalm 145*, 45).

been noticed.³⁹ Moreover, the possibility of going one letter further and reading מלכי, "my king," has not to my knowledge yet been considered, but it is a reading that has interesting implications for interpretation. The address of the text from verse 1 is resumed as a quasi-dedication of the psalm to God, "my king" or "the king par excellence." Simultaneously, the superscription operates as a signature of the psalm by the praying "I," the human king par excellence, King David. This deliberate poetic construction emphasizes one important metaphor for God in the history of prayer in the whole of its ambiguity. Psalm 145 remembers the connection of David and his God and at the same time constructs a new image of God's universal reign that comprises all generations and reveals all human power, all human kingship, in a different light. The picture of kingship drawn from the living environment of people continued to connect God and humans also in later times, as the texts of the New Testament show. Furthermore, the process of remembering and constructing continues, as times and thus perceptions of kingdom and power are changing.

From the center of the psalm—effectively, gazing from the kingdom of God—the eyes of the reader are drawn in two different directions: up toward a respectable collection of words and word combinations describing God's action, and down toward an ensemble of apparently more concrete pictures, illustrating how God's action ideally shows.

In the upper part, the accumulation of attributes that are brought into relation with God via possessive suffixes attracts attention. How can the relationship between the different attributes be described, and is there any possibility of bringing some organization to the accumulation of terms? They construct a semantic field of God's remembered and hoped-for deeds or actions. Among them, first and foremost, the term נפלאות requires explanation. Forms of the roots גדל and גבר, as well as the passive participle of ירא, are often found in parallel with the root פלא, being essential for the discourse on the topic of miracles/wonders in the Hebrew Bible, which could be further explored on the basis of Ps 145.⁴⁰ It seems to be about a theology that tries to describe God through his actions, portrayed as

---

39. See also Neumann, *Schriftgelehrte Hymnen*, 47–48.

40. On the often-unattended topic of miracle/wonder in the Hebrew Bible, see now the stimulating analysis of Friedhelm Hartenstein, "Wunder im Alten Testament: Zur theologischen Begrifflichkeit für das Außerordentliche in der Hebräischen Bibel (plʿ, päläʿ und niflaʿot)," in *Wunder*, ed. Elisabeth Gräb-Schmidt and Reiner Preul, MJT 28 (Leipzig: Evangelische Verlagsanstalt, 2016), 1–30.

special in more than one way. Accounts of these actions are to be found in narratives, to be assumed in the background of so-called abstract nouns as well as in (often poetic) texts with confessional character. These different facets meet in Ps 145 and are both especially important for a differentiated characterization of the biblical account of wonders/miracles. In this very play on words that we often simply check off as abstract nouns, we can instead examine theological reasoning as a work of remembering and constructing. It reshapes the past in tying together God's sameness in his actions in different realms (e.g., history and creation) and situations. Thus entire narratives such as that of the exodus are literally "brought to a term." These abstract nouns have the potential to be again unfolded into (new) narratives in the life of the praying community.

The accumulation of attributes is flanked by three verses combining God's name with a prefixed description, thus forming confession-like phrases. What can only be mentioned here is that with these short descriptions whole traditions are remembered, transformed, and brought together. Verse 3 is a kind of refrain of the psalms of YHWH's kingdom (see Ps 48:2a and Ps 96:4a), now culminating not in Zion but in God's greatness itself. Verse 8, combined with the term נפלאות and the crucial role of God's רחם, points to the events of the exodus, especially to the passage Exod 32–34 with its description of God's wrath and his benefaction to the people of Israel. A whole library of other memories could be added.[41]

Gazing down from the center of the psalm, one faces the tangible connection of the human neediness described earlier and God's acts responding to it. The characteristics and attributes introduced in the upper part are realized in some of God's deeds for the benefit of certain groups of people, which seems to contradict the universal character of the text and has challenged commentators throughout the ages. Especially striking is verse 20b, where the elimination of all evildoers is described, whereas elsewhere enemies, evildoers, or other adversaries of God or the praying individual do not seem to play any role in Ps 145. This passage is additionally highlighted by the use of the one single *yiqtol* form from God's side that the text offers. Once again, the nod to the comprehensive character of the text is important, since it does not allow us to ignore the menacing realities that are also in the background of other verses.

---

41. For a number of intertextual references, see Neumann, *Schriftgelehrte Hymnen*, 49–94.

Already with the reference to גדולות, נפלאות, גבורות, and נוראות, which may also allude to God's acts in creation, and with the mention of God's creatures as מעשה and כל חי (see Gen 3:20 with Eve as mother of "everything that is alive"), another vast and important tradition is connected to the psalm and newly embellished: God as creator, the world as creation. This can be seen to be starting with verse 3, where the aforementioned refrain of the psalms of God's kingdom is combined with a description of the inscrutability of God's magnitude. The seldom-used phrase אין חקר occurs, sometimes in parallel with forms of גדל and פלא, in important statements about and within contexts of creation (Isa 40:28; Job 5:9; 9:10; Prov 25:3). In the second part of the psalm, the topic of creation is recalled both by terms like חי and בשר and by the fundamental motif of the divine care for every living being, particularly for endangered life. In the Jewish tradition, this aspect survived in the prominent role of verse 16 in common prayer.[42] Psalm 104 merits discussion here, being closely connected to Ps 103, which has the one and only other occurrence of מלכות in the Hebrew Psalter. Psalm 104 has a lot of interesting parallels with Ps 145 in addition to the often-quoted grace (Ps 104:27).[43] To simply give a glimpse: Psalm 104 shows the functioning of creation in an all-encompassing, preferentially phenomenological mode with a characteristic style resonant of wisdom. God's action as creator and sustainer of the world may be observed and expressed, according to Pss 104 and 145, even if there are limits to the human capacity. Moreover, Ps 104 inaugurates a series of twenty-four exclamations of "Hallelujah!" in the Psalter, coming to their summit in the final *hallel* psalms, 146–50, and experiencing a special prelude to that in the תהלה לדוד.

Both parts recall known traditions and put them together into a new picture, describing God and humans against the background of God's kingdom and thus giving an interpretation of the image of God as king.

---

42. Noted, e.g., by Avrohom C. Feuer, *Psalms 73–150*, vol. 2 of *Sefer Tehillim: A New Translation with a Commentary Anthologized from Talmudic, Midrashic, and Rabbinic Sources*, ATS (Brooklyn: Mesorah, 1985), 1696.

43. Included among the different temporal aspects are the topics of the elimination of evildoers and the fundamental order of supply for all creatures. Besides, Ps 104 belongs to Pss 101–106, the group of psalms that comprises an "integrative-elementary conception of the מלכות יהוה." See Martin Leuenberger, *Konzeptionen des Königtums Gottes im Psalter: Untersuchungen zu Komposition und Redaktion der theokratischen Bücher IV–V im Psalter*, ATANT 83 (Zürich: TVZ, 2004), 248–60.

This very same מלכות that is found in the center of Ps 145 is in itself an example of remembering and constructing, interestingly showcasing different kinds of identity formation in the Second Temple period and beyond.

In the history of ancient Israel and its literature, a plenitude of concepts of divine and human power, in negative and positive senses, has evolved, sprouting from the root מלך, and growing on a semantic field of which we find significant parts in Ps 145 and the texts surrounding it, in terms of both Psalter composition and theological discourse. With the remembering and constructing of Ps 145, we find ourselves on a special stage in the history of the image of God as king, in which common traditions are reshaped and, together with other texts, important fundamentals are provided for later constructions of theologies and anthropologies relating to God's kingdom. The abstract noun מלכות, which only occurs in late texts of the Hebrew Bible, and even there quite infrequently, holds a central position concerning the formal composition and thus also the content of the psalm. For example, Anna Maria Schwemer, in her exploration of the Songs of the Sabbath Sacrifice from Qumran, was able to show the developing popularity of this term and the connected yet varying concepts tied to it.[44] One also has to take note of the existence of other interesting texts operating with the term מלכות/βασιλεία—for example, the Wisdom of Solomon, the Psalms of Solomon, and, not least, the continuation of kingship theology in the New Testament. Without being able to get into detail with specific texts, of which a noteworthy group are prayer texts, I want to note how tradition is condensed through one term remembered, through being applied in different contexts—be it through integration into a special constellation of motifs, a specific political situation, or a cosmological description as in the Songs of the Sabbath Sacrifice—may construct new realities and thus new identities. We get deeper into the history of this term if we successfully colocate these different contexts and explore their relationship to one another.

---

44. Anna Maria Schwemer, "Gott als König und seine Königsherrschaft in den Sabbatliedern aus Qumran," in *Königsherrschaft Gottes und himmlischer Kult im Judentum, Urchristentum und in der hellenistischen Welt*, ed. Martin Hengel and Anna M. Schwemer, WUNT 55 (Tübingen: Mohr Siebeck, 1991), 45-118. Compare with Odo Camponovo's different conclusion, which assumes that the topic of God's kingdom is important but not vivid in Qumran, in *Königtum, Königsherrschaft und Reich Gottes in den frühjüdischen Schriften*, OBO 58 (Freiburg: Universitätsverlag, 1984).

4. Psalm 145: Israelite Identity?

In the limited possibilities of this essay, I can only vaguely pose the question of what function Ps 145 had in a *special* time of identity formation—namely, in the rising and changing Judaism of the Persian and Hellenistic periods—and also, therefore, in a special literary context, the Psalter, for which this was the formative period of compilation.

Nowhere in Ps 145 is Israel mentioned—neither Jerusalem, nor Zion, nor the people, nor the temple. In fact, as we have already seen, an eminently universal character distinguishes the text. One must assert, however, that even in a text of such inclusiveness, there still may be construction of identity—not only Israelite identity—albeit in a special way.

This happens first and foremost through every contextualization of a motif such as the מלכות יהוה but also of an individual text, whether in the context of the Masoretic Psalter or the Psalter of the LXX, in manuscripts from Qumran and the Judean Desert, in the Mishnah, or in Christian liturgical books, where there may be new ways of constructing identities. A text such as Ps 145 unfolds its whole theological potential in the synopsis of its different points of contextualization. First and foremost, it does this in the processes of remembering and constructing between these points. Let me turn to the contextualization we normally start with when attempting to write the histories of a psalm and its contexts. The position Ps 145 was given by the formative redaction of the Psalter more closely exemplifies at this point the immediate context of Ps 145.[45] The last psalms of David begin with the praise of a praying individual in God's sanctuary (היכל קדשך) in Ps 138, then reflect the situation of the human being *coram Deo* in a way that is more concentrated on the individual in Pss 139–144, and end in a beatitude of the people in Ps 144:15. Psalm 145 follows, so that an identification of the collective addressed in Ps 145 with this very people stands to reason. Thereafter, Ps 145 opens the door to the finale of the Psalter, in which we encounter the perspective of universal praise as well as different groups and demarcations. Strikingly prominent is the group of the חסידים, known from Ps 145.[46] This term, with only thirty-four appearances in the Hebrew Bible, is in need of further explanation, even

---

45. For the part Ps 145 plays in the formation of the Psalter, see especially Leuenberger, *Konzeptionen*, 367–87.

46. See Neumann's interpretation, which may be complemented by considering the interaction of different groups, God's kingdom, and universal delineations in other

if Ps 148:14 implies a possible identification with the people of God. Concerning Ps 145, it is important that the חסידים, who occasionally appear in combination with ברך, are brought in parallel with "all deeds" and are framed by two occurrences of חסד referring to God and thus again pointing to the crucial correlation of theological and anthropological statements. If we expand our sight a little toward the psalms between the מעלות Psalter and the last Davidic Psalter, the dramatic interplay of individual and collective, of universal and particular predications, becomes even more intense: the twin psalms Pss 135 and 136 praise the deeds of God's חסד in creation and history and the חסד that seems actually to collide with the situation of political impotence, being theologically reflected in the Song of Zion, Ps 137. A blanket of silence unfurls over the terms *Zion* and *Jerusalem* throughout the whole last David Psalter and plays an important role in this psalm. The silence is not broken until Pss 146 and 147, with their conception of God the King on Mount Zion and the reconstruction of Jerusalem. Psalm 145 is itself part of this silence. It seems to confront the missing identification marks with a new factor, the מלכות יהוה, completed by universal praise by humanity, thus referring to a transmission of the knowledge about God's sameness in his action throughout history.

5. Conclusion

Looking at Ps 145 from the perspective of the topic of this volume suggests different observations that may at least raise new questions about the text and its history of contextualization. This history is capable of creating ever new constructions of identity. Moreover, the exploration of one individual text may possibly hint, at least, at feasible answers to the main questions of this volume:

- What difference does it make if theological and anthropological insights are offered in the form of prayers?
- Which transformations may be traced in the multivocal prayer texts of the Persian and Hellenistic periods?

---

texts from the Second Temple Period and the interesting reception history of these dynamics (Neumann, *Schriftgelehrte Hymnen*, 70–71).

- What are the functions of prayer texts like Ps 145 in the viral discourses of times that are significantly marked by dynamics of remembering and constructing?

The main arguments brought forth in this essay show the interconnectedness of these questions with the careful study of a single text, its different contexts, and its multifarious history. Even though only a couple of aspects of Ps 145, with its special stage in the history of the image of God as king, could be elaborated in this essay, it became clear that this prayer is a vivid example of dynamics of remembering and constructing in late texts of the Hebrew Bible. Reflecting on these categories sheds light on the way a text such as Ps 145 provides insights into theology and anthropology. Its theological work consists of the reassessment of well-known traditions that are poetically concentrated into abstract nouns, citations, and dense formulations that hold the potential of being reactivated in new narratives and are open to ever new contextualization. With its intensive use of the noun מלכות—which is, as we have seen, significantly characterized by the aspects of time the text offers, as well as by the connectedness of divine and human action—Ps 145 constructs a unique picture of God's kingdom in the Hebrew Psalter. Psalm 145 is a prayer that tries to hold together the dynamics of universality and particularity, of God's incomprehensible might and human reality, and of the consciousness of tradition and ever-changing circumstances, which shows especially in the long reception history of Ps 145 and its central theme—God's kingdom.

The better part of what has been said can perhaps be assembled in a simple picture: if we imagine Ps 145 as a kind of literary devotional object, it is per se marked by the fact that it functions like an image incompletely merged with itself. By means of such a devotional object, a concept of God is remembered, envisioned, and constructed and is cast into a small format. It has a personal, individual, but still collective reference and thus reveals something about its bearer. In different contexts, it may attract different associations. Sometimes, the object is even passed on from one generation to another.

Bibliography

Berlin, Adele. "The Rhetoric of Psalm 145." Pages 17–22 in *Biblical and Related Studies Presented to Samuel Iwry*. Edited by Ann Kort and Scott Morschauser. Winona Lake, IN: Eisenbrauns, 1985.

Blumenthal, David. "Psalm 145: A Liturgical Reading." Pages 13–35 in *Hesed ve-emet: Studies in Honor of Ernest. S. Frerichs*. Edited by Jodi Magness an Seymour Gitin. BJS 320. Atlanta: Scholars Press, 1998.

Booij, Thijs. "Psalm CXLV: David's Song of Praise." *VT* 58 (2008): 633–37.

Breed, Brennan W. *Nomadic Text: A Theory of Biblical Reception History*. Bloomington: Indiana University Press, 2014.

Brueggemann, Walter. *Israel's Praise: Doxology against Idolatry and Ideology*. 2nd ed. Philadelphia: Fortress, 1988.

Camponovo, Odo. *Königtum, Königsherrschaft und Reich Gottes in den frühjüdischen Schriften*. OBO 58. Freiburg: Universitätsverlag, 1984.

Dahmen, Ulrich. *Psalmen- und Psalter-Rezeption im Frühjudentum: Rekonstruktion, Textbestand, Struktur und Pragmatik der Psalmenrolle 11QPsa aus Qumran*. STDJ 49. Leiden: Brill, 2003.

Duhm, Bernhard. *Die Psalmen*. 2nd ed. KHC 14. Tübingen: Mohr Siebeck, 1922.

Feuer Avrohom C. *Psalms 73–150*. Vol. 2 of *Sefer Tehillim: A New Translation with a Commentary Anthologized from Talmudic, Midrashic, and Rabbinic Sources*. ATS. Brooklyn: Mesorah, 1985.

Gillmayr-Bucher, Susanne. "The Psalm Headings. A Canonical Relecture of the Psalms." Pages 247–55 in *The Biblical Canons*. Edited by J.-M. Auwers and H. J. de Jonge. BETL 163. Leuven: Peeters, 2003.

Hartenstein, Friedhelm. "Wunder im Alten Testament: Zur theologischen Begrifflichkeit für das Außerordentliche in der Hebräischen Bibel (plʿ, päläʿ und niflaʿot)." Pages 1–30 in *Wunder*. Edited by Elisabeth Gräb-Schmidt and Reiner Preul. MJT 28. Leipzig: Evangelische Verlagsanstalt, 2016.

Hossfeld, Frank-Lothar, and Erich Zenger. *Psalmen 101–50*. HThKAT. Freiburg im Breisgau: Herder, 2008.

Janowski, Bernd. "'Die Hindin der Morgenröte' (Ps 22,1): Ein Beitrag zum Verständnis der Psalmenüberschriften." In *Psalmen und Chronik—Aspekte ihres Verhältnisses*. Edited by Friedhelm Hartenstein and Thomas Willi. FAT. Tübingen: Mohr Siebeck, forthcoming.

———. *Konfliktgespräche mit Gott: Eine Anthropologie der Psalmen*. 4th ed. Neukirchen-Vluyn: Neukirchener Verlag, 2013.

———. "Ein Tempel aus Worten: Zur theologischen Architektur des Psalters." Pages 287–314 in *Der nahe und der ferne Gott*. BThAT 5. Neukirchen-Vluyn: Neukirchener Verlag 2014.

Kimelman, Reuven. "Psalm 145: Theme, Structure, and Impact." *JBL* 113 (1994): 37–58.

Kratz, Reinhard G. "'Blessed Be the Lord and Blessed Be His Name Forever': Psalm 145 in the Hebrew Bible and in the Psalms Scroll 11Q5." Pages 229–43 in *Prayer and Poetry in the Dead Sea Scrolls and Related Literature: Essays in Honor of Eileen Schuller on the Occasion of Her 65th Birthday*. Edited by Jeremy Penner, Ken M. Penner, and Cecilia Wassen. STDJ 98. Leiden: Brill, 2012.

Leuenberger, Martin. *Konzeptionen des Königtums Gottes im Psalter: Untersuchungen zu Komposition und Redaktion der theokratischen Bücher IV–V im Psalter*. ATANT 83. Zürich: TVZ, 2004.

Neumann, Friederike. *Schriftgelehrte Hymnen: Gestalt, Theologie und Intention der Psalmen 145 und 146–50*. BZAW 491. Berlin: de Gruyter, 2016.

Newsom, Carol Ann. *The Self as Symbolic Space: Constructing Identity and Community at Qumran*. STDJ 52. Leiden: Brill, 2004.

Nitzan, Bilhah. *Qumran Prayer and Religious Poetry*. Translated by Jonathan Chipman. STDJ 12. Leiden: Brill, 1994.

Ringgren, Helmer. "הלל I and II." *ThWAT* 2:433–41.

Rosenstock-Huessy, Eugen. *Die Sprache des Menschengeschlechts: Eine leibhaftige Grammatik in vier Teilen; Erster und zweiter Teil*. Vol. 1 of *Die Sprache des Menschengeschlechts: Eine leibhaftige Grammatik in vier Teilen*. Heidelberg: Schneider, 1963.

Schegg, Peter. *Achtundsechzigster bis hundertundfünfzigster Psalm*. Vol. 2 of *Die Psalmen: Übersetzt und erklärt für Verständnis und Betrachtung*. München: Lentner, 1847.

Schuller, Eileen. *Non-canonical Psalms from Qumran: A Pseudepigraphic Collection*. HSS 28. Atlanta: Scholars Press, 1986.

Schwemer, Anna M. "Gott als König und seine Königsherrschaft in den Sabbatliedern aus Qumran." Pages 45–118 in *Königsherrschaft Gottes und himmlischer Kult im Judentum, Urchristentum und in der hellenistischen Welt*. Edited by Martin Hengel and Anna M. Schwemer. WUNT 55. Tübingen: Mohr Siebeck, 1991.

Staubli, Thomas, and Silvia Schroer. *Menschenbilder der Bibel*. Ostfildern: Patmos, 2014.

Weber, Beat. *Die Psalmen 73–150*. Vol. 2 of *Werkbuch Psalmen*. Stuttgart: Kohlhammer, 2003.

Contributors

Hannes Bezzel is Professor of Old Testament at the Theological Faculty of Friedrich-Schiller-Universität Jena, Germany.

Dirk J. Human is Professor in Old Testament Studies and Head of the Department of Old Testament and Hebrew Scriptures, Faculty of Theology and Religion at the University of Pretoria, South Africa.

Susanne Gillmayr-Bucher is Professor of Old Testament Studies at the Catholic Private University of Linz, Austria.

Maria Häusl is Professor of Biblical Studies at the Technical University of Dresden, Germany, and Research Associate at the Department of Old Testament Studies, University of Pretoria, South Africa.

Scott C. Jones is Professor of Biblical Studies at Covenant College, Lookout Mountain, Georgia, USA.

Melody D. Knowles is Vice President for Academic Affairs and Associate Professor of Old Testament at Virginia Theological Seminary, Alexandria, Virginia, USA.

Christo Lombaard is Professor of Christian Spirituality at the University of South Africa, in Pretoria, South Africa.

Michael D. Matlock is Professor of Inductive Biblical Studies, Old Testament, and Early Judaism and Chair of the Inductive Biblical Studies at Asbury Theological Seminary, Wilmore, Kentucky, USA, and an Anglican Priest.

Ndikho Mtshiselwa is Associate Professor of the Old Testament in the Department of Biblical and Ancient Studies at the University of South Africa.

Nancy Rahn is Post-Doc and research assistant at the Faculty of Theology, University of Bern, Switzerland.

Ancient Sources Index

Hebrew Bible/Old Testament

Genesis
2–3	115
3:20	221
11:20	161
22	4, 115, 120–21
22:1–19	116, 119
22:15–18	116–17
29:17	157

Exodus
3:7	93–94
7:3	94
7:9	94
14:10	93–94
14:15	94
15:5	94
15:10	94
15:11	213, 214
20–23	73
20:20	114
24:3	73
24:4–8	73
32–34	220
34:16	21
34:6–7	44, 46–47
40:34–35	130

Leviticus
18:24–30	75
19:19	96
26	133
26:22–45	132
26:39–42	131

Deuteronomy
4	89, 133
4:25	89
4:26–31	132
4:27	89
4:28	89
4:29–30	88–90
4:29–31	131
6:22	94
7:1–4	76
7:3	21
7:9	69
7:12	69
8:2	114
10:21	213
12:10–11	130
17:16	21
17:17	22
26:7	93–94
26:19	213
28	132
29–30	89
29:21–30:10	89–90
29:23	89
29:26	89
30	132–33
30:1–4	70
30:1–10	88
30:2–4	130
30:6	96
34	89
34:4	91
34:10–12	89, 91

Judges

2	115
2:22	115
13	161

1 Samuel

1	154
1:5	157
1:5–7	150
1:6	157
1:7	157
1:10	150
1:10–13	151
1:11	150, 153
1:12–13	149–50
1:13	150, 161
1:14	150
1:15–16	151
1:17	151
1:18	152
1:21–28	152
1–2	5, 147, 149, 151, 159–61
2	148, 152, 155, 158, 160–61
2:1–10	153
2:3	159
2:5	159
2:6	156
2:10	148, 156, 158
2:11	148
8	100

2 Samuel

5:6	197
5:19	14
6:1	197
7	199–200
7:1–16	199
7:5–16	194
7:13	128–29
7:14	21
7:14–16	129
7:18–29	14
22	148–49, 161
22:51	148, 156
24:10	14

24:17	14
24:25	13

1 Kings

1–11	20
1:1–2:46	20–21
2:2–4	129
2:24	129
3:1–3	21
3:1–10:29	20
3:6	129
3:6–9	14
3:7	129
3:14	129
3:15	102
4:22–24	102
4:26	21
5:7–8	100
5:17	129
5:19	129
6–7	136
6:12–13	129
8	5, 28, 125, 126–27, 130, 133, 143–44
8:10–11	130, 138
8:12	138
8:13	138
8:14–21	14
8:16	128
8:17	129
8:17–20	138
8:18	129
8:19	136
8:20	128–29
8:22–30	128
8:22–54	196
8:22–53	14, 22, 141
8:23	69
8:23–26	129
8:27	138
8:28–30	139
8:29	138
8:32	134
8:34	134, 140
8:36	134, 140

8:37–40	23	15:3	197
8:39	134	15:28	197
8:40	140	16	147, 196
8:43	134	16:8	24
8:44–45	23	16:8–36	14, 29
8:46	133	16:35	215
8:46–53	23, 140	16:41	14, 28
8:49	134	17:1–15	199
8:51–53	131	17:13	21
8:56	130	17:16–27	13–14
8:58	131	21:8	13–14
8:62–64	137	21:17	13–14
8:65	102	21:26	13, 24
9:1–9	127	22–26	198
10:5	102	29:10–20	13–14, 24–25
10:28	21	29:23	22
11:1	21	29:25	22
11:1–40	20–21		
16:29–31	90	2 Chronicles	
19:4–5	35	1:1–9:31	17
22:32	13	1:2–3	22
21:27–29	37, 47	1:8–10	13–14
		2:1–7:22	22
2 Kings		5:2–7:11	28
20:2–3	23	5:13	14, 28
21	17–18	6:3–11	13–14
21:1	17	6:4	199
21:2–7	18	6:6	198
21:11–18	18	6:7–10	198
14:23–25	47	6:11	198
14:25	37, 46	6:14–39	13
14:25–27	36	6:14–42	12, 14, 20–22
19:15–29	23	6:16	198
		6:19–21	23
1 Chronicles		6:33	24
1–9	13	6:34–35	25
2:3–4:23	24	6:40–42	14, 28
4:10	13–14, 24	6:41	196, 198
5:20	13, 24, 26	6:41–42	6, 189, 195, 200
11:1–29:30	17	6:42	196, 198
11:4–5	197	7:1	196
13:2	197	7:3	14, 28
13:5	197	7:6	14, 28
13:6	197	8:11	21–22
14:10	13–14	10–36	13

2 Chronicles (cont.)		34:1–36:1	17
10:1–12:16	17	36:5–8	16
12:2–12	23	36:9–10	16
12:6	13, 20	36:11–14	16
13:1–14:1	17	36:23	197
13:13–21	23		
13:14	13, 26–27	Ezra	
14:1	13–14, 24–25	1–6	54, 76, 78
14:2–16:14	16	3:10–13	59
14:11	24	3:11–12	4
14:3	25	4:2–3	49
14:6	25	6:6–12	61
14:9–15	23	7	64, 76
17:1–21:3	17	7–8	62
18:28–19:1	23	7–10	54, 78–79
18:31	13	7:6	78
20:5–12	14, 24–25	7:6–9	64
20:6	25	7:9	78
20:12	26	7:27	65
20:21	14, 28	7:27–28	54, 59, 61, 63–64, 78
20:22	213	8:21	4
20:26	13, 19, 27	8:21–23	61, 65, 78
21:4–20	16	8:24	4
21:18–19	16	8:28	65
22:1–9	16	8:31	61
22:10–24:27	17	9	4, 147
25:1–28	17	9–10	49, 75, 78
26:1–23	17	9:2	96
27:1–9	17	9:3–5	74
28:1–27	16	9:5–15	53
29:1–32:33	17	9:6–9	75
30:8	197	9:6–15	54–57, 59, 73–74, 78
30:18–19	14, 23–24, 26	9:8	96
30:27	13, 19, 23	9:8–9	76
31:8	13, 19, 27	9:12	75–76
32:2	13, 23, 27	9:14–15	75
32:24	13, 27	10	75
32:31	114	10:3	73
33	17		
33:1–20	17	Nehemiah	
33:2–7	18	1	147
33:11–20	19	1–13	54, 78
33:12–13	12, 17, 19	1:1–7:3	62
33:12–14	13	1:2	76
33:21–25	16	1:4	61

1:5–7	69	9:5	71, 213
1:5–11	4, 53–57, 59, 68, 70–71, 77–78	9:6	89
		9:6–31	72
1:8	71	9:6–37	53–57, 59, 71–74, 77–78, 84, 87–94, 96–99, 102–5
1:8–9	131		
1:8–10	69	9:7–8	104
1:11	69	9:8	96
2:4	62, 71, 77	9:9–11	93
2:4–5	4, 62	9:9–15	93, 104
2:10	67	9:10	93–94
2:12	62	9:11	94
2:19	65	9:13–14	92–93
2:20	63	9:16–21	104
2:37	65	9:17	89
3:33	65	9:21	93, 104
3:36–37	4, 54, 58–59, 65, 67, 77	9:22–25	104
4:3	4, 62, 66, 71, 77	9:26–30	104
4:4–5	54, 58–59, 65, 67, 77	9:32	76
4:9	62, 66, 71, 77	9:32–37	72, 104
4:9–17	62	9:34	100
4:15	66	9:37	100
4:15–23	62	10	92, 104
5	67, 99, 100–103	10:1	73
5:3–5	103	10:1–40	72
5:5	100, 102–3	10:30	73
5:6–8	103	12:27–43	60
5:7	100	12:46	213, 215
5:8	100	13	67
5:13	67	13:14	4, 54, 58–59, 65, 67
5:17–18	100	13:22	4, 54, 58–59, 65, 67
5:19	4, 54, 58–59, 65, 67	13:25	49
6:14	4, 54, 58–59, 65–67, 77	13:28–30	49
6:16	63	13:29	4, 54, 58–59, 65, 67
8	92	13:31	4, 54, 58–59, 65, 67
8–10	49, 54		
8:1–12	92	Job	
8:9–18	60	5:9	221
8:10	96	9:10	221
8:13–18	96	23:10	114
9	4, 83–84, 86–87, 89–93, 96–100, 103–5		
		Psalms	
9–10	73, 79, 147	1	180, 184
9:1–2	61	3–14	181
9:2	96	6:8	151
9:3	92	8:5	218

Psalms (cont.)

9:5	215	37:28–29	174
10:14	151	37:29	173, 178
15–24	181	37:30	177
16	181	37:31	177
17:3	114	37:34	178
19	181	37:35	175
22	174	37:37	173, 177
23	181	37:38	180
25	181	38	181
26–32	181	38:16	182
26:2	114	39	181
31:8	151	39:9	182
33	181	40:5	182
34	181	40:14–18	182
34:2	214	40:18	174
35	180	41	181
35–41	180–81	41:6–8	182
35:1	181	41:13	183
35:10	174, 181	42:3	160
35:28	214	42:4	160
36 LXX	179	42:11	160
36:3	170	48:2	220
36:11 LXX	178	48:11	213
36:12	182	65:2	213
36:13	182	70:6	174
37	5, 168–72, 174–77, 179–81, 183–84	71:8	214
		71:14	214
37:1	174, 177	78:58	151
37:2	179–80	78:68	190
37:3	169, 177–78	78:70	190
37:5	182	78:89	190
37:7	174	79:13	214
37:9	173–74, 178	86:1	174
37:11	172–73, 178	87:2	190
37:12	174, 182	96	14
37:14	172–74	96:1–13	29, 196
37:17	174, 182	96:4	220
37:19	173, 180	100:4	213
37:20	174, 179	104:27	221
37:22	173, 177	105–106	14
37:25	179	105:1–15	29, 196
37:26	177, 179	106	57
37:27	177, 180	106:1	29, 196
37:28	174, 177	106:29	151
		106:47	215

106:47–48	29, 196	2:21–22	179
109:1	213	25:3	221
109:16	174		
118:1–4	167	Ecclesiastes	
120–134	189–90	1:14	177
132	6, 189–195, 197–98, 200	2:11	177
132:2	192	2:17	177
132:3–5	194, 199	2:26	177
132:8	193	4:4	177
132:8–10	6, 14, 28, 192, 194–95, 197	4:6	177
132:9–10	193	6:9	177
132:10	193, 198		
132:11	192	Isaiah	
132:11–12	194, 199	9:3	47
132:11–18	199	14:25	47
132:13	193	19:23–25	49
132:14	193	40:28	221
132:15	192	42:8	214
132:15–18	193	42:10	213
132:16	192	42:12	213
135	224	56:3	49, 61
136	57, 167, 224	60:6	214
137	224	60:18	215
138	223	62:7	213
139–144	223	63:7	213–14
144:3	217	66:1–2	138
144:9	215		
144:15	223	Jeremiah	
145	6, 204–16, 218, 220, 222–25	9	158
145:1–2	217	9:22–23	158
145:1–21	212	13:11	213
145:10	217	15:1	134
145:13	217	15:4	18
145:21	210, 212, 217	17:14	215
145:3	211	18:7	35
145:4	217	18:23	65
145:8	220	26:3	35
145:9	217	33:9	213
146	224	33:11	60
146–150	213, 221		
147	224	Daniel	
148:14	224	1:7	118, 119
		3	4, 115, 118–21
Proverbs		3:24–90 LXX	121
1–9	179	6	4, 115, 118, 120–21

Daniel (cont.)		Zephaniah	
9	147	2:11	49
9:4–19	56, 97	2:13	47
9:17–19	104	2:15	47
		3:19	214
Joel		3:9	49
2:13	35		
2:14	35	Zechariah	
2:17	35	13:9	114
		14:9	49
Jonah		14:16	49
1:1–2:11	38, 39		
1:5	39–40, 46	**Deuterocanonical Books**	
1:6	39–40		
1:8	34	Sirach	
1:14	34, 39–40, 45	39:5–8	167
1:16	40	44:1	214
2	36	44:11–15	214
2:2–10	42, 121	51:1–12	167
2:3–10	3, 33, 39, 41, 47	51:13–30	167
2:5	48		
2:7	46	Judith	
2:8	48	13:4	161
3:1–4:11	38, 43		
3:6	45, 47	Wisdom	
3:8	44, 46	4:3–5	180
3:8–10	35		
4:2	35, 45	**New Testament**	
4:2–3	3, 34, 44		
4:3	45	Matthew	
4:6	46	5:5	178
4:8	35		
4:9	3, 34, 45	1 Corinthians	
4:10–11	35	1:31	158
Nahum		**Dead Sea Scrolls**	
1:1	47		
1:13	47	1QHodayot[a]	168 n. 4, 175–76, 184
2:1	47	IX, 37–38	175
3:1	47	IX, 38	174
3:19	47	IX, 41	175
		X, 36	174
Habakkuk		XIII, 15–16	174
3:3	213	XIII, 23	174

4Q51 (4QSam)	158
4Q171 (4QpPs^a)	169, 174–75, 179
1–10 II, 10	175
1–10 III, 10	178
1–10 III, 10–11	169
1–10 III, 11	178
1–10 IV, 11–12	175
1–10 IV, 14	175
11QPs^a	167, 184

Ancient Jewish Writers

Pseudo-Philo, Liber antiquitatum biblicarum	
4:11	161
9:10	161
31:1	161
31:5	161
31:7	161
42:2	161
50–51	155
50:1	157
50:2	157
50:4	153
50:5	154–55, 161
51	156
51:3	159
51:4	159

Modern Authors Index

Aejmelaeus, Anneli   148 n. 5, 158 n. 43, 162
Albertz, Rainer   33 n. 3, 50, 117, 121 n. 15, 122
Allegro, John   169 n. 6, 179 n. 41, 184
Allen, James   176 n. 27, 184
Allen, Leslie   38 n. 16, 50
Assmann, Jan   176, 184
Auld, Graeme   148 n. 4, 162
Avioz, Michael   126 n. 3, 137 n. 32, 144
Balentine, Samuel   12, 13 n. 4, 28 n. 38, 30, 55, 79, 88, 95, 106
Baltzer, Klaus   69 n. 46, 79, 191 n. 4, 202
Bar-Efrat, Shimon   24 n. 29, 30
Bar-Tal, Daniel   2 n. 5, 7
Bauks, Michaela   179, 185
Bautch, Richard   56 n. 9, 57 n. 11, 79
Becking, Bob   57 nn. 10–11, 79
Bedford, Peter   103 n. 76, 106
Beentjes, Pancratius   12, 13 n. 4, 18 n. 21, 29 n. 40, 30, 168 n. 3, 185, 196 n. 11, 200
Begg, Christopher   153 n. 23, 162,
Begrich, Joachim   151–52, 163, 177, 185
Bellinger, William, Jr.   176, 185
Ben Zvi, Ehud   15, 18 n. 18, 19 n. 22, 30, 97 n. 52, 106, 133 n. 15, 141 n. 45, 144
Berlin, Adele   207, 225
Berquist, John   3 n. 8, 6, 140 n. 43, 144
Bezzel, Hannes   66 n. 36, 79, 149 n. 10, 151 n. 16, 162
Blenkinsopp, Joseph   63 n. 32, 79
Blumenthal, David   210 n. 14, 226
Boase, Elizabeth   115 n. 4, 122
Boccaccini, Gabriele   120 n. 13, 122

Boda, Mark   56–58, 72 n. 56, 79, 93 n. 37, 94, 106, 133 nn. 17 and 20, 134 n. 20, 140 n. 39, 144
Boer, Roland   86 n. 9, 102 n. 72, 103 n. 76, 106
Bogaert, Pierre-Maurice   153 n. 22, 162
Booij, Thijs   212 n. 19, 226
Botta, Alejandro   85 n. 7, 106
Braun, Roddy   21 n. 23, 30
Breed, Brennan   209 n. 11, 226
Brett, Mark   96 n. 49, 106
Brettler, Marc Zvi   2 n. 5, 3 n. 8, 7, 132 n. 11, 138 n. 35, 144
Bronner, Leila   149 n. 9, 150 n. 12, 162
Brown, Cheryl   153 n. 23, 159 n. 47, 162
Brueggemann, Walter   92 n. 29, 94 n. 41, 96, 99 n. 58, 106, 176 n. 28, 185, 210 n. 15, 226
Camponovo, Odo   222 n. 44, 226
Carr, David   49 n. 42, 50,
Cezula, Ntozakhe   96 n. 47, 99 n. 59, 100 n. 61, 106
Clines, David   92 n. 31, 107
Coats, George   116, 122
Collins, John   42 n. 23, 48 n. 36, 50
Cross, Frank Moore   158, 162, 192 n. 5, 200
Crow, Loren   190 n. 2, 200
Dahmen, Ulrich   214–15, 226
Davies, Philip   113 n. 1, 123
Deissler, Alfons   48 n. 36, 48 n. 38, 50
Deist, Ferdinand.   37 n. 15, 50
Denis-Constant, Martin   2 n. 6, 7
Deurloo, Karel   192 n. 5, 200
Di Lella, Alexander   167 n. 2, 187

Dietrich, Walter   34 n. 4, 50, 148 n. 5, 149 nn. 8–9, 152 n. 21, 159 n. 44, 162
Dietzfelbinger, Christian   153 n. 22, 155 n. 31, 156 n. 34, 161 n. 50, 162
Duggan, Michael   56 n. 9, 57, 71 n. 54, 72 nn. 55–56, 75 n. 63, 76 n. 67, 79
Duhm, Bernhard   183 n. 48, 185, 216 n. 30, 226
Englund, Robert   102 n. 75, 107
Eskenazi, Tamara Cohn   92, 93, 98, 104, 107
Eynikel, Erik   37 nn. 12–13, 47 n. 34, 50, 148 n. 6, 162
Falk, Daniel   88 n. 18, 107, 144
Feldman, Louis   153 n. 22, 158, 162
Feuer Avrohom   221 n. 42, 226
Fina, Anna de   2 n. 6, 7
Fischer, Irmtraud   66 n. 38, 80
Fishbane, Michael   83, 96 n. 48, 107, 132 n. 11, 144
Fox, Michael   176 n. 27, 179 n. 40, 185
Fretheim, Terence   190 n. 1, 200
Frevel, Christian   36 n. 11, 67 n. 39, 80
Galling, Kurt   58, 80, 147 n. 2, 163
Gamper, Arnold   142 n. 47, 144
Gélin, Albert   176 n. 24, 185
Gerstenberger, Erhard   57 nn. 11–12, 59 n. 20, 72 n. 57, 80
Gese, Hartmut   191 n. 5, 200
Gillingham, Sue   173 n. 16, 174, 185
Gillmayr-Bucher, Susanne   34 n. 5, 48 n. 35, 50, 215, 226
Goff, Matthew   168 n. 4, 185
Gottwald, Norman   86, 103 n. 76, 107
Grabbe, Lester   55 n. 5, 80, 100 nn. 60–61, 107
Graetz, Heinrich   172, 185
Groß, Walter   129 n. 6, 144
Gruber, Mayer   180 n. 43, 185
Gruen, Erich   154, 163
Gunkel, Hermann   151, 152 n. 20, 163, 177, 185
Haarmann, Volker   134 n. 23, 138 n. 33, 144
Hadot, Jean   153 n. 22, 163

Ḥakham, Amos   177, 178 n. 34, 179 n. 40, 185
Harrington, Daniel   154 n. 24, 163
Hartenstein, Friedhelm   138 n. 36, 145, 119 n. 40, 226
Häusl, Maria   53 n. 2, 80
Heckl, Raik   63 n. 32, 80
Hillers, Delbert   193 n. 7, 200
Hoppe, Leslie   135 n. 27, 145
Horgan, Maurya   169 n. 7, 175 n. 23, 178 n. 36, 185
Hossfeld, Frank-Lothar   171, 176, 180–81, 185, 190 n. 1, 200, 208, 212 nn. 17–18, 213 n. 22, 218 n. 37, 226
Human, Dirk   34 n. 5, 37 n. 14, 38 n. 17, 41 n. 22, 42 n. 26, 48 n. 36, 49 n. 41, 50
Hurvitz, Avi   191 n. 5, 201
Huwiler, Elizbeth   193 n. 7, 201
Jacobson, Howard   147 n. 3, 153 n. 22, 154 n. 24, 156 n. 35, 156 n. 37, 157 n. 41, 158 nn. 44–45, 163
Janowski, Bernd   206 n. 5, 208 n. 12, 212 n. 20, 216 n. 29, 226
Jansen, Herman   183 n. 48, 186
Japhet, Sara   15 n. 6, 24 nn. 30–31, 27 n. 37, 31, 73 n. 59, 80
Jeremias, Jörg   35 nn. 6–7, 36 n. 9, 44 n. 27, 51, 52,
Johnstone, William   24, 31
Jonker, Louis   15 n. 5, 31, 95, 98, 107,
Kalimi, Isaac   197 n. 15, 201
Karrer-Grube, Christiane   60, 68 n. 42, 80
Karrer, Christiane   54 n. 3, 56 n. 10, 58 n. 18, 60 n. 22, 62 nn. 31–32, 67 n. 40, 70, 73, 74, 80
Keel, Othmar   57 n. 12, 81
Kellermann, Ulrich   59 n. 19, 81
Kim, Yeong Seon   15 n. 6, 31
Kimelman, Reuven   217 n. 34, 218 n. 38, 226
Klein, Anja   72 n. 58, 81
Klein, Ralph   15 n. 6, 26, 28 n. 39, 31, 92 n. 31, 107, 196 nn. 10 and 13–14, 199 n. 19, 201

Knauf, Ernst Axel 33 n. 4, 48 nn. 37 and 39, 51, 149 n. 10, 163
Knoppers, Gary 15 n. 7, 18 n. 21, 31, 128 n. 4, 130 nn. 7-8, 131 n. 9, 132 n. 11, 134 n. 24, 137 n. 31, 145, 199 n. 20, 201
Knowles, Melody 136 n. 30, 141 n. 44, 145, 197 nn. 16-17, 201
Koch, Klaus 156 n. 38, 163
Köhlmoos, Melanie 33 n. 1, 48 n. 40, 51
Kratz, Reinhard 214 n. 24, 215 n. 26, 227
Kruger, 116 n. 7, 123
Kruse, Heinz 192 n. 5, 201
Laato, Antti 191 n. 5, 201
Lappenga, Benjamin 154-55, 163
Le Roux, Jurie 85 n. 5, 108
Lemche, Niels 120, 123
Leuchter, Mark 96 n. 50, 108
Leuenberger, Martin 33 n. 2, 51, 221 n. 43, 227
Levenson, Jon 141 n. 46, 145
Levin, Christoph 120, 123, 172-73, 186
Limburg, James 38 n. 16, 42 n. 25, 51
Linville, James 133, 145
Liverani, Mario 102 n. 72, 108
Loader, James 179 n. 40, 186
Lohfink, Norbert 183, 186
Lombaard, Christo 115 n. 3, 117 n. 8, 119 n. 12, 123
Luther, Martin 169-70, 186
Luz, Ulrich 178, 186
Maré, Leonard 168 n. 5, 186
Mathys, Hans-Peter 2 n. 7, 7, 42 n. 25, 51, 104 n. 79, 108, 136 n. 29, 145, 147 n. 2, 148 n. 5, 163
Matlock, Michael 31, 129, 134 n. 25, 145
Mbiti, John 95, 108
McCann, Clinton 195 n. 9, 201
McConville, Gordon 140 n. 42, 143 n. 51, 145
Hollman, Meredith 101, 110
Mettinger, Tryggve 191 n. 5, 201
Michael Chan 100 nn. 62-63, 110

Michaelis, Johann 117, 123
Miller, Cynthia 12 n. 2, 31
Miller, Patrick 33 nn. 1 and 3, 40 n. 20, 44 n. 29, 51, 105, 108
Moberly, R. Walter 116 n. 6, 123
Moffat, Donald 88 n. 18, 98 nn. 55 and 57, 99 n. 59, 108
Montgomery, James 117 n. 8, 123
Mosala, Itumeleng 85-86, 108
Mowinckel, Sigmund 58, 81
Mtshiselwa, Ndikho 83, 85 n. 6, 86 n. 10, 90 n. 25, 91 n. 26, 97 n. 52, 108, 110
Mülhaupt, Erwin 171 n. 9, 186
Müller, Hans-Peter 117 n. 10, 123
Muraoka, Takamitsu 138 n. 37, 186
Murphy, Frederick 156 n. 37, 157 n. 41, 163,
Neumann, Friederike 206 n. 4, 208 n. 9, 210 n. 14, 211 n. 16, 216 n. 31, 218 n. 37, 219 n. 39, 220 n. 41, 223 n. 46, 227
Newman, Judith 4 n. 1, 7, 87, 97 n. 51, 109, 126 n. 1, 132 n. 12, 134 n. 22, 147 nn. 31-32, 142 nn. 48-49, 145
Newsom, Carol A. 126 n. 2, 145, 168 n. 4, 175 nn. 21-22, 176 n. 25, 186, 204 n. 2, 227
Nihan, Christophe 34 n. 4, 51, 89, 109
Nitzan, Bilhah 204 n. 2, 227
O'Kennedy, Daniel 135 n. 26, 136 n. 29, 142 n. 47, 143 n. 53, 145
Oegema, Gerbern 153 n. 22, 163
Ohad, David 2 n. 5, 7
Oorschot, Jürgen van 138 n. 34, 146
Oswald, Wolfgang 54 n. 3, 55 n. 5, 81
Otto, Eckart 89-90, 109
Patton, Corrine 192 n. 5, 202
Perlitt, Lothar 191 n. 5, 202
Perry, T. 39 nn. 18-19, 40 n. 21, 42 n. 24, 51
Philonenko, Marc 155, 164
Pilarski, Ahida Calderón 85 n. 7, 109
Plöger, Otto 12, 25 n. 33, 32
Podechard, Emmanuel 175, 186
Potgieter, Henk 42 n. 25, 51

Pratt, Richard   16, 17 n. 16, 21 n. 24, 23 n. 27, 25 n. 34, 32
Rad, Gerhard von   58, 81
Rahlfs, Alfred   172, 186
Ramose, Mogobe   95 n. 42, 109
Rautenberg, Johanna   53 n. 1, 81
Reif, Stefan   3 n. 9, 7
Reindl, Joseph   184 n. 50, 186
Reinmuth, Titus   54, 81
Rendsburg, Gary   191 n. 5, 202
Ritschl, Albrecht   171, 187
Rogerson, John   2 n. 7, 7
Rohde, Michael   138 n. 35, 139 n. 38, 146
Rosenstock-Huessy, Eugen   203 n. 1, 227
Rothenbusch, Ralf   76 n. 65, 81
Said, Edward   88 n. 19, 109
Schart, Aaron   35 n. 6, 52
Schegg, Peter   217 n. 33, 227
Schmid, Konrad   35 n. 8, 36 n. 9, 48 n. 38, 52, 90 n. 25, 91, 109, 176 n. 26, 187
Schmitt, Hans-Christoph   33 n. 4, 52
Schmitz, Barbara   53 n. 1, 55, 81
Schniedewind, Willia   18, 32, 133 n. 16, 146, 199 n. 20, 202
Schottroff, Willy   58, 81
Schroer, Silvia   210 n. 13, 227
Schuller, Eileen   1 n. 3, 7, 168 n. 4, 175 n. 22, 187, 215 n. 27, 227
Schunck, Klaus-Dietrich   54 nn. 3 and 5, 56 n. 10, 59 n. 19, 81
Schwemer, Anna   222, 227
Segovia, Fernando   85 n. 7, 109
Seow, C. L.   173 n. 15, 187, 191 n. 5, 202
Seybold, Klaus   190 n. 2, 202
Skehan, Patrick   167 n. 2, 187
Smith-Christopher, Daniel   91 n. 27, 109
Soll, William   183 n. 47, 184, 187
Spieckermann, Hermann   167 n. 1, 187
Staubli, Thomas   210 n. 13, 227
Stegemann, Hartmut   168 n. 4, 178, 187
Steins, Georg   15 n. 7, 32
Stipp, Hermann-Josef   132 n. 11, 146
Stoebe, Hans Joachim   151 n. 15, 164
Tajfel, Henri   2 n. 4, 7

Talstra, Eep   56 n. 10, 69 nn. 46–48, 70, 81
Tanzer, Sara   168 n. 4, 187
Throntveit, Mark   16 n.11, 25 n. 33, 32, 87 n. 15, 92–93, 104, 110
Tsevat, Matitiahu   191 n. 5, 202
Tucker, W. Dennis   38 n. 16, 52
Van der Woude, Adam   36 n. 8, 46 n. 31, 52
Van Deventer, Hans   113, 117, 120 n. 13, 123
Van Seters, Jan   116, 123, 199 n. 20, 202
Veijola, Timo   191 n. 5, 202
Venter, Pieter   83, 84 n. 3, 88 nn. 14–15, 95, 96 n. 46, 97, 104 nn. 78–79 and 81, 105 n. 83, 110
Wagner, Andreas   1 n. 2, 7
Wallace, Howard   196 n. 12, 202
Weber, Beat   206 n. 5, 227
Weinfeld, Moshe   136 n. 29, 146
Werline, Rodney   56 n. 9, 79, 81, 88, 95, 96 n. 45, 110, 135 n. 28, 142 n. 50, 143 n. 52, 146
Wesselius, Jan-Wim   117, 123
West, Gerald   84 n. 4, 85 n. 5, 110
Wette, Wilhelm de   174 n. 27, 176, 177 n. 29, 187
Wilke, Alexa   147, 164
Williamson, Hugh   15 n. 5, 23 n. 28, 27 n. 36, 32, 55 nn. 5–6, 66, 82, 93 n. 36, 97, 110, 196 n. 11, 197 n. 15, 202
Witte, Markus   1 n. 2, 7, 178, 187
Wolff, Hans Walter   35 n. 7, 36 n. 8.9, 38 n. 17, 42 n. 25, 52, 91 n. 27, 110
Wright, Jacob   54 n. 4, 55 n. 5, 82, 92 n. 31, 100 n. 62.63, 101, 110, 199 n. 20, 202
Yee, Gale   102, 103, 110
Zastrow, Klaus   56 n. 9.10, 82
Zenger, Erich   36 n. 11, 42 n. 25, 46 n. 31, 52, 171, 176, 180–81, 185, 190 n. 2, 191 n. 4, 192 n. 5, 195, 202, 208 n. 8, 212 nn. 17 and 18, 213 n. 22, 218 n. 37, 226
Zimran, Yisca   16 n. 9.14, 32

Subject Index

blessing 17, 19, 23–25, 27, 117, 120, 128, 130, 151, 198
communication 4, 62, 70, 121, 142, 209
  communicative intent 115, 118
confession 29, 40, 43, 45, 56 n. 10, 57, 61, 69, 72, 74–75, 87–88, 92, 104–5, 134 n. 22, 210, 220
  Jeremiah's 65, 68
cult 29, 197, 198
  activity 22
  action 59, 71, 74
  context 62, 196
  deed 43
  encounter 136
  initiative 195
  manner 14
  organizer 199
  performance 54
  personnel 14
  practice 76
  protest 116
  ritual 68
  setting 105
  terminology 214
dedication 60, 127, 128 n. 11, 137–38, 143, 197, 219
  Solomon's dedication prayer 23
  temple dedication prayer 20–22, 25, 125
disobedience. See obedience
fasting 39, 43, 61, 68, 71–72
forgiveness 5, 75, 88, 126, 133–35, 142, 197
guilt 25 n. 33, 56 n. 10, 57 n. 11, 65–66, 72, 74–76, 133–34

hymn 159, 161, 167–68, 174–75, 207
  hymnal 204, 209, 211, 214
identification 96, 118, 172, 184, 223–24
  identification theory 172
  identify with 169, 171 n. 11, 206
identity 2–6, 14, 34, 42, 49, 98, 141, 143, 169, 172, 189–90, 195, 200, 211, 214,
  communal identity 6, 195, 199–200
  group identity 5, 33, 169–71, 174–75
  Hebrew identity 3
  identity construction 168, 190, 223–24
  identity formation 15, 95, 168, 222
  identity forming 27
  identity shaping 209
  inclusive identity 49
  individual identity 95
  Israelite identity 2, 4, 33–35, 37, 41, 189, 204, 223
  Judean identity 4, 84, 87, 92–93, 95–99, 103–5
  national identity 96, 197
  religious identity 49, 200
joy 33, 59–60, 192–93
justice 5, 105, 125, 169, 175–77, 181
  social 4, 83–84, 87, 95, 103–6
  economic 99
lament 6, 61, 71–72, 151, 160, 207, 211, 216
  communal 57
  corporate 25
  individual 151–52, 172
liturgy 98, 191 n. 4, 195, 211
  books 223
  context 211

Subject Index

liturgy (cont.)
   expression 46
   items 127
   plan 71
   prayer 215
   procession 189
   reality 3, 11
   setting 209
mercy 36, 39, 41, 44–48, 50, 68, 72, 74–77, 104–5, 129 n. 6, 133, 217
mourning 43, 68, 70
musician 29, 60
oath 189, 192, 194
obedience 17, 117, 129
   disobedience 92–93, 96, 104
penitential prayer 4, 19–20, 54, 56–57, 72, 83–84, 86–90, 92–99, 103–5, 133 n. 17, 135 n. 28, 142
petition 23, 25, 28, 40 n. 20, 44 n. 29, 61, 66 n. 36, 88, 104, 127–29, 131–35, 139–40, 143, 192–94, 199
petitionary prayer 24, 54, 59, 61, 65, 67, 73, 75
   petitioner 24, 129, 134, 142
piety 17, 24–25, 116, 118, 154, 161, 171, 174, 199
pilgrimage 141, 195, 197, 200
poor, the 2, 5, 86, 91, 99, 152, 166–76, 179–80
praise 6, 25, 29, 42–43, 54, 59, 63–64, 71–72, 128, 130, 152, 159, 183, 205, 207–8, 210–11, 212 n. 17, 213–18, 223–24
   psalm of praise 59–61, 63–65, 67
punishment 20–21, 37, 65, 68, 71–72, 74–75, 132–34
redemption 36, 43, 119
   redeem 34 n. 4, 36, 43
   redeeming quality 16–17
religious practice 6, 189, 192
repentance 18, 37, 47, 74, 88, 105, 133, 135
ritual 43–44, 59, 61, 68, 70, 197
sacrifice 38, 40, 43, 60, 116, 127, 137, 141, 196–97, 222

salvation 36, 43, 45, 47, 50, 151, 174, 193
singer 29, 60, 161, 198, 215
temple 5–6, 12, 15, 22, 25–26, 28–29, 41–43, 49, 59–61, 64, 66, 76, 97, 105, 125–32, 134–43, 189, 194–200, 209, 223
thanksgiving 60
   hymn 168
   prayer 25, 39, 148
   psalm 152, 155, 167
   song 41–42, 153
torah 15, 20, 22, 26, 44, 47–48, 60, 71–73, 75, 77–79, 89–93, 97, 104–5, 133 n. 20
vow 38, 40, 43, 67, 150, 152–54, 189–90, 192, 194, 199
worship 15, 22–23, 26, 28, 30, 33, 89, 105, 134, 141, 183, 197
   of foreign gods 18, 22, 89–91

www.ingramcontent.com/pod-product-compliance
Lightning Source LLC
Chambersburg PA
CBHW022005220426
43663CB00007B/965